Research Strategies in Psychotherapy
by Edward S. Bordin

The Volunteer Subject
by Robert Rosenthal and Ralph L. Rosnow

Innovations in Client-Centered Therapy
by David A. Wexler and Laura North Rice

The Rorschach: A Comprehensive System, in two volumes
by John E. Exner

Theory and Practice in Behavior Therapy
by Aubrey J. Yates

Principles of Psychotherapy
by Irving B. Weiner

Psychoactive Drugs and Social Judgment: Theory and Research
edited by Kenneth Hammond and C. R. B. Joyce

Clinical Methods in Psychology
edited by Irving B. Weiner

Human Resources for Troubled Children
by Werner I. Halpern and Stanley Kissel

Hyperactivity
by Dorothea M. Ross and Sheila A. Ross

Heroin Addiction: Theory, Research, and Treatment
by Jerome J. Platt and Christina Labate

Children's Rights and the Mental Health Profession
edited by Gerald P. Koocher

The Role of the Father in Child Development
edited by Michael E. Lamb

Handbook of Behavioral Assessment
edited by Anthony R. Ciminero, Karen S. Calhoun, and Henry E. Adams

Counseling and Psychotherapy: A Behavioral Approach
by E. Lakin Phillips

Dimensions of Personality
edited by Harvey London and John E. Exner, Jr.

The Mental Health Industry: A Cultural Phenomenon
by Peter A. Magaro, Robert Gripp, David McDowell, and Ivan W. Miller III

Nonverbal Communication: The State of the Art
by Robert G. Harper, Arthur N. Wiens, and Joseph D. Matarazzo

Alcoholism and Treatment
by David J. Armor, J. Michael Polich, and Harriet B. Stambul

A Biodevelopmental Approach to Clinical Child Psychology: Cognitive Controls and Cognitive Control Theory
by Sebastiano Santostefano

Handbook of Infant Development
edited by Joy D. Osofsky

Understanding the Rape Victim: A Synthesis of Research Findings
by Sedelle Katz and Mary Ann Mazur

Childhood Pathology and Later Adjustment: The Question of Prediction
by Loretta K. Cass and Carolyn B. Thomas

Handbook of Minimal Brain Dysfunctions
edited by Herbert E. Rie and Ellen D. Rie

Intelligent Testing with the WISC-R
by Alan S. Kaufman

INTELLIGENT TESTING
WITH THE WISC-R

INTELLIGENT TESTING WITH THE WISC-R

ALAN S. KAUFMAN
University of Georgia

JOHN WILEY & SONS

New York • Chichester • Brisbane • Toronto • Singapore

Library of Congress Cataloging in Publication Data

Kaufman, Alan S
    Intelligent testing with the WISC-R.

    (Wiley series on personality processes)
    "A Wiley-Interscience publication."
    Bibliography: p.
    Includes index.
    1. Wechsler intelligence scale for children.
I.   Title.
BF432.5.W42K38   153.9'32   78-31174
ISBN 0-471-04971-9

Printed in the United States of America

10 9 8

For my sweet lady

Nadeen

with love and admiration

until the twelfth of never

About the Author

Dr. Alan S. Kaufman is associate professor of educational psychology at the University of Georgia, where he has been training school psychologists since 1974. Prior to his academic appointment he was assistant director of The Psychological Corporation's Test Division. In that capacity, he worked closely with Dr. David Wechsler in the revision of the WISC and then supervised the standardization, data analysis, and manual preparation of the WISC-R. Dr. Kaufman has published over 40 articles on assessment in a wide variety of professional journals in the fields of clinical psychology, school psychology, educational psychology, and special education. More than 10 of these studies deal directly with the WISC-R, concentrating on the application of psychometric techniques to the clinical analysis of profiles. Dr. Kaufman has also coauthored, with his wife, the book *Clinical Evaluation of Young Children with the McCarthy Scales,* and is on the Editorial Board of the *Journal of Consulting and Clinical Psychology.*

Series Preface

This series of books is addressed to behavioral scientists interested in the nature of human personality. Its scope should prove pertinent to personality theorists and researchers as well as to clinicians concerned with applying an understanding of personality processes to the amelioration of emotional difficulties in living. To this end, the series provides a scholarly integration of theoretical formulations, empirical data, and practical recommendations.

Six major aspects of studying and learning about human personality can be designated: personality theory, personality structure and dynamics, personality development, personality assessment, personality change, and personality adjustment. In exploring these aspects of personality, the books in the series discuss a number of distinct but related subject areas: the nature and implications of various theories of personality; personality characteristics that account for consistencies and variations in human behavior; the emergence of personality processes in children and adolescents; the use of interviewing and testing procedures to evaluate individual differences in personality; efforts to modify personality styles through psychotherapy, counseling, behavior therapy, and other methods of influence; and patterns of abnormal personality functioning that impair individual competence.

IRVING B. WEINER

Case Western Reserve University
Cleveland, Ohio

Preface

The intelligence testing scene is currently in turmoil, highlighted by litigation, legislation, and outbursts by well-intentioned professionals. Advocates of both sides are polarized, and many of the arguments are emotional and uncompromising. One goal of this book, exemplified by the notion of "intelligent testing," is to present a rational integration of the arguments for and against intelligence tests, and to synthesize a sensible approach to the interpretation of the WISC-R. Until new and better instruments are developed, we must learn to apply existing psychological theories and neuropsychological research findings to the interpretation of contemporary intelligence tests. Cries for a moratorium on intelligence testing, if heeded, will create havoc on the assessment scene, because there is nothing of value to replace these well-constructed (albeit imperfect) instruments. In this book I attempt to take a realistic look at the limitations of intelligence tests and to show that these flaws are not debilitating. In addition, I demonstrate how the results of a WISC-R administration can be meaningful both theoretically and rationally if interpreted in the context of clinical observations, developmental theory, research on cognitive style, Black dialect, theories of intelligence, brain research, and so forth.

In the process of applying psychological theory and research to WISC-R interpretation, a systematic and step-by-step method of profile attack is advanced. This method reflects a synthesis of my experiences in working closely with Dr. David Wechsler in the revision of the WISC and standardization of the WISC-R, in conducting numerous research investigations with the revised battery, and in training school psychologists in individual assessment at the University of Georgia for the past 5 years. The interpretive approach begins with analysis of the Full Scale IQ and V-P discrepancies, continues with exploration of the diverse meanings of the distractibility factor, and ends with concrete suggestions for deriving meaning from fluctuations in the subtest profile. Comprehensive psychological case reports and illustrative WISC-R profiles are sprinkled throughout the book to enhance and illuminate the proposed method of interpretation.

The main goal of this book, therefore, is to integrate the theoretical with the practical so as to make the WISC-R a valued tool rather than a feared weapon. Although the proposed procedure for WISC-R interpretation is derived from factor analytic and psychometric considerations, the actual detective work advocated for competent analysis represents more of a *logical* than a *quantitative* endeavor. Examiners are urged to understand and use simple psychometric guidelines and then to go far beyond the statistics to formulate useful hypotheses about each child's strengths and weaknesses. The book is thus geared especially for practitioners, i.e., for any professionals who routinely or occasionally administer the WISC-R, whether in the fields of school psychology, clinical psychology, counseling, learning disabilities or special education in general, reading, neuropsychology, psychiatry, or medical psychology. Graduate students in school or clinical psychology and allied fields who are learning the WISC-R should find the step-by-step procedure of profile attack, along with the theoretical and clinical correlates of fluctuations in WISC-R profiles, of particular value. The juxtaposition of theory and research with clinical practice also makes this book a pertinent resource for nonpractitioners in fields such as educational psychology, psychometrics, and special education.

Athens, Georgia   ALAN S. KAUFMAN
February 1979

Acknowledgments

I wish to thank Dr. Mary M. (Peggy) Wood and Dr. J. C. Mullis for their permission to include the adapted case reports in this book. I am also grateful to Dr. Cecil R. Reynolds for his pertinent comments about portions of the manuscript, and to Dr. Kathleen D. Paget for her conscientious and excellent job of preparing the indexes. Finally, I am indebted to my wife, Dr. Nadeen L. Kaufman, for allowing me to adapt her case reports and incorporate them into the text, and for the considerable time she spent in discussing with me many of the topics that are treated in the book. Her contributions were indeed valuable.

A. S. K.

Contents

List of Tables

CHAPTER 1

Intelligent Testing

This is a book about the Wechsler Intelligence Scale for Children-Revised (WISC-R), which, as almost any graduate student in education or psychology knows, is an IQ-yielding intelligence test. But neither the IQ nor the concept of intelligence is the focus of the chapters that follow. The focus is the child, with interpretation of the WISC-R and communication of the test results in the context of the child's particular background, behaviors, and approach to the test items as the main goals. Global scores are deemphasized, flexibility and insight on the part of the examiner are demanded, and the test is perceived as a dynamic helping agent rather than as an instrument for placement, labeling, or other types of academic oppression. In short, *intelligent* testing is the key, and the WISC-R is the vehicle.

In an age where intelligence tests are at the center of heated controversies, both public and professional, and are frequently the focus of litigation and legislation, it is not possible to discuss test interpretation in a vacuum. Polarization is rampant. Arguments that intelligence tests are racially biased and dangerous (Hilliard 1975, 1976; Williams 1972, 1974a, 1974b) contrast with the assertions of researchers (Jensen 1976) who staunchly defend the importance of the *g* factor for blacks and whites. Cries for a moratorium on intelligence testing or the replacement of IQ tests with criterion-referenced measures (Bosma 1973; Bransford 1974; Cardon 1975; Hobbs 1975b; Laosa 1973; *Larry P.* v. *Riles* 1972; Meisgeier 1976; Reynolds 1974, 1975; Rudman 1977) stand in direct opposition to the state government and local school-district officials who demand the use of rigid cutoff points for diagnosis and placement and who apparently believe the term "standard error" pertains to baseball. The writing of computerized and depersonalized case reports (Alcorn and Nicholson 1975; Flynn, Vitelli, et al. 1978; Shapiro 1974) is antithetical to the type of individualization required for preparing individual education programs and to the humanistic pleas of concerned and socially aware professionals such as Florence Halpern (1974, p. 325) urging clinicians to "recognize that intelligence and cognition do not comprise the total human being!"

Current court cases and pending legislation dramatically reflect the polarization and may ultimately lead to a moratorium on intelligence testing or the abolition of all ability tests. A middle ground is needed before such drastic steps are taken. The potential benefits of well-standardized and carefully developed intelligence tests, with their rich research heritage and clinical−neurological applications, demand to be preserved. At the same time, rampant test abuse, in the form of deification of the test itself, overvaluation of global IQs, equation of test scores with genetic potential, and interpretation of low IQs as a call to passive placement rather than active intervention, must be squelched. The flaws of intelligence tests need to be understood by all test users—not to impel examiners to reject the tests, but to facilitate a more incisive interpretation of what the scores mean. Test administrators must not be subservient to the tests they use or to the scores that their instruments yield.

Jane Mercer (1973, 1974, 1977), a cogent and insightful advocate of intelligent testing, provides a good illustration of a middle-road approach. She outspokenly criticizes standardized intelligence tests as being culture specific and Anglo oriented, yet she acknowledges their potential value by including the WISC-R and Wechsler Preschool and Primary Scale of Intelligence (WPPSI) in her comprehensive SOMPA (system of multicultural pluralistic assessment) package (Mercer and Lewis, 1978). She thus encourages psychologists to administer a Wechsler scale to Anglo, black, and Chicano youngsters, so long as they use it in the context of other measures (e.g., adaptive behavior, gross motor coordination) and interpret the IQs not only with regard to national norms, but also in relation to the child's sociocultural background.

Mercer's approach is sensible and highly congruent with the push for pluralistic measurement and multifactored unbiased assessment (Engin, Leppaluoto, et al. 1977; Oakland 1977) that is accompanying the implementation of PL 94−142 (Education for All Handicapped Children Act, 1975). Indeed, considering an intelligence test as but one of several measures necessary for competent evaluation is a practice well accepted by psychologists and educators actively engaged in psychoeducational evaluation; so is the individualization of assessment that characterizes Mercer's whole technique.

The method of attack proposed in this book stresses the fact that the WISC-R is an *individual* intelligence test. If administration is individual, so should be the interpretation of the profile of scores for each child tested. Continuing the trend toward individualization begun by psychoeducational diagnosticians (Bush and Waugh 1976; Myers and Hammill 1976) and by Mercer and her associates, and consistent with the individualization of instruction that has become so prevalent in educational practice (Birch 1974; Cronbach 1967; Hobbs 1975a; Keislar and Stern 1970; Klausmeier, Morrow, et al., 1968; Snow 1976, 1977), the focus of the WISC-R interpretation presented here is one of personalization. From this vantage point one does not equate IQs with academic potential and, indeed, one may declare the WISC-R IQs to be irrelevant or inaccurate information for understanding some childrens' functioning. The key is to understand *why* the youngsters scored the way they did, not to stress how well they performed. For example, the Verbal–Performance (V–P) dichotomy may be useful for describing the Verbal Comprehension and Perceptual Organization abilities of most children, but a different division of Wechsler's tasks [such as Bannatyne's (1971, 1974) or Meeker's (1969, 1975b) recategorizations] may describe more efficiently the intellectual skills of the specific individual who was just tested in a school or clinic. Finding the hypotheses that explain the pattern of scores obtained for each new child evaluated becomes the crux of individualized WISC-R interpretation and also the goal of this book.

WHERE INTELLIGENCE TESTS FALL SHORT

Criticisms of individually administered and group intelligence tests are certainly commonplace, appearing with regularity in professional journals, popular magazines, and local newspapers. Many of the negative comments are more emotional than empirically defensible, focusing on the thorny issues of culture fairness and test bias. Some critics claim intelligence tests are biased because of the inclusion of some apparently unfair items or because of the difference in mean scores obtained by whites and blacks. As Thorndike (1971) and many others (Cleary, Humphreys, et al. 1975) point out, unequal mean scores for different groups is an unreasonable and oversimplified definition of bias. Test bias has many varied empirical definitions, most of which stress predictive, content, or construct validity (Angoff 1972; Cleary, Humphreys, et al. 1975; Cronbach 1976; Flaugher 1978; Hunter and Schmidt, 1976; Thorndike 1971). Numerous studies of the differential validity of ability tests for blacks versus whites have generally revealed similar empirical results for the instruments under study (Cleary 1968; Flaugher 1974, 1978; Kaufman and Di Cuio, 1975; Mitchell 1967; Merz 1970). Furthermore, the lack of systematic bias against blacks in studies of the various types of validity has specifically been supported for the WISC, WISC-R, and WPPSI [Jensen (1976), using data collected by Jane Mercer; Kaufman and Hollenbeck (1974); Lambert (1978); Reschly and Reschly (in press); Reschly and Sabers (in press); Reynolds and Hartlage (1978); Ryan (1973); Silverstein (1973); Thorne (1974)].

Largely because of the unfair educational consequences of the misuse and abuse of intelligence tests and the scores they yield, critics have damned the tests. They frequently seek to force intelligence tests into an early retirement, despite the logical arguments against such a ban put forth in the introduction of the American Psychological Association's *Standards for Educational and Psychological Tests* (Davis 1974). Unfortunately, many staunch defenders of the faith are equally lacking in objectivity; they unquestioningly accept "what intelligence tests measure'' as an adequate definition of the construct of intelligence, pay homage to global IQs, and perceive these IQs to be immutable reflections of the magical *g* factor.

The tests do have flaws, but the shortcomings are not debilitating and do not justify turning the WISC-R and Binet into historical relics. Rather, their lacks need to be understood well by test users to facilitate both test interpretation and the selection of supplementary measures. Test publishers also need to be directly aware of the limitations to impel them to change some of their current policies and to spend the money necessary for the research and development of greatly improved tests of cognitive functioning.

One major limitation of intelligence tests is their failure to grow conceptually with the advent of important advances in psychology and neurology. The items in the Stanford–Binet (Terman and Merrill 1973) are essentially the tasks that were developed by Binet and his collaborators Henri and Simon in France near the turn of the century. Wechsler's Verbal subtests are close analogs to tasks conceived in Binet's laboratory; some of his Performance subtests also resemble Binet items, and all of them have their roots in the nonverbal test batteries in use about a half century ago. This historical perspective is not intended to demean the genius of Alfred Binet or the innovative contributions of David Wechsler. But the fact remains that the impressive findings in the areas of cognitive develop-ment, learning theory, and neuropsychology during the past 25–50 years have not invaded the domain of the individual intelligence test. Stimulus materials have been improved and modernized; new test items and pictures have been constructed with keen awareness of the needs and feelings of both minority-group members and women; and advances in psychometric theory have been rigorously applied to various aspects of test construction, norming, and valida-tion. However, both the item content and the structure of the intelligence tests have remained basically unchanged.

Piaget's theory of the development of intelligence and his experimental obser-vations indicate that children at different stages of development differ qualita-tively rather than quantitatively in their mental organization. To best assess each youngster's intelligence, the specific type of task in terms of both process and content must vary with the age and cognitive stage of the child. The implication is that different tests will be needed to measure intelligence across a broad age range. In the Wechsler series of scales, however, virtually the same subtests are used to assess preschoolers, school-age children, and adults. In the Stan-ford–Binet, the content and process of the test items do differ dramatically across the range from 2 years to adult, but the changes do not coincide with any known theory. Indeed, many of the fluctuations in item content from age to age seem to be arbitrary or a function of empirical expedience. For example, using Sattler's (1965, 1974) system for categorizing Binet items, one finds only a single Numerical Reasoning item below year IX, and only one Visual–Motor item above year VII; furthermore, an examination of the Reasoning items between years II and VI reveals that all 10 demand nonverbal rather than verbal reasoning.

Serious questions about the nature or breadth of the content of intelligence tests arise as well from disciplines other than developmental psychology. Intelligence quotients are used to predict ability to learn in school, and the close theoretical relationship between intelligence and learning ability is indisputable. Yet the only item types that may be thought of as actual "learning" tasks in the Wechsler scales are Animal House/Coding/Digit Symbol, and these do not require high-level mental processing. Over a half century ago, Thorndike (1926) bemoaned the fact that the then-available intelligence tests did not measure directly an individual's ability to learn more things, or the same things more quickly, than another individual. Estes (1974, p. 740) explained prudently that Thorndike's words are still true in the present: "Little has changed with respect either to the basic method of measuring intelligence by the sampling of performance or to our inability to improve on this procedure by more direct measurement of learning abilities." No attempts have been made to incorporate into intelligence tests any of the numerous learning or concept-formation tasks in the experimental psychology literature or to use a comprehensive learning system such as Gagne's (1977) hierarchy as a blueprint or guideline for determining the processes to be measured in tests purporting to predict learning ability. However, Estes (1974) has advised that we do not necessarily need to replace or revise existing instruments. He proposes an "alternative route," namely, the interpretation of the *processes* involved in the test behavior from the vantage point of learning-theory concepts and the utilization of this information to isolate the sources of poor performance.

Guilford's (1967) theory of intelligence posits five mental processes: cognition, memory, convergent-production, divergent-production, and evaluation. One does not have to join Guilford's search for the more than 100 factors or even be a devotee of his theory to realize that his hypothesized intellectual operations are both sensible and comprehensive and that his structure-of-intellect (SOI) system provides a useful means of categorizing and organizing intellectual tasks. From the standpoint of Guilford's model, the operations of divergent−production and memory are clearly underrepresented in the Stanford−Binet and in Wechsler's tests (Kaufman 1973). Equally important are the differences in the mental processes measured by diverse intelligence tests. For example, the operation of evaluation is assessed by 70% of the WPPSI subtests, which is strikingly higher than the 30% found for the Stanford−Binet tasks at years II−XII. The failure of intelligence tests to measure some abilities adequately and the differences between the tests themselves are difficult to explain in view of the contentions that each test is a measure of the individual's global intelligence.

The entire issue of global intelligence becomes even more pertinent when reviewing the exciting findings of neuropsychologists regarding the specialization of function of the cerebral hemispheres. A mounting body of evidence has shown the left hemisphere of the brain to specialize in sequential processing, which is analytical and successive in nature, and to be particularly well suited for handling linguistic and numerical stimuli; in contrast, the right hemisphere (long the forgotten part of the brain) excels in multiple processing, which is holistic and simultaneous in nature, and handles visual–spatial and musical stimuli with facility (Bogen 1975; Gazzaniga 1975; Ornstein 1972, 1973, 1978).

To understand human intelligence, one must consider the specialization of the hemispheres, the integration between them, and probably the individual's ability to shift from one hemisphere to the other depending on the demands of a problem. To measure intelligence globally, a test should be constructed that utilizes the processing approach of each hemisphere separately and in unison and that taps or at least samples thoroughly the multiplicity of verbal, symbolic, nonverbal, aesthetic, and creative skills that are in the domain of both halves of the brain. These issues have been treated elsewhere in more depth (Kaufman in press a).

The study of "split-brain" patients by Roger Sperry and his associates (Bogen, Fischer et al. 1965; Gazzaniga 1970; Gazzaniga and Sperry 1967; Sperry 1968), which led to understanding of the lateralization of cerebral functions, was obviously too recent to have influenced the structure and format of current intelligence tests. But the time has come for these instruments to be revised in accordance with what we know about the brain, or for entirely new tests to be constructed. These innovations are particularly necessary because the present test batteries do not coincide with the division of mental functions in the brain. The Stanford–Binet is basically a language-oriented left-brain test with the exception of years III, III-6, and V, in which visual–spatial right-brain tasks predominate. At first glance Wechsler's scales seem like a perfect dichotomy reflecting left (Verbal) and right (Performance) hemispheric functioning, but this is not the case. The Verbal and Performance Scales differ in terms of content (verbal vs. visual–concrete stimuli). However, many leading neuropsychological researchers (Bever 1975; Bogen 1969; Krashen 1975; Ornstein 1978) have argued cogently that the key difference between the hemispheres is the mode of processing the stimuli (analytic vs. holistic) rather than the specific nature of the stimuli. Whereas the Verbal Scale requires primarily left-brain processing, the Performance Scale does not uniformly correspond to right-brain functioning. Picture Arrangement, for example, has a definite right-hemisphere component (Reitan 1974, pp. 44–45), but the temporal sequencing required for solving the problems is clearly in the domain of the left hemisphere. Similarly, Coding requires analytic and sequencing skills that are associated with the left half of the brain. Further evidence that the Performance Scale demands a good deal of interhemispheric integration, rather than pure right-brain activity, comes from the fact that the examinee needs good verbal comprehension to understand the lengthy oral directions to a number of nonverbal subtests (e.g. Animal House, Block Design, Picture Arrangement).

The underrepresentation of right-brain assessment in intelligence tests may be particularly penalizing to black children. Ornstein (1972) suggests that entire cultures may place a primary emphasis on different types of skills. Some cultures may be left brained and verbal in their orientation, whereas others are right brained and nonverbal. The emphasis on music and movement among blacks (Weems 1975) implies a right-brain preference, as does the central role attributed to nonverbal and gestural communication within the black community (Carter 1977). According to Carter (1977, p. 25), nonverbal communication among blacks "is a way of expressing love, contempt, admiration, strength, sadness, and many other emotions which only people of equivalent experiences understand." Abrahams (1973) notes further that Black Dialect is not merely a linguistic system, but also an expressive system that combines movement with sound to create a dynamic interaction among the speaker and listeners. Clearly, conventional intelligence tests do not assess the effectiveness of a child's nonverbal communication or the combination of "verbal discord and non-verbal behavior (Carter 1977, p. 24)" that characterizes communication among blacks. Empirical evidence of a possible right-brain leaning comes from findings that black children outscore whites on certain visual-spatial tasks such as pattern recognition and figure completion (Bogen, DeZure, et al., 1972; Pines 1973) and on the nonverbal creative skills of figural fluency and flexibility (Kaltsounis 1974). Torrance (1977) presents an impressive array of evidence to support black children's strengths in presumed right-hemisphere activities such as music, visual arts, and creative movement and dance. From studies of black children's WISC-R profiles comes additional support for a possible right-hemisphere preference: two samples of black children referred for evaluation (Vance and Engin 1978; Weiner and Kaufman in press) and a sample of black severely emotionally disturbed youngsters (Morris, Evans, et al. 1978) all earned two of their three highest mean scaled scores on Picture Completion and Object Assembly, the WISC-R tasks that seem to be most dependent on the right-brained processing style.

As a final thought, consider that the right hemisphere is deemed to be very *intuitive*, in contrast to the computer-like logic of its counterpart (Ornstein 1978; Sage 1976). It is, therefore, conceivable that the right half of the brain may be responsible for common sense in dealing with people and for functioning adaptively within a specific subcultural environment. Thus intelligence tests may measure a large chunk of the overall mental ability of children or adults raised in left-brained environments, but are likely to assess a much smaller portion of the intellectual functioning of individuals from cultures that stress nonverbal communication and other types of right-brained processing.

The preceding portion of this section concerns the need for improvement in intelligence testing. Note, however, that the items constituting the tests are not considered unfair or biased; rather, the potential unfairness stems from areas and items that are *not* included as part of a person's IQ. Biased assessment does not result from the use of an intelligence test per se, but it may easily be the product of decisions made by test users who consider the IQs as direct reflections of a child's brain power and who hence pay nothing more than lip service to the need for supplementary tests and observations.

Two problems with intelligence tests that do not relate to item content merit attention. First is the adherence to the term "intelligence" test and the retention of IQs as the principal scores that are derived. These labels have clearly become offensive to a substantial portion of professionals and lay persons alike. The terms are emotion laden because of the claims of extremists regarding genetic implications and because of rampant test abuse in educational institutions. McCarthy (1972) showed sensitivity to the issue by using the term *general cognitive index* (GCI) for the overall mental score yielded by the McCarthy Scales of Children's Abilities. However, by using a mean of 100 and standard deviation of 16 for the GCI and by calling children "Mentally Retarded" if they score below 70 on the index, she did not really sidestep the emotional issue. Why test authors and publishers should cling to the historical terms is not clear. Wesman (1956, 1968) argued convincingly that tests of intelligence, aptitude, and achievement differ more in the purposes for which they are used than in the uniqueness of their item content. Lennon (1978, p. 20) noted that a strong case can be made for the elimination of the term "IQ" "on the grounds that it now carries, in professional and lay minds alike, an insupportable freighting of emotional and otherwise irrelevant connotations." In addition, in view of the preceding theoretical and neuropsychological points raised, there certainly must be reasonable doubt regarding the assignment of the label "general intelligence" to the summative scores yielded by mental ability tests. The term "IQ" is even more difficult to accept as an unalterable label in view of the fact that it has been years since a *quotient* actually has been obtained in the procedure for scoring the tests.

The final problem to be discussed regarding intelligence tests is the use of the categories "Mentally Deficient" (Wechsler 1974) and "Mentally Defective" (Terman and Merrill 1973) to define IQs below 70. These labels, like McCarthy's (1972) term "Mentally Retarded," correspond to actual diagnostic classifications and imply that diagnosis of mental retardation is possible based solely on the results of an intelligence test. In view of the necessity of using a measure of adaptive behavior in conjunction with an intelligence test to diagnose retardation (as demanded by PL 94–142), it is imperative that the category systems used by test authors be modified to contain a more neutral term for the "below-70" group. Such a modification would actually be consistent with the category labels used for IQs of other ability levels; for instance, the term "Very Superior" is used for IQs of 130 and above, rather than its diagnostic counterpart ("Gifted"). Ideally, stigmatizing labels such as "retardate" and "defective" should be abandoned altogether, even for individuals who are well below average in both intellectual functioning and adaptive behavior [as suggested by the Board of Directors of the American Psychological Association (1970, p. 268)].

The abuses surrounding intelligence tests are a problem of obvious magnitude (Hobbs 1975b; Hunt 1969), and it is incumbent upon test publishers to take swift steps to curtail abuse to the extent possible. To hasten the publication of improved intelligence tests, critics in all walks of life should continue to be vocal in their expression of dissatisfaction with existing measures and in their suggestions for improved assessment.

IN DEFENSE OF INTELLIGENCE TESTS

Intelligence tests are clearly far from ideal, but they remain the best instruments available for revealing an individual's mental functioning. The items may date back to Binet, but at least they have stood the test of time. They are known quantities, both clinically and psychometrically, and have been the subject of literally thousands of research investigations in psychology, education, and neuropsychology. The IQ does not reflect a global summation of the brain's capabilities and is certainly not an index of genetic potential, but it does predict school achievement effectively. Typical correlations between aptitude and achievement are in the 0.50–0.60 range overall, with values of about 0.70 usually obtained in elementary school (Thorndike and Hagen 1977, p. 326). For the WISC, correlations between Full Scale IQ and a wide variety of objective achievement measures averaged 0.61 (Sattler 1974, p. 156). Coefficients of a similar magnitude have been obtained for the WISC-R Full Scale IQ for groups of white or predominantly white children (Hale 1978; Schwarting and Schwarting 1977), for groups of minority or primarily minority youngsters (Hartlage and Steele 1977; Reschly and Reschly in press; Reynolds and Hartlage 1978), and for exceptional populations (Raskin, Bloom, et al. 1978).

As Lennon (1978, p. 11) stated: "Ironically, these relationships have sometimes been so strong as to lead to the criticism that the two types of tests really were not measuring anything different." Vocal critics of intelligence tests have indeed claimed that the criteria of achievement are as culture specific as the intelligence tests and thus do not really provide evidence of validity (Jackson 1975; Mercer 1977). Consequently, Goldman and Hartig (1976) correlated WISC IQs with teacher ratings for Anglos, blacks, and Chicanos aged 6–11 years. The correlations between Full Scale IQ and academic grade point average were very low for all groups (0.12 for Chicanos, 0.14 for blacks, 0.25 for

Anglos). However, no conclusions can be drawn from their study because of the subjective nature of teacher ratings and hence the unknown reliability of the criteria employed; the fact that no attempt was made to correct for the different grading styles of different teachers (e.g., hard vs. easy markers); and the inexplicable inclusion of subjects such as music, art, and physical education in the academic grade-point average. Furthermore, only Full Scale IQ was analyzed, a score of dubious value for Chicanos.

It is difficult to see how standardized measures of reading and arithmetic achievement can be dismissed so unquestioningly by some researchers. Reading achievement is surely a high-priority goal of formal schooling, especially at the elementary-school level; the fact that ability tests—including some such as the WISC-R or Binet that require virtually no reading—can correlate so high with reading success is indeed impressive. Flaugher (1978, p. 672) makes an extremely valid point on this general topic: "Achievement tests are certainly capable of being poorly composed, but when the many carefully constructed and widely used tests are actually inspected for content, almost always that content is found to consist of legitimate samplings of quite uncontroversial educational goals."

Test publishers were criticized here for not spending the money necessary for developing intelligence tests that incorporate psychological theory and neurological research. Nevertheless, they have maintained the psychometric excellence of the existing instruments and have gone to considerable pains (including financial) to conduct rigorous item analyses, consider carefully comments from critics in the field, provide stable measurement of the IQ, and obtain representative nationwide standardization samples. The relatively small standard errors of measurement of the overall IQs that emerge as by-products of the psychometric rigor indicate that whatever is being measured by the summative scores is at least being assessed accurately. Even though the numbers yielded by the intelligence tests do not correspond to known developmental or neuropsychological constructs, the tasks that constitute the test batteries align closely with a variety of theoretical approaches. Using Wechsler's scales and subtests as illustrations, a correspondence with Cattell's (1971) crystallized (Verbal) and fluid (Performance) abilities is readily apparent. The coordination with Piaget's experimental tasks is evident in areas such as judgment and reasoning (Comprehension), logical classification (Similarities), space (Geometric Design, Object Assembly), and number (Arithmetic). Similarly, some Wechsler subtests are clearly classifiable as right brain (Picture Completion, Object Assembly) or left brain (Vocabulary, Similarities), and the three WISC-R factors (Kaufman 1975) are each definable from the perspective of Guilford's SOI *content* dimension: Verbal Comprehension (semantic); Perceptual Organization (figural); Freedom from Distractibility (symbolic). Furthermore, each Wechsler and Binet task may be defined in terms of one or more Guilford factor (Meeker 1969), and examiners with a Guilford orientation may interpret conventional intelligence tests entirely from the SOI model if they choose (Meeker 1975b).

There is thus a reasonable amount of overlap between the abilities reflected in IQs and the abilities posited by various theories, despite their separate and independent roots. The commonalities substantiate the value of intelligence tests and the potential meaningfulness (in a practical, if not a theoretical, sense) of the scores they yield. The differences reinforce the necessity of interpreting IQs in the context of other tests or behavior-related information before inferring an individual's overall mental functioning; they also indicate the prudence of re-grouping subtests in accordance with contemporary practical or theoretical systems to gain insights into the dynamics of a person's cognitive behavior.

AN APPROACH TO WISC-R INTERPRETATION

The limitations and assets of intelligence tests, taken together, suggest that the tests should be used by examiners who are sufficiently knowledgeable to interpret them intelligently. The burden is on test users to be "better" than the tests they use. Training in psychological theory must be put to good advantage when interpreting a profile of scores on an intelligence test. With the WISC-R, the three IQs and 12 scaled scores should be the raw materials for understanding an individual's cognitive functioning. By regrouping the subtests in specified or novel ways and by carefully analyzing "wrong" responses from different vantage points, the examiner can apply knowledge of Piaget, Guilford, Cattell, cerebral specialization, and so on to produce a theoretically relevant WISC-R profile interpretation. This type of psychological sophistication and flexibility of profile analysis, coupled with awareness of the tests' limitations, is essential for breaking an examiner's overdependency on the obtained scores. Psychologists, learning-disabilities specialists, or counselors who routinely call upon their theoretical knowledge of development and learning to interpret WISC-R profiles clearly set up a hierarchy where they are at a considerably higher level than the intelligence tests they use.

The approach to WISC-R interpretation outlined in this book rests on the following premises concerning what the test measures:

1. *The WISC-R subtests measure what the individual has learned.* This is a point stated simply, but elaborated cogently, by Wesman (1968) in his article on intelligent testing. From this vantage point, the intelligence test is really a kind of achievement test; not the same type of achievement test as reading or science, but a measure of past accomplishments that is predictive of success in traditional school subjects. When intelligence tests are regarded as measures of prior learning, the issue of heredity versus environment becomes irrelevant. Since learning occurs within a

culture, intelligence tests obviously must be considered to be culture loaded—a concept that is different from culture biased. Treating the WISC-R as an achievement test may actually have vital social implications. Flaugher (1978, p. 672) notes that poor performance on a test viewed as an index of *achievement* pressures society to apply additional educational resources to improve the children's achievement; in contrast, poor performance on a test interpreted as a measure of *aptitude* "may be seen as a justification of the *withdrawal* of educational resources."

2.) *The WISC-R subtests are samples of behavior and are not exhaustive.* As samples of behavior, one must be cautious about generalizing the results to other behaviors or to performance under different circumstances [see Cronbach (1970) for a thorough treatment of the issue of generalizability]. The other implications of this assumption regarding behavior sampling are: (a) the WISC-R should be administered along with other measures, and the IQs interpreted in the context of the other test scores; and (b) the Full Scale IQ should not be interpreted as an estimate of a child's global or total intellectual functioning.

3.) *The WISC-R assesses mental functioning under fixed experimental conditions.* The standardized procedures for administration and scoring of the WISC-R help ensure objectivity in evaluating a child, but they sacrifice the in-depth understanding of a youngster's cognitive processing that may be obtained from a technique such as Piaget's probing *methode clinique*. The rigidity of test instructions, the use of materials such as a stopwatch, and the recording of most words spoken by a child add to the artificial nature of the situation and make the standardized intelligence test scores comparable to data obtained in a psychological experiment. My suggestion is *not* to deviate from required administration procedures or add nonpermissible probes to elicit a correct response from the child (except when testing the limits). I am a firm believer in strict adherence to standardized procedures, for otherwise the obtained scores—derived from normative data collected painstakingly—are utterly meaningless. But interpretation is another matter, one that demands flexibility and awareness of the limitations of the standardized procedures so as to make the most sense out of the numerical scores.

Thus the finding by Hardy, Welcher, et al. (1976) that urban children really "know" the answers to some WISC questions they get wrong, based on a testing-the-limits procedure, is of considerable interest. However, their conclusion that "a standardized test, in this instance the WISC, may not be a valid estimate of the intellectual capabilities of innercity children" (Hardy, Welcher, et al 1976, p. 50) follows logically only if the intelligence test is viewed as a criterion-referenced measure rather than as a sampling of abilities assessed under carefully specified conditions. Realization of the experimental nature of the testing process will prevent an examiner or researcher from interpreting a child's IQs as evidence of maximum performance or capacity.

When an examiner is able to relate observations of the child's behaviors in the testing situation to the profile of obtained scores (e.g., by noting that the child's anxiety disrupted test performance on all timed tasks), two things occur: (a) the examiner learns important information about the child that can be translated to practical educational suggestions, thereby enhancing the value of the intelligence test, and (b) the actual IQs earned by the child may become gross underestimates of his or her real intellectual abilities. In general, the actual IQs are valuable because they provide evidence of a child's mental functioning under a known set of conditions and permit comparison with youngsters of a comparable age. The value of the scores increases when the examiner functions as a true experimenter and tries to determine why the child earned the particular profile revealed on the record form; the IQs become harmful when they are unquestioningly interpreted as valid indicators of intellectual functioning and are misconstrued as evidence of the child's maximum or even typical performance.

Based on these three premises, the guidelines and procedures for conducting a nondiscriminatory evaluation (Rehabilitation Act of 1973, Section 504) follow logically. For example, the WISC-R, when administered alone, should never form the basis for decisions such as diagnosis or placement. These types of decisions require the administration of several measures in addition to an intelligence test and should reflect the consensus of a multidisciplinary team that includes the child's parents (as directed by PL 94–142).

When the WISC-R is used as part of the decision-making process, the IQs should not be used rigidly. Precise cutoff points, formulas, or minimum IQ requirements distort the meaning of what is measured and prevent intelligent test interpretation. An instrument as reliable as the WISC-R still has a standard error of measurement of about 3 or 4 points (depending on the child's age, and whether the Verbal, Performance, or Full Scale IQ is being considered). A child whose IQ is near the cutoff point, even 6 or 8 points away, may be labeled or placed because of the chance error surrounding his or her true IQ. Apart from errors of measurement, the fact that IQs may not be valid assessors of a child's real functioning because of mitigating factors (e.g., behavioral or subcultural variables) provides another strong argument for avoiding rigid cutoff points. A clerk can interpret an intelligence test when only the precise magnitude of the IQ is considered. A thoroughly trained professional, knowledgeable in testing and psychology, is needed when intelligence tests are used appropriately, that is, as tools for helping to understand the child's strong and weak areas of functioning so that appropriate decisions can be made. It is important to be a good clerk when scoring the WISC-R and computing scaled scores and IQs, but the examiner's role as clerk ends when the final computation is made.

When the precise IQs obtained by an individual are given too much stress, even when supplementary tests are administered, then the test is put in the role of punisher. The intelligence test serves better as a helping agent. It is of greater interest to know what children can do well, relative to their own level of ability, than to know how well they did. Finding out that a girl with a Full Scale IQ of 63 did poorly, compared to other children her age, in all abilities tapped by the WISC-R leads to a dead end. Discovering that she has strengths in nonverbal reasoning and short-term memory, relative to her own level of functioning, provides information that can be used to help write her individualized education program.

Intelligence tests are good predictors of school achievement, providing one justification for using them in an academic setting. However, intelligence test scores should result ultimately in killing the prediction. The fact that most children who score very poorly on the WISC-R will also do poorly in school should not be accepted as a statement of destiny. Judicious test interpretation and translation of test findings to action can alter what is sometimes treated as inevitable; when cast in this role, the intelligence test can justifiably be termed a "helping agent." Psychologists in clinics and in other nonacademic settings have traditionally used Wechsler scales as a means for helping to understand an individual's presenting symptoms and as an essential ingredient in planning for treatment. With the implementation of PL 94-142, intelligence test examiners within school systems will necessarily follow suit.

When working from the perspective outlined in the preceding paragraphs, the examiner's main role is to generate hypotheses. These hypotheses, which require verification with other tests and supplementary observations, may take many forms: explanations of low IQs, V-P differences, or peaks and valleys in the scaled-score profile; speculations about the child's learning style and optimum learning environment; interpretations of the child's behaviors observed during the testing session in the context of how they interact with test performance; and inferences about the impact of known background variables in light of test scores and behavioral observations. The WISC-R provides the astute examiner with an excellent set of stimuli for generating hypotheses. The tasks are divided about equally into the auditory-vocal and visual-motor channels of communication, providing reliable data about these two major modalities for processing information. Items include socially relevant as well as abstract content, and the subtests range from school-related achievement to the kinds of achievement (such as short-term memory or psychomotor speed) that are usually not formally trained. The emotional content of some items, such as the violent stories in Picture Arrangement, permit the examiner to obtain clinical information about the child that cannot be revealed by the profile of scores. In addition, some of the tasks are known to be especially vulnerable to the effects of distractibility and anxiety, thereby enhancing their potential for providing the examiner with useful information.

Hypotheses derived from the WISC-R and other tests, behavioral observations, and background data constitute the essence of individualized test interpretation. The hypotheses explaining the scores, rather than the scores themselves, form the basis for making recommendations. For some individuals, the Verbal and Performance IQs of the WISC-R may provide great insight into their mental functioning. For others, the best explanations may come from the three factors yielded by factor analysis, from Bannatyne's (1971, 1974) or Meeker's (1969, 1975b) division of WISC-R subtests, from developmental or neuropsychological theory, from clinical analysis of test data, from knowledge of Black Dialect and its impact on test performance, or from a novel set of hypotheses that is applicable only to one specific youngster.

Individualizing WISC-R interpretation requires effort. It is fairly easy to look at the three IQs, along with the extremely high and low scaled scores, and come up with some predictable statements about the child's general intellectual functioning and specific strengths and weaknesses. This type of cookbook interpretation does not meet the pressing needs of an aware and concerned public and is not compatible with the intent of recent federal legislation. Individualization demands a flexible examiner, one who is not wedded to a particular approach—such as a conventional cookbook method, the strict reliance on factor scores, or the use of Meeker analysis. Thorough knowledge of each different technique for interpreting the WISC-R is important, as is mastery of the core areas of psychology, since these are the inputs necessary for interpreting a child's test profile. With experience, a well-trained examiner will be able to shift from one approach to another to find the best explanations for the observed fluctuations in a child's profile. Experience is also a prime requisite for interpreting children's behaviors during the testing session and for inferring cause−effect relationships between behaviors and test performance.

The technique of matching the type of interpretation given to a WISC-R profile with the nature and background of the child tested (i.e., personalized test interpretation) is applicable to all children, regardless of their racial group or exceptionality, and shifts the focus from the group to the individual. This approach accords well with Oakland and Matuszek's (1977, p. 55) logic for determining the applicability of a test or its norms for a minority youngster: "We must avoid the notion that all minority or lower socioeconomic children are, by definition, significantly different from those in the standardization sample. This position is prejudicial and unwarranted. . . . The decision as to whether a child's acculturation patterns are similar to those generally reflected in the test's standardization sample may be made for each child individually and only after a thorough knowledge of the child's background."

Group differences in obtained scores are not meaningful for individualized test interpretation, although the examiner's complete familiarity with the characteristics of the pertinent group is essential. Thus the fact that hearing-impaired children, as a group, score below average on intelligence tests is of limited importance. However, the examiner's understanding of the impact on test scores of variables such as living in an institution or of the role of auditory feedback in the learning process is necessary for effective test interpretation, as is the ability to communicate directions to deaf or partially deaf youngsters and to comprehend their efforts at responding to test items.

Similarly, examiners who test cerebral-palsied children and others with physical handicaps need much experience interacting with these youngsters to develop the clinical ability to estimate the degree to which failure on a test item is a function of mental ability versus physical disability. Emotionally disturbed children sometimes perform very poorly on mental tasks because their disorder interferes with and disrupts their cognitive processing; it takes an exceptionally perceptive and experienced examiner to distinguish between valid and invalid estimates of an emotionally disturbed child's intellectual functioning. Gross underestimates of the intelligence of normal preschool youngsters are also quite frequent when examiners are inexperienced in deciphering immature speech or in gaining rapport with individuals who are uninterested in their performance and tend to be impulsive.

To individualize WISC-R interpretation of a black school-age child, examiners must understand the rules of Black Dialect and respect this dialect as being different but not deficient (Baratz 1970; Labov 1970; Stewart 1970); be familiar with the child's subculture and homelife, but not in the stereotypical sense; and be able to determine the inhibiting effect that language and culture may have on the profile of scores of black children at all ability levels. Labov (1970) gives a fascinating account of an 8-year old black boy whose (white) examiner dramatically underestimated the verbal capacity and fluency he later displayed in a relaxed, informal discussion with a black adult. Reports such as Labov's reinforce the importance of rapport-related variables when testing intelligence and underscore the need to be cautious before inferring that a child's low scores reflect deficient ability.

The language and cultural factors that loom so large when interpreting the WISC-R for black youngsters are also vital for interpreting the test scores of Spanish-speaking and other bilingual children. Understanding the meaning of the V−PIQ discrepancies of Spanish-speaking youngsters (see pp. 31−34 and the case study of Jose on pp. 65−69) is especially crucial for proper interpretation of their mental functioning. Again, it takes a very experienced examiner with a special linguistic and cultural background to interpret the WISC-R competently for a child who does not use English exclusively.

Cautious, insightful WISC-R interpretation by well-trained and appropriately experienced examiners leads to true *individual* intelligence testing and helps reduce test abuse. But from both a legal and practical standpoint, much more is needed. To fully comprehend a youngster's ability spectrum and learning potential, the IQs and scaled scores must be interpreted in the context of (and in conjunction with) scores from other measures. In neuropsychological batteries examiners supplement intelligence tests with perceptual–motor, speech, language, memory, and motor tests; projective measures make suitable adjuncts when emotional disturbance or maladjustment is suspected. Adaptive behavior scales are necessary supplements whenever a diagnosis of mental retardation is in question, and measures of creativity help in the identification of gifted children. Criterion-referenced tests also make important contributions to the complete understanding of a child's functioning (Hively and Reynolds 1975), as does Bersoff's (1973) psychosituational assessment, a technique devised to evaluate an individual's intellectual functioning under real-life conditions. Budoff's (1972) test–train–retest paradigm, which is intended to get at children's learning potential by assessing their ability to profit from experience, also has considerable value. Although proponents of criterion-referenced measurement, psychosituational assessment, and test–train–retest paradigms often see these approaches as *alternatives* to intelligence tests, I see them as useful *supplements* to the data yielded by conventional standardized instruments.

The use of adaptive behavior measures is of special importance when assessing black and Spanish-speaking children. Mercer (1973) found that many blacks and Chicanos who scored at the retarded level on intelligence tests were decidedly not retarded in their adaptive behavior; this finding did *not* hold for white children. Now that Mercer's Adaptive Behavior Inventory for Children (Mercer and Lewis, 1978) is available for youngsters aged 5–11 years, it might be wise for examiners to routinely assess the adaptive behavior of each black and bilingual child assessed within this age range. Although time consuming to obtain, adaptive behavior is an aspect of intellectual functioning that is not tapped by the WISC-R. In addition, Mercer's adaptive behavior inventory spans the entire ability range (rather than merely distinguishing between normal and abnormal) and guarantees parental involvement in the assessment process—two factors that enhance the value of Mercer's scale as a supplement to the WISC-R.

If the examiner is able to administer the entire SOMPA package (Mercer and Lewis 1978), then information about the child's sociocultural modality, visual–motor and gross motor coordination, and health history will be obtained along with the assessment of adaptive behavior and intelligence. All these data greatly facilitate the examiner's task of individualizing test interpretation. The sociocultural modality information, besides presenting a quantified picture of the child's socioeconomic background, may be entered in regression equations to convert the white, black, or Latino child's WISC-R IQs to estimated learning potentials (ELPs). The ELPs indicate the child's intellectual ability in comparison to youngsters from a similar racial and socioeconomic background, rather than merely considering the youngster's performance in terms of national norms. Much research needs to be conducted to help interpret the meaning and value of ELPs. However, the concept is so potentially important when it is used to *supplement* scores based on national norms, that examiners would be wise to compute ELPs for blacks, Chicanos, and working-class whites whenever feasible. These scores reflect the child's ability compared to the abilities of children having similar opportunities and experiences; when examined in light of the child's actual IQs, observed behaviors, and specific background, the ELPs should enhance individualized interpretation of the child's WISC-R profile.

The approach to interpretation described in this section may be impractical for some practitioners in the field. School psychologists and psychometrists, faced with long waiting lists and inordinate numbers of cases that must be tested each week, cannot usually administer very many tests as supplements to the WISC-R or find the time to administer the parent interview portion of the SOMPA battery. Psychologists or learning disabilities specialists in a clinic have to assess an urban bilingual Puerto Rican youngster referred for evaluation whether or not they speak Spanish or have any knowledge whatsoever of the child's Puerto Rican subculture. These realities force evaluations of school-age children to be less than ideal in some instances, but they should not be used as excuses for fostering inadequate test interpretation or other types of test abuse. As new federal guidelines are set up, implemented, and enforced, unwieldy case loads will have to be reduced to permit compliance with the regulations. Similarly, rigid use of intelligence test scores in reaching diagnostic or placement decisions will necessarily have to give way to a more flexible and clinical interpretation of the test results.

In the interim, and regardless of case loads, there is much the conscientious examiner can do to facilitate intelligent testing: (a) try to enlighten school administrators about the pros and cons of intelligence tests and their proper use; (b) treat the tasks in intelligence tests as samples of behavior which measure, under fixed experimental conditions, what the individual has learned; (c) not overvalue the IQs or treat them as a magical manifestation of a child's inborn potential; (d) learn and truly internalize a method of interpretation, such as the one presented in this book, that promotes flexibility, focuses on ipsative (*intra*individual) more than normative measurement, provides a systematic method of attacking profiles, and encourages going beyond the scores to understand the individual's functioning; (e) spend time interacting in the neighborhoods that are serviced by the examiner's school or clinic as a first-hand means of learning local pronunciations and dialects and of gaining insight into the backgrounds and subcultural customs of the children who will be referred for evaluation; (f) become closely involved with teachers by observing their classrooms, working with them to follow up and modify recommendations made in psychological reports, and using the teacher-administered American Association on Mental Deficiency (AAMD) Adaptive Behavior Scale (Lambert, Windmiller, et al. 1975) when it is unfeasible to use Mercer's parent-administered adaptive behavior inventory; (g) be alert to the potential benefits of existing and new tests in a variety of assessment areas, particularly short-to-administer measures of skills such as short-term memory and creativity that are barely tapped by the WISC-R; (h) be constantly aware of the limitations of the test and especially of the examiner's ability to interpret the test for certain individuals because of limited exposure to them and their environments; and (i) keep abreast of new research and theories in psychology and related areas, since they may provide novel insights into profile interpretation.

An examiner who follows these suggestions (several of which are stated in the federal guidelines on nondiscriminatory evaluation) will be an intelligent tester despite a crowded schedule or rigidities in the policies of school administrators or state officials.

Intra individual

CHAPTER 2

Interpreting the IQs and Verbal–Performance Discrepancies

Interpretation of a child's WISC-R profile requires a systematic method of attack. One sensible approach is to begin with the most global score and work from the general to the specific until all meaningful hypotheses about the child's abilities are unveiled. This technique, which also provides a useful logic for writing WISC-R reports, corresponds to the organization of Chapters 2−6; Chapter 2 proceeds from the Full Scale IQ to the major WISC-R factors and focuses on understanding V−P IQ differences; Chapter 3 provides an interpretation of the distractibility factor, and Chapters 4−6 are concerned with analysis of the subtest profile.

FULL SCALE IQ

As the most global score yielded by the WISC-R, the Full Scale IQ merits the examiner's immediate attention. By converting it to an ability level and percentile rank (Wechsler 1974, pp. 25−26) and bounding it by a band of error (Sattler 1974, pp. 554−556), examiners will put the IQ in better perspective and enhance its meaning to the reader of their case reports. Confidence intervals for the Full Scale IQ, based on data for all children in the standardization sample and rounded to the nearest whole number, are:

Percent Confidence	Band of Error
68%	±3
85%	±5
90%	±5
95%	±6
99%	±8

I consider 85−90% to be an appropriate confidence level for most testing purposes.

Beginning test interpretation with the Full Scale IQ does not elevate this global score into a position of primacy. Rather, the Full Scale IQ serves as a target at which the examiner will take careful aim. In fact, as examiners explore peaks and valleys in the WISC-R profile while attempting to reveal the underlying dynamics of a child's ability spectrum, they are, in effect, trying to declare the Full Scale IQ ineffectual as an explanation of the child's mental functioning. Large V−P IQ differences, numerous fluctuations in the scaled-score profile, or inferred relationships between test scores and extraneous variables (e.g., fatigue, anxiety, subcultural background) greatly diminish the importance of the Full Scale IQ as an index of the child's level of intelligence.

Even if youngsters obtain Verbal, Performance, and Full Scale IQs that are fairly similar and display only a few unremarkable fluctuations in their scaled scores, it would be inappropriate to attribute too much value to the Full Scale IQ. For such a child, the global IQ is surely a good summary score of his or her performance in about a dozen samples of behavior and reflects relative level of ability under the standardized conditions prescribed by the WISC-R Manual (Wechsler, 1974). As elaborated in Chapter 1, the Full Scale IQ is an incomplete measure of the various mental capacities of the human brain and must be supplemented by additional measures. For example, when assessing black children, tests of memory, creativity, and adaptive behavior are valuable supplements. Although these aspects of intelligence are not assessed very well by the WISC-R Full Scale IQ, research studies have shown that black children, including those from disadvantaged backgrounds, tend to perform quite well on measures of short-term memory (Jensen 1969), creative thinking (Torrance 1977), and social adaptive behavior (Mercer 1973).

As a first step in deemphasizing the Full Scale IQ, one needs a rationale for inferring a child's level of functioning in separate skill areas. Wechsler provides one type of rationale by his grouping of the WISC-R subtests into the Verbal and Performance Scales. However, this armchair dichotomy provides a less impressive justification for profile interpretation than do the results of the empirical technique of factor analysis. It is to the three WISC-R factors that we now turn in an attempt to formulate a rationale for WISC-R interpretation.

FACTORS UNDERLYING THE WISC-R

In a factor-analytic study of data from the WISC-R standardization sample at 11 age levels between 6½ and 16½ years, Kaufman (1975) identified the three factors tabulated as follows:

Cognitive (handwritten)

behavioural. or affective (handwritten)

Verbal Comprehension	Perceptual Organization	Freedom from Distractibility
Information	Picture Completion	Arithmetic
Similarities	Picture Arrangement	Digit Span
Vocabulary	Block Design	Coding
Comprehension	Object Assembly	
	Mazes	

Left brain (handwritten)   *Right brain* (handwritten)

The results of three different methods of factor analysis for each age group yielded the preceding pattern with striking consistency, thereby reinforcing the robustness and meaningfulness of the three factors for all youngsters within the 6–16-year age range. In analyses of the standardization data that I conducted for separate samples of males and females, and also for discrete samples of blacks and whites, the identical three factors were isolated for both sexes and racial groups (unpublished data). Cross-validation of these findings with other normal populations of whites (Reschly 1978) and blacks and whites combined (Shiek and Miller 1978) again produced the three well-known factorial dimensions. Furthermore, verbal, perceptual, and distractibility factors composed of the same or virtually the same subtests as the factors listed in the preceding table were identified for mentally retarded youngsters (Van Hagen and Kaufman 1975), children referred for learning or behavioral disorders (Lombard and Riedel 1978; Stedman, Lawlis et al. 1978; Swerdlik and Schweitzer 1978), adolescent psychiatric patients (De Horn and Klinge 1978), and Chicanos in grades 1–9 (Reschly 1978). For a few samples, such as the urban blacks and rural Native Americans studied by Reschly (1978), only the Verbal Comprehension and Perceptual Organization factors emerged.

In Vance and Wallbrown's (1978) hierarchical factor analysis of the WISC-R for 150 black children and adolescents referred for psychoeducational evaluation, clear-cut Verbal Comprehension and Perceptual Organization factors emerged along with a surprisingly small general factor, but no distractibility factor was obtained. However, the failure of a Freedom from Distractibility factor to emerge was conceivably a function of the methodology used; that is to say, the hierarchical approach did not produce a distractibility dimension for the WISC-R standardization sample (Wallbrown, Blaha, et al. 1975), even though this factor was consistently isolated for the same group when several other methodologies were employed (Kaufman 1975).

The Verbal Comprehension and Perceptual Organization factors bear a clear resemblance to Wechsler's Verbal and Performance Scales, respectively. Although the correspondence between the factors and scales is not identical, it is close enough to justify assigning a primary role in WISC-R interpretation to the Verbal and Performance IQs and to consider these IQs as good estimates of the child's Verbal Comprehension and Perceptual Organization abilities. As presently defined, the first two factors are in the cognitive domain, whereas the distractibility dimension is in the behavioral or affective domain. A thorough treatment of the third factor, including a discussion of its possible cognitive component, appears in the next chapter.

INTERPRETING V–P IQ DIFFERENCES

The clinical history of Wechsler's scales is rich with various interpretations of discrepancies between a child's Verbal and Performance IQs. One of the key applications of the emergent WISC-R factor structure is to provide strong empirical evidence of the construct validity of both the Verbal and Performance Scales. The robust Verbal Comprehension and Perceptual Organization factors for all age groups and for a variety of supplementary samples of exceptional and minority-group children indicate that the Verbal and Performance IQs reflect a child's performance on real and meaningful dimensions of mental ability. Thus the discrepancy between these IQs may well suggest important differences in the child's learning style and ability to handle different types of stimuli. If the factor structure of the WISC-R had produced a factor pattern that was totally at variance with Wechsler's dichotomous division of subtests, the Verbal and Performance IQs (and the difference between them) would have been of little psychological value. Even with the 1949 WISC, the $V - P$ IQ discrepancy was not as meaningful as it is for the WISC-R. Unlike the WISC-R analyses, factor analyses of the 1949 WISC (Cohen 1959) usually found the Verbal Comprehension factor to split in two and the Perceptual Organization factor to contain high loadings primarily by the Block Design and Object Assembly subtests.

Although not perfect, the relationship between the two largest WISC-R factors and the Verbal and Performance Scales is unmistakeable. The five subtests that contribute to the Verbal IQ had the five highest loadings on the Verbal Comprehension factor (although Arithmetic was a distant fifth) and, among Performance subtests, only Coding failed to load significantly on the Perceptual Organization factor. If the examiner chooses to administer Mazes instead of Coding as the fifth Performance subtest [a permissible substitution according to Wechsler (1974, p. 8)], the Performance IQ is a precise reflection of the child's Perceptual Organization ability. However, even if the examiner prefers not to administer Mazes, it is recommended that the Verbal and Performance IQs be used as factor scores for the first two WISC-R factors. These IQs are computed automatically when scoring the WISC-R and have meaning to the experienced clinician, as does the discrepancy between the IQs. The extra clerical work of computing separate factor scores by averaging scaled scores on the pertinent subtests or by entering a convenient table developed by Sobotka and Black (1978) is usually not justified because of: (a) the very high correlations that necessarily exist between a Verbal or Performance IQ and its corresponding factor score and (b) the confusion that often reigns when there are too many global scores to interpret. (For an exception to this rule, see pp. 43–46).

The V and P IQs are both rather reliable and stable across the age range, with average coefficients of 0.93–0.94 and 0.90, respectively (Wechsler 1974, pp. 30–33). The bands of error for the Verbal and Performance IQs are tabulated as follows for different confidence levels (data based on the total standardization sample; values rounded to nearest whole number):

			Confidence Level		
Scale	68%	85%	90%	95%	99%
Verbal	±4	±5	±6	±7	±9
Performance	±5	±7	±8	±9	±12

As with the Full Scale, I consider 85–90% to be an appropriate confidence band in most testing situations.

The size of V−P IQ differences required for statistical significance is 9 points ($p<0.15$), 12 points ($p<0.05$), and 15 points ($p<0.01$). For V−P comparisons, I consider 12 points to be a difference that is worthy of explanation. Although 85–90% confidence is usually ample when banding an IQ with error, difference scores are notoriously unreliable; hence 95% confidence is sensible for V−P discrepancies. Insisting on a 15 point V−P IQ discrepancy before inferring a meaningful difference between a youngster's verbal and nonverbal abilities seems extreme. The name of the WISC-R interpretation game is to generate useful hypotheses via flexibility; 99% confidence is too conservative to permit flexible interpretation.

Research on V−P discrepancies has abounded through the years, with literally hundreds of investigators searching for characteristic differences in the Wechsler profiles of a wide variety of exceptional and minority-group populations. Occasionally a consistent finding emerges, such as the P> V IQ discrepancy noted for numerous populations of delinquents (Andrew 1974; Dean 1977a; Wechsler 1944; Zimmerman and Woo-Sam 1972). In general, however, the results have been contradictory with clear-cut findings few and far between (Matarazzo 1972; Zimmerman and Woo-Sam 1972).

Large V−P differences have frequently been associated with possible brain damage, with differences exceeding 25 points considered suggestive of neurological dysfunction (Holroyd and Wright 1965). Black (1974b) found an index of neurological impairment to be significantly related to the absolute magnitude of the WISC V−P discrepancy and also discovered larger V−P differences in children with documented brain damage than in children with suspected neurological impairment or in normal youngsters (Black 1974a, 1976). He concluded that differences exceeding 15 points may be predictive of neurological dysfunction. Assertions such as those made by Holroyd and Wright or by Black must be tempered by contradictory findings [Bortner, Hertzig, et al. (1972), for example, found the WISC V−P discrepancies of brain-damaged children to be comparable to the V−P differences of normal youngsters], by the fact sizable V−P differences can be traced to a variety of causative factors other than neurological impairment (Simensen and Sutherland 1974), and by data on normal children (see Table 2−1) showing that V−P differences as large as 17 points cannot be considered "abnormal" by any reasonable statistical standard (Kaufman 1976c; Seashore 1951).

Without question, the literature is teeming with contradictory findings regarding the relationship of V−P discrepancies to organic impairment. The lack of definitive studies with children stems from the difficulty in finding children with well-localized brain lesions and in obtaining refined neurological criterion information (Reed 1976). However, there is also much confusion and a variety of contradictions within the adult neuropsychological literature as well (Matarazzo 1972). One conclusion is warranted: V−P IQ discrepancies should not be used to infer neurological dysfunction without convincing support from supplementary data and observations.

As indicated earlier, virtually the entire V−P literature—not just the studies pertaining to brain dysfunction—is beset by contradictions and a lack of success in identifying characteristic patterns for various groups. Poorly defined samples or samples that fail to control for essential variables are probably partially responsible for the inconsistencies. However, another likely source of the problem is the fact that a V−P discrepancy may signify quite different things for different individuals. Also, some V−P discrepancies may be misleading and not indicative of differential verbal and nonverbal skills, or they may be totally meaningless. Finally, some of the contradictory research results may be due to the investigators' unawareness of the magnitude of V−P discrepancies for normal individuals. These topics bear greatly on the issue of individualized WISC-R interpretation and are treated in the following sections.

Diverse Explanations for V−P IQ Differences

A half-dozen children may have identical V−P discrepancies of 15 points in the same direction, and yet each may have an entirely different reason for manifesting this discrepancy in his or her ability spectrum. For example, a child with a previously undetected visual or hearing problem may score very poorly on the Performance or Verbal Scale, respectively, merely because of the sensory loss. No judgment about that child's relative verbal and nonverbal abilities can be made until a retest is arranged after the child has been examined by a physician

Table 2–1. Percentage of Normal Children Obtaining WISC-R V-P Discrepancies of a Given Magnitude or Greater, by Parental Occupation

Size of V–P Discrepancy (Regardless of Direction)	Parental Occupation					Total Sample
	Professional & Technical	Managerial, Clerical, Sales	Skilled Workers	Semi-skilled Workers	Unskilled Workers	
9	52	48	48	46	43	48
10	48	44	43	41	37	43
11	43	40	39	36	34	39
12	40	35	34	31	29	34
13	36	33	31	28	26	31
14	32	29	29	25	24	28
15	29	25	26	21	22	24
16	26	22	22	19	19	22
17	24	19	18	15	16	18
18	20	16	16	14	15	16
19	16	15	13	12	14	14
20	13	13	12	10	13	12
21	11	11	8	9	10	10
22	10	9	7	7	9	8
23	8	8	6	6	8	7
24	7	7	5	5	6	6
25	6	6	4	4	5	5
26	5	5	3	3	4	4
27	4	4	2	2	3	3
28–30	3	3	1	1	3	3
31–33	2	2	<1	<1	2	2
34+	1	1	<1	<1	<1	<1

and given the appropriate corrective devices. Without exhausting the possibilities, a number of other plausible explanations for significant differences in the Verbal and Performance IQs are discussed in the following paragraphs.

Verbal versus Nonverbal Intelligence

The discrepancy may mean what it is supposed to convey according to Wechsler's logic in dichotomizing the subtests and be consistent with the Verbal Comprehension and Perceptual Organization factors that have been identified. In other words, individuals may simply have a significantly different facility in expressing their intelligence vocally, in response to verbal stimuli, than manipulatively in response to visual—concrete stimuli. Such individuals are not likely to have wide scatter on either the Verbal or Performance Scale; if they do have highly discrepant scaled scores, these discrepancies are likely to be on Arithmetic, Digit Span, or Coding, which tend to group together and often do not evidence strong relationships to their designated scales.

True differences in verbal and nonverbal intelligence may reflect greater dependency on one or the other cerebral hemisphere. The left hemisphere is specialized for processing linguistic stimuli, and the right hemisphere is adept at handling visual—spatial stimuli. Consequently, P>V may suggest a better-developed right hemisphere, and V>P may imply an especially efficient processing system in, or dependence on, the left hemisphere. Numerous studies with brain-damaged children or with children suspected of neurological dysfunction have been conducted in attempts to link Verbal scores to left-hemisphere functioning and Performance scores to right-brain functioning. The results of many investigations have been promising. For example, Rourke, Young, et al. (1971) found that 9–14-year-old learning-disabled children with V>P on the WISC performed better than did disordered youngsters with P>V on verbal, language, and auditory perceptual tasks; in contrast, the P>V group was superior on visual—perceptual tasks. In addition, Fedio and Mirsky (1969) found that in a group of temporal-lobe epileptics aged 6–14 years, the direction of the WISC V–P discrepancy was predictive of whether the lesion was in the right or left hemisphere. Other neuropsychological studies supportive of significant Verbal IQ/left hemisphere and Performance IQ/right hemisphere relationships were conducted by Kershner and King (1974), Rourke and Telegdy (1971), Rudel and Teuber (1971), and Rudel, Teuber, et al. (1974).

As one might predict from the typical contradictions in the neuropsychological literature, however, there are at least as many studies with children that do *not* support a direct linkup between Wechsler's Verbal and Performance Scales and the cerebral hemispheres (Binder 1976; Wener and Templer 1976). These inconsistencies are probably due to a variety of reasons, such as the plasticity of a child's brain (e.g., the functions of a left hemisphere damaged in infancy may be assumed by the right hemisphere) or to the fact that the two Wechsler scales do not correspond in a 1:1 fashion to the differential specialization of the left and right hemispheres (see pp. 6–7). Nevertheless, the positive findings with the WISC are encouraging, and neuropsychological investigations with the WISC-R are needed. Even more important is research with *normal* populations, perhaps using the dichotic listening (Freides 1977) or conjugate lateral eye movement (Day 1964; Galin and Ornstein 1974; Reynolds and Kaufman 1978) technique, to establish relationships between WISC-R V−P IQ differences and the hemispheric specialization of individuals with presumably intact brains.

Regardless of the degree to which V−P discrepancies can be traced to brain functioning, it is clear that real intraindividual differences in styles of thinking and learning are a fact of life. These differences are reflected in significant V−P IQ discrepancies and should be respected and utilized in educational planning; they should not be subverted by focusing on the artificial midpoint of these disparate skill areas (i.e., the Full Scale IQ).

Fluid Versus Crystallized Ability

Differences in Verbal and Performance IQs may be indicative of discrepancies in fluid and crystallized ability rather than in verbal and nonverbal thinking. The comprehensive Cattell–Horn theory of fluid and crystallized intelligence relates to Hebb's (1949) distinction between Intelligence A and Intelligence B and involves aspects that pertain to the heredity–environment issue, differential rates of development, and the effects of brain damage (Cattell 1968, 1971; Horn 1968, 1970; Horn and Cattell 1966). Without going into detail, "fluid ability" involves problem solving where the key is adaptation and flexibility when faced with unfamiliar stimuli; "crystallized ability" refers to intellectual functioning on tasks calling upon previous training, education, and acculturation. Vocabulary and Block Design are prototypes of crystallized and fluid ability tests, respectively. Although the theory has been primarily applied to adults, factor-analytic studies have been conducted that basically support the fluid–crystallized distinction within children as well as adults (Cattell 1963, 1967; Undheim 1976).

The match between the V−P and fluid–crystallized dichotomies is not perfect. Whereas the Verbal Scale (excluding Digit Span) can be thought of as a good measure of crystallized thinking, the Performance Scale assesses fluid thinking, Broad Visualization (a Cattell–Horn factor akin to Perceptual Organization), and some lesser abilities.

A child from a very advantaged background whose parents place great stress on school achievement may demonstrate V>P, as may any youngster who achieves school success through excessive effort. For these children, V>P may well reflect high intelligence in the crystallized, specifically trained skill areas but a poor ability to cope with the fluid tasks that Cronbach (1977, p. 287) terms "intellectual surprises." One cannot discount the possibility that the exceptional school achievement (reflected in the high Verbal IQ) has been accomplished by intensive, mostly rote, learning in the absence of the development of a flexible understanding of pertinent underlying concepts.

It is not unusual for learning-disabled children to obtain P > V on the WISC or WISC-R (Anderson, Kaufman, et al. 1976; Smith, Coleman, et al. 1977b; Zingale and Smith 1978). Similarly, a review of over 20 studies of children with reading problems (Rugel 1974b) revealed that on the WISC these youngsters characteristically scored higher on Bannatyne's nonverbal Spatial category (Block Design, Object Assembly, Picture Completion) than on his Verbal Conceptualization category (Vocabulary, Similarities, Comprehension). Since a reading or learning problem reflects a deficiency in education-related tasks, it is conceivable that P > V in these youngsters may be related to a discrepancy between their fluid and crystallized abilities. Note, however, that one cannot infer causality between performance on crystallized tasks and poor school achievement. Whereas low crystallized intelligence can lead to a poor prognosis in school-related subjects, failure in school may well be the cause of low scores on Verbal subtests such as Information and Arithmetic.

P > V scores for culturally disadvantaged children may suggest true intellectual ability ("potential") despite inadequate learning experiences. The poor school achievement that typically accompanies cultural deprivation is, almost by definition, consistent with the low Verbal IQ (reflecting a deficiency in crystallized thinking). However, the significantly higher Performance IQ suggests that the child may have an adaptive, flexible problem-solving approach that can lead to successful school achievement in learning environments that actively encourage and utilize these skills. Illustrations of these environments are Montessori's (1964) approach to education; Piaget-based methods and curriculums (Schwebel and Raph 1973; Varma and Williams 1976; Wadsworth 1978); and programs for the gifted, especially those stressing creative problem solving (Stanley, George, et al. 1977). Thus the fact that crystallized ability is considerably better than fluid ability as a predictor of conventional school achievement should not lead to pessimism for a child (culturally disadvantaged, learning disabled, or otherwise) who has P > V. Insightful educators should be able to channel good fluid ability and use it to develop the basic tool skills that may be deficient.

One should not imply from the preceding discussion that crystallized thinking is learned but fluid thinking is not. As indicated in Chapter 1, a basic premise of intelligence tests is that they measure what the individual has learned. Whereas crystallized ability reflects direct and deliberate training, fluid ability develops through incidental learning, gained indirectly from life's experiences. From this perspective, the crystallized—fluid distinction may tie in directly with left-versus right-hemispheric specialization since Luria and Simernitskaya (1977) have shown that incidental learning is primarily a right-brain function.

Inference of a discrepancy in fluid and crystallized thinking should certainly not accompany the finding of a significant V > P difference. The remainder of this chapter makes it abundantly clear that such differences may reflect an inordinate number of causative factors. As stated earlier, the Performance Scale seems to be largely a measure of both fluid ability and Broad Visualization; furthermore, most mental tasks call upon *both* fluid ability and crystallized thinking, so the Verbal and Performance Scales are far from pure measures of these abilities. For example, the Similarities subtest requires some fluid ability for success, and the Object Assembly and Mazes subtests surely measure crystallized ability for children with much direct practice with puzzles and maze tracing. Before inferring that a V−P discrepancy corresponds to the crystallized−fluid dichotomy, examiners have to have considerable knowledge about the child's cultural background and specific educational experiences, and they have to relate this knowledge to the problem-solving approach he or she evidenced while responding to the various verbal and nonverbal tasks. Assessment on supplementary instruments is also essential, particularly on tasks that are more pure measures of fluid intelligence such as Raven's (1956, 1960) Progressive Matrices or group tests such as Figure Exclusion and Figure Analogies (Guilford and Hoepfner 1971).

Psycholinguistic Deficiency

A child who has a learning disability may well be deficient in one or more aspects of psycholinguistic functioning (Kirk and Kirk 1971). Such deficiencies may be fairly global and involve an entire modality (channel of communication) or level of organization, or they may be specific and affect a single psycholinguistic process. When these communication problems occur in children, intelligence test scores will undoubtedly suffer. For example, a child with a deficiency in the auditory−vocal channel of communication will probably perform quite poorly on most verbal subtests and may have difficulty with the nonverbal subtests that demand comprehension of lengthy instructions spoken by the examiner. Similarly, a child with a problem in the visual−motor modality, such as poor visual reception, is likely to have considerable difficulty with most tasks on the Performance Scale. Research support for the relationship between the Illinois Test of Psycholinguistic Abilities (ITPA) channels of communication and the WISC V−P dichotomy was provided by two studies involving learning-disabled children (De Boer, Kaufman, et al. 1974; West, 1973). De Boer, Kaufman, et al. (1974), for example, found that Performance IQ correlated 0.51 with scores on ITPA visual−motor subtests but only 0.32 with ITPA auditory−vocal scores; in contrast, Verbal IQ correlated higher with auditory−vocal than visual−motor scores (0.42 vs. 0.25). In a study of children with suspected learning disabilities, Polley (1971) found that the auditory−vocal channel correlated significantly higher with WISC Verbal IQ than Performance IQ, but found no reciprocal relationship for Performance IQ.

From the vantage points of research and the experience of clinicians, children with serious psycholinguistic problems in one or the other major modality may evidence V−P discrepancies of substantial magnitude. When this type of causality can be inferred (by supplementary testing with instruments designed to assess psycholinguistic ability and by clinical observations), the V−P IQ difference does *not* necessarily reflect a discrepancy in the child's verbal versus nonverbal intelligence. Children with receptive problems do not have the opportunity to demonstrate their intelligence in the affected channel, whereas children with expressive problems are unable to communicate their thought processes. In both cases the children's intelligence on the scale with the depressed IQ must remain a question mark, pending a more subtle type of mental assessment by the experienced clinician who can select cognitive tasks that circumvent the psycholinguistic deficiency.

The WISC-R assesses verbal and nonverbal intelligence via the vehicles of the auditory−vocal and visual−motor channels of communication. When one of these vehicles is damaged, some or most of the battery is no longer measuring intelligence for that individual. Thus for a youngster whose V−P discrepancy can be traced to, or assumed to result from, a psycholinguistic deficiency, the Full Scale IQ becomes a totally meaningless statistic. Since some psycholinguistic problems (e.g., auditory reception) can affect scores on both the Verbal and Performance Scales, even the higher of the Verbal and Performance IQs may be an underestimate of the child's level of intellectual functioning. Primarily for this reason, rules stipulating that a learning disabled child must have ''normal'' intelligence (based on scores on conventional intelligence tests) are unfair and potentially hazardous to the child's educational welfare.

Bilingualism

Spanish-speaking children who learn English as their second language or who learn two languages simultaneously during their childhood are likely to score significantly higher on the Performance than on the Verbal Scale. A variety of investigators have found Mexican−American children and Puerto Rican children living in the United States to score significantly higher on nonverbal than on verbal measures of mental ability (Altus 1953; Christiansen and Livermore 1970; Fitch 1966; Gerken 1978; Phillipus 1967; Shellenberger and Lachterman 1976; Silverstein 1973; Talerico and Brown 1963). Not infrequently, Spanish-speaking youngsters score very close to the normative mean on nonverbal measures of intelligence, while scoring at a Borderline to Low Average level of functioning on the verbal portions of the same test batteries (Fitch 1966; Gerken 1978; Shellenberger and Lachterman 1976; Silverstein 1973). Clearly, an overall score such as the Full Scale IQ is totally meaningless in such instances and should never be used for categorization or labeling.

The low Verbal scores by many Spanish-speaking youngsters cannot be considered as reflecting an intellectual deficit because of the obvious interaction of scores on crystallized tasks with variables such as language ability, culture, and cognitive style. Nevertheless, the P > V for these youngsters does not merely reflect a difficulty in understanding the meaning of the test items or instructions spoken by the examiner. Bilingual children who speak English quite adequately are often found to show a marked superiority on nonverbal than verbal tasks (e.g., see the case report for Jose on pp. 65–69), and P > V differences have been observed for bilingual children when the tests are administered in Spanish (Guzman, 1976; Palmer and Graffney 1972; Shellenberger 1977). Nor is the nonverbal–verbal discrepancy likely to be solely a function of cultural differences. Sizable P > V differences were found on the McCarthy Scales of Children's Abilities (Shellenberger and Lachterman 1976), a battery that does not seem to be as culture loaded as the Wechsler tests (Kaufman and Kaufman 1973). In addition, Shellenberger and Lachterman (1976) found that bilingual Puerto Rican children who spoke English adequately were no more deficient in highly culture-loaded tasks (WISC-R or WPPSI Information and Comprehension subtests) than in tests of verbal memory and verbal concept formation. Finally, Shellenberger (1977) administered a Spanish translation of the McCarthy Scales to bilingual Puerto Rican children living in Pennsylvania and to monolingual youngsters living in Puerto Rico and found a sizable nonverbal–verbal discrepancy for the bilingual American youngsters, but *not* for the monolingual Spanish-speaking children in Puerto Rico (whose culture is extremely different from Anglo–American culture).

These studies are not meant to minimize the importance of language and cultural differences. Indeed, the pitfalls of using direct translations of American tests are known (De Avila 1973; Sechrest, Fay, et al. 1972). Also, it has been shown that Chicano children instructed in English and Spanish at home have a measurable intellectual advantage over those instructed only in Spanish (Spence, Mishra, et al. 1971) and that higher IQs are obtained by Puerto Rican youngsters when examiners encourage the children to actively participate, verbalize, and persevere (Thomas, Hertzig, et al. 1971). Thus the investigations discussed here should be kept in perspective; at the same time, they show that simple answers such as language or cultural differences are not satisfactory for the question regarding V–P discrepancies in bilingual children. Additional research is needed to help clarify the psychological, sociological, and educational meaning of the two disparate indexes of intellectual functioning for the bilingual Spanish–American child. Shellenberger (1977) speculated that the strength in nonverbal skills evidenced by the Pennsylvania Puerto Rican children may reflect a compensation they developed to help them cope with the communication barriers encountered in an English-speaking school, may be the result of more nonverbal stimulation in the United States than in Puerto Rico, or may indicate that test performance suffers in both languages when two languages are learned simultaneously. Regardless of why bilingual Spanish-speaking children obtain relatively low Verbal scores, it is quite clear that Verbal IQs or other indexes of verbal ability—although they may be meaningful for understanding the children better—do not reflect their intellectual potential.

Despite the verbal orientation of most American schools and the fact that Verbal IQ is by far the best predictor of achievement for Anglo−American children, verbal ability may not be the best predictor of school achievement for Spanish-speaking youngsters in the early school grades. Mishra and Hurt (1970), studying Chicanos, found the verbal subtests of the Metropolitan Readiness Test to have a lower predictive validity than the tasks such as Numbers that require less English. Phillipus (1967), also investigating Chicano children, found the WISC Performance Scale and Raven's Coloured Progressive Matrices to be much better predictors of school achievement than either the WISC Verbal or Full Scale. Finally Shellenberger (1977), in her investigation of Puerto Rican children with the Spanish McCarthy, found that for Spanish-speaking children in both cultures, the best predictors of school achievement were nonverbal and quantitative tasks; verbal measures were the least important predictors of achievement and added little or nothing to the prediction that was obtained from other types of tasks (including gross motor tests for the Pennsylvania group).

The ethical, legal, and practical issues involved in assessing Spanish-speaking children have been well documented (Oakland 1977). Children have to be tested in their primary language, and appropriate intelligence tests need to be developed and standardized (Diana v. State Board of Education, 1970; Guadalupe Organization, Inc. v. Tempe Elementary School District No. 3, 1972). According to PL 94−142 (Education for All Handicapped Children Act, 1975), "materials or procedures shall be provided and administered in the child's native language or mode of communication, unless it clearly is not feasible to do so" (p. 15). Based on present research, discrepancies between nonverbal and verbal skills may well be present for many bilingual Spanish-speaking children whether they are tested in English or Spanish, and even if English is the only language spoken in their homes; such discrepancies may ultimately be found to exist in the culture-relevant tests that will presumably be developed in the future. The examiner should be keenly aware of the research findings for bilingual Spanish-speaking children, especially that verbal ability is apparently an ineffectual measure of intelligence or predictor of achievement for youngsters who face the extra stresses required to learn two languages and to overcome the communication barriers encountered in school.

When the WISC-R is deemed an appropriate instrument for use with a bilingual child [cf. Oakland and Matuszek (1977) and Tucker (1977) for appropriate guidelines], the examiner is advised not to compute or interpret the Full Scale IQ. The fact that all three WISC-R IQs, including Full Scale IQ, were found to be quite reliable for a sample of Mexican – American children (Dean 1977b) does not alter the inadvisability of computing an overall IQ for bilingual youngsters. The Perceptual Organization and Freedom from Distractibility factors should be stressed for estimating their intellectual functioning and school-related potential. Whereas a verbal deficit cannot be ignored for educational planning, it should never penalize a Spanish-speaking child during the diagnostic process. Hence V – P IQ discrepancies require sensitive interpretation for bilingual children; supplementary tests have to be given to facilitate profile analysis. Spanish-speaking children who evidence school learning problems need a remedial program that capitalizes on the nonverbal strengths they have developed both for teaching school subjects and for improving verbal areas of functioning.

Black Dialect

Psychologists and educators have not dealt very well with the assessment and placement of bilingual Spanish-speaking children, but at least they recognize that the youngsters may be taught a different language at home. A similar type of awareness has been slow to emerge regarding the language development of black children. Too frequently, the pronunciations, grammatical structure, or vocabulary of the black youngster is considered deficient or inferior and in need of substantial improvement—despite the careful research and cogent arguments of linguists and psycholinguists regarding "Negro Nonstandard English" (Black Dialect). Baratz (1970), for example, cites numerous studies showing that Black Dialect is a rule-governed linguistic system that is different from standard English but decidedly *not* deficient. Linguists assume that any verbal system used by a community that is well ordered with a predictable sound pattern, grammatical structure, and vocabulary is a language, and that no language is structurally superior to any other language (Baratz 1970, pp. 13 – 14). The internal consistency of Black Dialect and the predictability of its phonological and grammatical rules has been supported empirically (Marwit, Marwit, et al. 1972) and also by the results of ethnographic investigation (Bauman 1971).

Black Dialect should gain the respect that it rightfully deserves, and the language-deficiency stigma must be removed from children who use this systematic language. Furthermore, the differences between standard English and Black Dialect should be understood well by teachers and psychologists. Since these differences span grammar, phonology, syntax, semantics, and "soul" (Carter 1977), the necessary task of learning the black student's language demands conscientious effort.

Even when the examiner is familiar with black language and culture, the impact of Black Dialect on WISC-R IQs is likely to be felt. The words to be spoken are in standard English, which may lead to comprehension problems. Whereas Performance IQ as well as Verbal IQ may be depressed because of the lengthy verbal instructions for some Performance subtests, Verbal IQ is the most vulnerable. The Performance tasks involve concrete visual stimuli, and most tasks include demonstration items, so that black children typically understand the aim of each subtest despite the highly verbal instructions. When examiners do not know Black Dialect, the influence of language differences on Verbal IQ may be profound. Because of pronunciation differences, the black child may have special difficulty with words that are not in context, such as the stimuli for Vocabulary and Similarities. Also, the youngster may use subcultural slang words and concepts that are specific to black culture when answering verbal items. An unaware examiner may regard these responses as wrong or fail to query them appropriately, even though the answers are partially or completely correct. The lack of verbosity that often characterizes blacks (Labov 1970) may also penalize their scores on the more subjectively scored verbal items; white children who tend to give longer (although not necessarily more correct) responses are more likely to be given the benefit of the doubt in questionable cases. Thus when a black child scores much higher on the Performance than on the Verbal Scale, the possibility that the Verbal score was depressed due to a linguistic difference must be considered. Although discrepancies of this sort are not typical for black children (Cole and Hunter 1971), as they are for Spanish-speaking youngsters, the implication is the same. In other words when a P > V discrepancy for a black child can reasonably be traced to a language difference, the Verbal Scale (and hence the Full Scale) is not an adequate measure of the intellectual functioning of that individual.

The finding by some researchers that black children show little improvement on standardized ability tests (Quay 1971, 1972) or achievement tests (Marwit and Neuman 1974) that have been translated into Black Dialect merely points out that a simple solution to a complex problem will not usually work. The fact that translating a test into Black Dialect facilitates the performance of a few individual children on standardized tests, despite nonsignificant differences in group means, is still an important finding. Furthermore, a few studies involving nonstandardized measures have shown that Black Dialect does significantly affect a child's performance. Baratz (1970), for example, showed that although whites were superior to blacks when repeating sentences in standard English, blacks far exceeded the performance of whites when repeating sentences spoken in Black Dialect. Crowl and MacGinitie (1974) found that experienced white teachers assigned significantly higher grades to the responses given by white boys to typical school questions than to the responses given by black boys, even though they gave answers with identical wording. The language problem is clearly important to consider when assessing a black child.

Coordination Problem

A higher Verbal than Performance IQ does not necessarily mean that the examinee has better developed verbal than nonverbal mental ability. Some of the

Performance tasks demand a considerable amount of motor coordination for successful performance; a child with exceptional nonverbal reasoning skill may score quite low on the Performance Scale primarily because of poor motor development. Since coordination problems (which may be due to neurological factors) are outside the domain of cognitive abilities, they may serve to reduce the Performance IQ to an underestimate of nonverbal thinking.

By coincidence, the amount of coordination needed for each of the five regularly administered Performance subtests is approximately inversely proportional to their order of administration. Picture Completion requires virtually no coordination, and its items may even be answered vocally. Picture Arrangement demands some motor coordination to organize the pictures, but the emphasis is on discovering the correct sequence; the straightness of the line formed by the picture cards and the proximity of the cards to each other are both irrelevant. Block Design and Object Assembly require good coordination to rapidly align the blocks or pieces to form the correct product. However, the role of nonverbal thinking for both of these tasks is sufficiently important to take precedence over motor coordination in determining the scaled scores of most children. Nevertheless, poor coordination is especially penalizing to adolescents on Block Design and Object Assembly (particularly the latter subtest) because of the increasingly important role played by time bonuses in determining the scaled scores of older children (see pp. 119–123). In contrast, Coding is more of a clerical than an intellectual task, thereby elevating motor coordination as a primary element for successful performance at all ages. Unlike the three Performance subtests that precede it, a child cannot use quick nonverbal thinking to compensate or partially compensate for poor coordination when responding to the Coding items.

The amount of coordination needed for Mazes probably fits somewhere between the amount for Picture Arrangement and Block Design. Coordination is certainly important for drawing with a pencil between parallel lines, but the scoring system does not penalize for corners that are "cut" or for lines that stray somewhat from the intended path; also, bonus points for rapid correct performance are not given for Mazes. A sample Performance profile for a child with good nonverbal intelligence and poor motor coordination is tabulated as follows:

Subtest	Scaled Score
Picture Completion	15
Picture Arrangement	13
Block Design	8
Object Assembly	9
Coding	5
Mazes	10

Whenever the examiner notices that the child's scaled scores on the first five Performance subtests decrease fairly steadily, the possibility of a motor problem should be considered. If no coordination difficulty was apparent during the examination, particularly during the Performance subtests, the hypothesis probably requires quick rejection. Similarly, a hypothesized motor problem would be rejected if the examiner had different explanations for the relatively good performance on the first two tasks and the poor performance on Coding. For example, the scores on Picture Completion and Picture Arrangement may have been elevated by the child's good verbal ability (see pp. 46−48), and the low Coding score may have been due to factors such as extreme distractibility, obvious fatigue, and anxiety.

When a hypothesis of a motor problem cannot be easily rejected, supplementary observations and test scores are needed. Assessment of the child's performance during cognitive tasks requiring good coordination (e.g., the Bender−Gestalt), along with examination of his or her profile of scores on an instrument like the Purdue Perceptual Motor Survey (Roach and Kephart 1966), should help identify or isolate the nature of the problem. Administration of a nonverbal test requiring little or no motor coordination, such as the Columbia Mental Maturity Scale (Burgemeister, Blum, et al. 1972) or Progressive Matrices Test (Raven 1956, 1960), is useful to provide a more accurate description of motor-impaired children's nonverbal intelligence than is portrayed by their Performance IQ.

Time Pressure

Like coordination difficulties, the child's inability to do well under time pressure can lead to significant V > P discrepancies. All Performance subtests are timed, with bonus points awarded for Picture Arrangement, Block Design, Object Assembly, and Coding A; furthermore, speed is so important an element of success for Coding B that virtually no one completes all items. In contrast, only Arithmetic on the Verbal Scale requires a stopwatch. Thus children who have difficulty working within time limits will be extremely penalized on the Performance Scale and may well score significantly higher on the Verbal Scale, even if their nonverbal intelligence per se is on a par with or possibly superior to their verbal intelligence.

Inferring that a depressed Performance IQ may be largely explained by factors related to time is contingent on the examiner's perceptiveness and his or her ability to integrate background information and behavioral observations with test scores. From the WISC-R profile, one would expect a child to score relatively low on the Arithmetic subtest, in addition to obtaining a depressed Performance IQ; otherwise, hypotheses concerning the importance of time factors are conceivably not correct. If the examiner is aware of cultural or subcultural influences that may impel a child to work slowly due to caution or noncompetitiveness, such background knowledge can certainly support a hypothesis regarding the role of time. More typically, however, support comes from the child's behavior. Some youngsters will make obvious negative gestural responses to the stopwatch or make an anxious comment about it, whereas others may be totally oblivious to the watch or the fact that timing is important.

Some of the major causes of poor performance on timed items (other than poor motor coordination) are immaturity, anxiety, distractibility, reflectiveness, and compulsiveness. An immature child often pays no attention to the watch, or, if aware of it, either does not understand its implications or does not care. Irrelevant comments during a timed task are frequent for immature youngsters, and examiners may have to redirect children who have interrupted their performance with a story or lengthy discourse. Immature physical behavior and silliness are often noted throughout the test, but the impact of these actions on untimed verbal tasks is usually less pronounced. An anxious or distractible child is likely to evidence the pertinent behaviors from time to time during the testing session. The perceptive clinician who notes these behaviors should scrutinize carefully the child's profile of scaled scores. Depressed scores on highly speeded tasks, on Digit Span, and on any other subtest during which the distractible or anxious behaviors were specifically observed, would help corroborate a cause–effect relationship between those behavioral variables and a child's low Performance IQ.

Reflective children, who may respond deliberately because of their characteristic style of approaching ambiguous problems (Kagan 1966), may fail Performance items because they do not solve them correctly within the allowable time limit. Many cross-sectional and longitudinal studies have shown that children typically become more reflective with age (Messer 1976). Whereas older reflective children may have no difficulty completing items before the time limit expires, and indeed be very accurate problem solvers, they may still obtain depressed Performance IQs because of their failure to earn bonus points for quick perfect performance. (See pp. 119–123 for a discussion of the vital role that quick responding plays in the Performance scores of adolescents.) Interestingly, the polar opposite of reflectivity may also lead to a lowered Performance IQ. Plomin and Buss (1973) showed that errors on the Matching Familiar Figures Test (indicative of impulsivity) were more related to WISC Performance IQ than to Verbal IQ.

Like the highly reflective child, the compulsive youngster—that is, one who may be observed copying the Coding symbols in painstaking fashion or aligning the Block Design cubes and Object Assembly pieces until the fit is "perfect"— commonly gets items right on overtime. Although credit is never given for these belated correct responses, this behavioral observation can be crucial for test interpretation, and it has obvious implications for the type of nonpressured learning environment that may be optimum for such a youngster. Ironically, reflective or compulsive behavior on the Verbal Scale may have an effect opposite to that observed on the Performance Scale. Scores on Verbal Comprehension subtests may be elevated substantially by children who give a string of responses of varying quality (Similarities) and who respond to probing with a variety of ideas (Comprehension) or with much elaboration (Vocabulary). The combined effect of the child's reflective cognitive style or compulsive tendencies on the WISC-R profile may thus be to inflate V > P discrepancies or to produce no V−P difference for the child who really has a nonverbal superiority. (See the case report of David S. for an illustration of the latter phenomenon on pp. 59−65.)

Testing the limits (Glasser and Zimmerman 1967; Sattler 1974) after the entire WISC-R is administered provides one method of estimating a child's nonverbal problem-solving ability in the absence of time pressure. With the stopwatch removed, the examiner can again present items the child failed or present the more difficult items that may not have been reached and observe the child's performance. Since correct responses obtained during the testing-the-limits procedure do not "count" and do not affect the IQs, the examiner can modify the instructions if need be ("Now take as much time as you need to put these pictures in the right order to tell a story; there's no hurry") or use other means to calm an anxious youngster. Children who far surpass their previous nonverbal or arithmetic performance in the more informal setting were probably unduly penalized by the influence of the clock on the timed WISC-R subtests.

Another method of trying to estimate the nonverbal intelligence of a child believed to be overly bothered by the stopwatch is to administer supplementary tests. The Columbia and Raven (mentioned in the section on coordination problems) are good supplements because they assess nonverbal reasoning without imposing time limits on the child. One word of caution: the examiner should not be too surprised if testing the limits and administering supplementary tests fail to result in improved performance. It is important to remember that quick performance is not just related to behavior or personality, but also bears a clear relationship to problem-solving ability. Children who solve nonverbal problems quickly do better on similar problems than do youngsters who solve them more slowly (Kaufman in press b). For example, children in the standardization sample who solved a given Block Design item correctly in a brief time solved more Block Design items perfectly than did children getting the same item correct with a longer response time. Similar relationships between speed of performance and problem-solving ability were obtained for all Object Assembly items and for most Picture Arrangement items, suggesting that quickness of perfect performance is an aspect of mental ability and that the inclusion of time-bonus points has empirical justification.

Field Dependence/Field Independence

It is quite possible that a V−P discrepancy, in either direction, may reflect a dimension of behavior that is far more pervasive than a mere distinction between verbal and nonverbal intelligence. A substantial body of research has accumulated regarding the cognitive style of field dependence versus field independence (Witkin, Dyk, et al. 1974), with several studies directly pinpointing the relationship of this bipolar cognitive style to scaled scores on various Wechsler batteries (Coates 1975; Goodenough and Karp 1961; Karp 1963).

Like other cognitive styles, field dependence–field independence deals with the process or form of a cognitive activity (e.g., *how* we perceive, learn, relate to people), rather than the content; it is pervasive, spanning the intellective and personal–social domains, and is stable over time; and, unlike extremes of intelligence, each pole has adaptive, positive value in specified circumstances (Witkin, Moore, et al. 1977). The tools for measuring individuals on this bipolar cognitive style continuum are two laboratory tasks involving spatial orientation (Rod-and-frame test and Body-adjustment test, described by Witkin, Moore, et al. 1977), and the nonverbal, perceptual Embedded Figures Test (Witkin, Oltman, et al. 1971). Success on all tasks depends on "the extent to which the person perceives part of a field as discrete from the surrounding field as a whole, rather than embedded in the field" (Witkin, Moore, et al. 1977, pp. 6–7). People who can adjust a rod to an upright position regardless of the tilt of the frame surrounding it, adjust their own body to an upright position when placed in a disoriented environment, and locate a simple figure that has been embedded in a complex geometric design are said to be *field independent*. Inability to perform well on these tasks, presumably because of the power the field exerts on an individual's perception of its components, characterizes *field-dependent* people.

Based on summaries and discussions of numerous research investigations, Witkin, Moore, et al. (1977) paint the following picture of individuals at the two poles of the cognitive style continuum. Field-independent people are flexible in problem-solving situations, impose structure where it is lacking when dealing with perceptual and verbal materials, have an impersonal orientation, are interested in the abstract and theoretical, and use specialized defense mechanisms such as intellectualization. In contrast, field-dependent individuals are well attuned to the social aspects of their environment, make use of prevailing social frameworks, do not spontaneously structure stimuli but leave them "as is," are drawn to people and like being with them, are better liked, have a global (rather than a distinct) body concept, and use nonspecific defenses such as repression.

The analytic mode of perceiving that characterizes field-independent people facilitates performance on the Wechsler Picture Completion, Block Design, and Object Assembly subtests, and these tasks have been shown to load substantially on the same factor as the field-independent measures, namely, the Rod-and-frame test, Body-adjustment test, and Embedded Figures Test (Goodenough and Karp 1961; Karp 1963). In a study of the WPPSI, Block Design and Geometric Design loaded on a factor with the Preschool Embedded Figures Test (Coates

1975). Consequently, it is possible that sizable V > P discrepancies on the WISC-R may be indicative of a more pervasive field-dependent cognitive style, with P > V differences signifying field independence.

Hypotheses regarding this cognitive style may be checked out in a number of ways. First, the child's subtest profile should be scrutinized; the Picture Completion, Block Design, and Object Assembly scaled scores should cluster together and be substantially different (either higher or lower) than the mean of his or her other scaled scores, both nonverbal and verbal. Next, the Embedded Figures Test might be administered to get a purer measure of field independence, and other supplementary measures such as the Rorschach test also relate to this cognitive style (Witkin, Dyk, et al. 1974; Witkin, Moore, et al. 1977). Finally background information and behavioral observations pertaining to cognitive, social, and personal aspects of the child's functioning should be integrated and studied carefully to determine whether his or her pattern of behavior aligns closely with the "typical" pattern of field-dependent or field-independent individuals (Witkin, Moore, et al. 1977; Witkin and Goodenough 1977).

If a hypothesis relating to this cognitive style can be supported, examiners will have far more important information at their disposal than mere knowledge of a V−P discrepancy on the WISC-R. Witkin, Moore, et al. (1977) have enumerated many valuable educational implications and suggestions pertaining to field dependence that should aid the examiner in making practical recommendations for a child who is judged to fall near either extreme of the bipolar cognitive style. In addition, it is of interest to note that mentally retarded youngsters have consistently scored higher on the three field-independent Wechsler subtests than on Verbal Comprehension tasks (Kaufman and Van Hagen, 1977; Keogh and Hall 1974; Keogh, Wetter, et al. 1973; Silverstein 1968; Witkin, Faterson, et al. 1966), as have children with reading problems (Rugel 1974b). Since several of these studies were specifically investigating Bannatyne's (1971) grouping of WISC subtests (see pp. 73−74) or were not tied to any theoretical framework, the relationship of these exceptionalities to Witkin's field-dependent/field-independent framework is still largely speculative. Continued investigation of this cognitive style with exceptional populations is necessary to gain greater insight into the psychology and education of mentally retarded, reading-disabled, and other handicapped children. In addition, assessment of field dependence/field independence for different cultural groups is a fruitful avenue of research (Ramirez and Price-Williams 1974). The results of studies that have assessed Witkin's cognitive style for Mexican−American children are particularly provocative and are discussed in Chapter 5 (see pp. 155−156). Finally, better understanding of the relationship between field dependence/field independence and intelligence in children is needed (Cronbach 1970, p. 297; Riley and Denmark 1974), as is the relationship of the bipolar cognitive style to hemispheric specialization (Cohen, Berent, et al. 1973; Hoffman and Kagan 1974; Kaufman in press a).

Guilford's Operation of Evaluation

The Verbal and Performance Scales differ on yet another dimension—the degree to which they assess Guilford's operation of *evaluation*, the ability to make judgments in terms of a known standard (see Table 3–1). This mental process is required for success on all five regularly administered Performance subtests, but only on one Verbal subtest (Comprehension). Therefore, it is possible that some children obtain significant V–P discrepancies because of either very good or very poor evaluation ability, rather than because of differences between their Verbal Comprehension and Perceptual Organization skills. This hypothesis becomes a viable explanation of a significant V–P difference when two conditions are met: (a) there is very little variability in the Performance scaled scores, and (b) the Comprehension scaled score differs significantly from the mean of the child's Verbal scaled scores (see p. 55) and is consistent with the Performance scaled scores.

Whereas one cannot be sure that this pattern implies either a strength or weakness in evaluation, the likelihood should be considered since such a finding may have remedial implications (Meeker and Shadduck 1973). An examiner with a Guilford orientation may wish to follow up the evaluation hypothesis by administering tasks that are "purer" measures of this operation (each of the regular Performance subtests assesses evaluation along with one other operation). The SOI Learning Abilities Test (Meeker, Mestyanek, et al. 1975) should prove useful for this purpose. It would also be wise to conduct a more thorough SOI analysis, since the examiner may discover that Guilford's classification scheme is more beneficial than Wechsler's dichotomy for the individual in question (see pp. 71–73).

Interestingly, the results of several research investigations may be explainable from the Guilford model. In three studies of reading- or learning-disabled children, the mean Comprehension scaled score was substantially higher than the other Verbal subtest scores and more in line with the Performance scores (Anderson, Kaufman, et al. 1976; McManis, Figley, et al. 1978; Vance, Gaynor, et al. 1976). Furthermore, a factor analysis of the WISC-R for mentally retarded children revealed that the Comprehension subtest was the only Verbal task to load substantially on *both* the Verbal Comprehension and Perceptual Organization factors (Van Hagen and Kaufman 1975). These findings are conceivably related to the Guilford operation of evaluation, although any such inference must remain purely speculative pending the outcome of systematic empirical investigation.

Socioeconomic Influences

Part of the reason for a V−P discrepancy may stem from a child's socioeconomic background. Research has shown that children from professional families tend to score higher on the Verbal Scale, with the reverse holding true for the children of unskilled workers; this finding was observed both for the 1949 WISC (Seashore 1951) and the WISC-R (Kaufman, 1976c). Although there is considerable variability within each socioeconomic category, the trends are worthy of note since they suggest that a child's background experiences can help shape his or her relative skills in the verbal and nonverbal spheres. Recognition of this possibility should facilitate interpretation of V−P differences when they are in the predicted direction; awareness of the research findings enables the examiner to consider as noteworthy any significant V−P discrepancies that are opposite in direction to the typical findings for a child from a particular socioeconomic background.

When V–P IQ Differences are Meaningless

In the preceding portion of this chapter, numerous explanations for V−P discrepancies were offered. These explanations each focused on a way in which the scales differ and stressed that V−P IQ differences can have diverse meanings. In virtually all instances, however, the Verbal and Performance IQs were each presumed to correspond to reasonably unitary dimensions. Sometimes the dimension did not correspond to a cognitive ability, but instead was indicative of the impact of language background, motor coordination, or a personality variable such as anxiety; nevertheless, in each case the V−P difference told us something meaningful about the individual. In this section attention is given to instances where the V−P IQ discrepancy is meaningless or of limited value for interpretive purposes.

Intelligence Quotients Do Not Correspond to Factor Scores

The Verbal and Performance IQs are used as factor scores for Verbal Comprehension and Perceptual Organization, respectively, but as indicated elsewhere (pp. 22−23), the fit between IQ scale and factor is not perfect. Arithmetic does not really belong on the verbal factor, and Coding has no empirical support for inclusion on the perceptual dimension. Usually these slight incongruencies have little or no bearing on V−P interpretation, but the examiner has to be alert for the occasions when competent profile analysis rests on these differences. In the following table, consider the impact of Arithmetic on the V−P discrepancy shown in Example A and the role played by Coding in Example B.

Example A

Verbal	Scaled Score	Performance	Scaled Score
Information	12	Picture Completion	8
Similarities	9	Picture Arrangement	9
Arithmetic	5	Block Design	7
Vocabulary	13	Object Assembly	10
Comprehension	10	Coding	8

Verbal IQ = 98.   Performance IQ = 88.

Example B

Verbal	Scaled Score	Performance	Scaled Score
Information	7	Picture Completion	11
Similarities	10	Picture Arrangement	8
Arithmetic	8	Block Design	10
Vocabulary	11	Object Assembly	9
Comprehension	8	Coding	16

Verbal IQ = 92.   Performance IQ = 105.

In Example A the V−P discrepancy of 10 points is *not* significant at the 0.05 level, implying no real difference between the child's verbal and nonverbal abilities. However, Arithmetic pulled down the Verbal IQ substantially, rendering the Verbal IQ as an inaccurate estimate of the Verbal Comprehension factor score. When the scaled scores of only the four Verbal Comprehension subtests are averaged, the resulting percentile rank of 63 far outstrips the percentile rank of 31 for the four Perceptual Organization subtests administered. When factor scores are computed based on the four factor-related subtests in each scale (Sobotka and Black 1978, Table 1), one obtains a Verbal IQ equivalent of 106 and a Performance IQ equivalent of 89 yielding a significant 17-point discrepancy. Examiners are advised *not* to mention these prorated IQ equivalents in a case report because they will confuse rather than clarify, but they are obligated to point out that an individual really does have meaningful differences in his or her verbal and nonverbal abilities, despite a nonsignificant V−P IQ discrepancy.

Example B shows how a significant V−P difference of 13 points may exist even though the child actually has no difference between his or her Verbal Comprehension and Perceptual Organization skills. In this example Coding has inflated the Performance IQ, thereby overestimating the perceptual factor score. When only the four Perceptual Organization and four Verbal Comprehension subtests are considered, prorated IQ equivalents of 96 (Performance) and 94 (Verbal) are obtained; the 2-point discrepancy is trivial and nonsignificant. [Examiners may use Sobotka and Black's (1978) table or follow Wechsler's (1974) procedures for prorating to obtain the IQ equivalents which serve as factor scores.]

Sometimes Arithmetic and Coding may both deviate substantially from the mean of their respective scales, leading to more dramatic results. Consider Example C:

Example C

Verbal	Scaled Score	Performance	Scaled Score
Information	9	Picture Completion	14
Similarities	8	Picture Arrangement	12
Arithmetic	17	Block Design	15
Vocabulary	12	Object Assembly	11
Comprehension	11	Coding	4

Verbal IQ = 108.   Performance IQ = 108.

Here the Verbal IQ and Performance IQ are the same, suggesting equal functioning in the verbal and nonverbal spheres. However, Arithmetic elevates Verbal IQ while Coding depresses Performance IQ, creating the illusion of similar intellectual behavior. When prorated IQs are computed based on the factor-relevant subtests, a significant P > V discrepancy of 21 points is obtained (Performance IQ = 121, Verbal IQ = 100)—a strikingly different picture from the one portrayed by the original IQ comparison. Whereas extremely different performance on Arithmetic and Coding is not frequent (both subtests load together on the distractibility factor), it certainly does happen. Although more likely to occur with Coding A, which is not closely associated with the third factor, an extreme discrepancy with Arithmetic sometimes is observed for Coding B as well. It is important to remember that the Arithmetic and Coding subtests each assess a number of separate abilities, not just the shared abilities that cause them to load together on the third factor (see Chapter 4).

However, it should be noted that the procedure described here for inferring real verbal−nonverbal differences despite nonsignificant V−P IQ discrepancies cannot be applied indiscriminately or arbitrarily. If a child has a very deviant score in, say, Similarities or Block Design, the examiner generally has no right to decide not to count this score in the verbal or perceptual factor. Arithmetic and Coding are the only two subtests that have empirical support, from numerous factor-analytic investigations, to justify the technique for any child tested. Occasionally, the examiner may find good reason for using the procedure for a different subtest. For example, a black child may score very low on Comprehension and the examiner may infer from the child's responses and from knowledge of his or her background that subcultural differences largely accounted for the depressed scaled score. Or some children may score uncharacteristically high on Object Assembly and subsequently explain to the examiner that their hobby is putting together puzzles, of which they have a collection of over 100. In both of these instances, the examiner would have justification for eliminating the test in question when computing factor scores, since the factor scores are presumed to reflect an underlying verbal or nonverbal ability that transcends any particular task. However, without a well-supported rational justification, examiners would be just as wrong to eliminate a deviant subtest from factor score computation as they would be to call an 11-point V−P difference meaningful merely because "it's so close to being significant."

One method of avoiding some of the problems associated with the match-up between IQs and factor scores is to substitute Mazes for Coding when computing Performance IQ (Wechsler 1974, p. 8). This suggestion, which was also made earlier (p. 23), renders the Performance Scale congruent with the Perceptual Organization factor. Examiners who choose this permissible substitution would nevertheless be wise to administer all six Performance subtests because of the unique contributions Coding makes to the overall assessment procedure. (See discussion of *Coding* v. *Mazes* in Chapter 4.)

Verbal Compensation of Performance Deficit

Youngsters with exceptionally well-developed verbal skills can sometimes use their strength to compensate for relatively deficient nonverbal ability. Picture Completion and Picture Arrangement are two Performance subtests that frequently are influenced by good verbal skills; indeed, both have secondary loadings of about 0.30 on the Verbal Comprehension factor. Active use of verbal mediation facilitates the arrangement of pictures to tell a sensible story, and the use of verbal responses for Picture Completion can classify this task in the visual−vocal rather than visual−motor modality. Highly verbal children are sometimes observed to vocalize their problem-solving strategies and even to direct their hands to perform a series of movements during Block Design, Object Assembly, and Mazes. Such mediating processes may improve scaled scores on these subtests, although undue emphasis on verbalization can be costly in view of the speed component inherent in the tasks. Coding is less likely to be helped very much by compensatory efforts on the part of the verbally bright youngster.

A sample profile illustrative of verbal compensation is tabulated as follows:

Verbal	Scaled Score	Performance	Scaled Score
Information	15	Picture Completion	14
Similarities	13	Picture Arrangement	16
Arithmetic	12	Block Design	9
Vocabulary	13	Object Assembly	10
Comprehension	17	Coding	9

Verbal IQ = 124. Performance IQ = 111.

Even though a significant V > P discrepancy of 13 points is observed, the magnitude of the difference grossly underestimates the degree of verbal superiority that probably characterizes the above child. It would be inappropriate to compute any type of modified Perceptual Organization factor score for this youngster because of the fragmentation of the Performance Scale. Despite the inability to quantify the child's true verbal−nonverbal discrepancy, the hypothesis of spontaneous verbal compensation should be featured in the case report (if there is behavioral support to the hypothesis, such as vocalization while solving some problems), and tied in to educational plans that will take full advantage of this strength.

It would be most advisable for the examiner to test the limits after completing the WISC-R by administering nonverbal items under modified conditions to better understand the apparent strength. For example, the examiner can instruct the child to verbalize aloud when solving Block Design items if the child did not seem to make use of his or her verbal skills for that task, or the examiner can prohibit the child from vocalizing on Picture Arrangement items if he or she seemed too dependent on that compensatory technique. Any marked changes in problem-solving ability during the testing-the-limits session would give support to the verbal compensation hypothesis and would enhance the examiner's ability to make educational recommendations.

Also desirable would be the administration of supplementary nonverbal tasks under standard and adapted conditions to determine the facilitating effect of verbal ability on visual−motor performance. Some tasks that are especially facilitated by application of verbal skills are Raven's (1956, 1960) Progressive Matrices, Arthur's (1947) Stencil Design, and the Visual Association subtest in the ITPA (Kirk, McCarthy, et al. 1968). Tests that emphasize visual−motor coordination and are usually less amenable to verbal compensation, such as the Bender−Gestalt test or the Motor Speed and Precision subtest in the Detroit Tests of Learning Aptitude (Baker and Leland, 1967), are also worthy supplements. Since the typical kind of profile for a child using verbal compensation during the Performance Scale may be identical to the profile of a youngster with motor coordination problems (see pp. 35–37), it is essential that behavioral observations made during the WISC-R and that scores and observations based on supplementary measures be used as corroborating evidence.

Scatter in Profile

Whenever there is considerable scatter in the WISC-R scaled-score profile within the Verbal and/or Performance Scales (see Chapter 6), the V–P discrepancy often becomes meaningless. Scatter among the Verbal subtest scores means that the child's overall Verbal Comprehension ability was not primarily responsible for his or her scaled scores on the Verbal subtests, but that other variables loomed more important; hence the Verbal IQ represents an overview of a few diverse abilities or traits and does not correspond to a unitary entity. The same logic applies to scatter on the Performance Scale. If either of the scales does not reflect a reasonably unitary ability, the V–P IQ discrepancy for the youngster may not be a very meaningful concept. Keogh and Hall (1974), for example, pointed out that the lack of significant V–P differences in the WISC profiles of the mentally retarded children they studied masked the significantly higher scores these youngsters obtained on the Analytic Field Approach factor (composed of the three field-independent subtests) than on Verbal Comprehension.

Whenever the examiner speculates that the V–P dichotomy is inefficient for understanding a given child's profile, some reorganization of the subtests is needed. One type of regrouping has already been discussed (pp. 43–46): the elimination of Arithmetic and Coding from their respective scales, based on the empirical results of factor analysis, to create a better correspondence between the Verbal and Performance IQs and the factors they represent. Other regroupings may come from Meeker's (1969, 1975b) application of Guilford's structure of intellect model or Bannatyne's (1971, 1974) category system, both of which are described in Chapter 3 and applied to profile interpretation in Chapters 5 and 6. In addition, numerous other supplementary explanations may make sense out of a profile filled with scatter if one of the more "established" reorganizations of Wechsler's subtests does not tie the loose ends together. Most of these potential explanations come from a thorough understanding of what each subtest measures (Chapter 4), coupled with systematic and energetic detective work (Chapters 5 and 6).

Effects of Retesting

It is not uncommon for a child to be tested on the WISC-R and then to be retested within a few months. Second testing sessions are arranged when the child scores lower than the examiner might have anticipated, when mitigating circumstances are subsequently discovered (such as the recent divorce of his or her parents) that may have influenced the child's test performance, when the initial scores are challenged by a parent or teacher, and so forth. In clinics a child is occasionally tested on the WISC-R, despite being given the same test fairly recently. The child referred to the clinic may have been tested by a school psychologist, but the results may not be available or complete. To benefit from clinical observations of the child's test performance, the psychologist in the clinic may wish to retest a youngster even if the first record form is available, or the psychologists may discover, to their surprise, that the child was recently given the WISC-R based on the innocent statement during Object Assembly, "I can't wait until we get to the car puzzle."

Whenever children are retested on the WISC-R after one or several months, their V−P discrepancy and Full Scale IQ obtained on the second administration are suspect. All children within the entire age range covered by the WISC-R may be expected to gain about 7 points in their Full Scale IQ on a retest after a month has elapsed (Wechsler 1974, pp. 29−33). However, this gain—which occurs despite the lack of feedback regarding correct responses—is not divided evenly across the Verbal and Performance Scales. Rather, the gain is 3½ points in Verbal IQ and a striking 9½ points in Performance IQ. [Similar results were obtained for the 1949 WISC; see Zimmerman and Woo-Sam (1972).] Thus a child may be expected to achieve a relative gain of 6 points on the Performance Scale, compared to the Verbal Scale, merely by taking the WISC-R for a second time. A gain of this magnitude can convert a trivial discrepancy in favor of Performance IQ into a significant difference or a barely significant P > V discrepancy into a substantial one, and it can totally mask a legitimate V > P discrepancy.

Probably the larger gain in Performance IQ relates to the relative familiarity of the tasks. School-age children are quite used to a barrage of questions closely similar to Verbal items, but they are not usually asked to rapidly assemble blocks to match a design or to tell a story with pictures. The experience gained with the use of the concrete test materials probably leads to the increase in scores of Performance subtests, rather than recall of specific items; the only exception to this generalization may involve the Object Assembly puzzles.

It is difficult to interpret V−P discrepancies, as well as Full Scale IQ, when a retest is given a few months after the initial battery. An average gain of 7 points on the Full Scale may mean 1 point or 13 points when a reasonable amount of error is considered, and similar bands of error surround the gains for Verbal and Performance IQ. When feasible, a different retest instrument such as the Stanford−Binet or the McCarthy Scales of Children's Abilities (McCarthy 1972) should be administered. If the WISC-R is given, the best solution to the practice−effect problem is cautious interpretation, highlighted by not placing undue stress on the specific Full Scale IQ obtained or on the precise magnitude of the V−P discrepancy. A V > P discrepancy that is almost significant should be considered as probably reflecting a meaningful difference, and a P > V discrepancy that is barely significant should be ignored. When large P > V discrepancies are found, the hypothesis that the magnitude is partly due to retesting must remain viable. Supplementary administration of other well-normed nonverbal tests that differ in content from Wechsler's subtests is advised.

When determining the child's overall level of performance on the WISC-R, both the original and new set of scores should be examined (if the old scores are available). If the current scores are higher than the first scores by the expected margin (up to about 12 points on the Full Scale), the gains are probably due primarily to the retest factor, and the original scores should be interpreted as the valid estimates of mental functioning. If the latest scores are substantially higher than the previous values, it might be wise to take the *average* of corresponding IQs and scaled scores on the two administrations for the most accurate guess as to the child's true performance. The main exception to the latter rule is when the examiner feels reasonably certain that the first set of scores is predominantly invalid. In such cases, which may occur when the examiner is aware of an important external variable that interfered with performance or when the second set of scores is very much (say, 30 IQ points) higher than the first set, the examiner should simply ignore the first testing.

A word of warning applies to the situation where a child is retested because of surprisingly low scores the first time. In that instance, the retest effect along with the statistical phenomenon of regression to the mean will jointly serve to inflate the second profile of scores; under such circumstances, extreme caution in interpreting gains is needed.

Normal or Expected V–P Discrepancies

Statistical criteria, based on the standard error of measurement of the difference between IQs on the Verbal and Performance Scales, have been provided by Wechsler (1974, p. 35) to help the examiner identify significant V−P discrepancies. The values required for significance, as stated earlier (p. 24), are 9 points ($p < 0.15$), 12 points ($p < 0.05$), and 15 points ($p < 0.01$). When examiners use these values they determine whether any particular discrepancy is "real," as opposed to purely a function of chance error; the level of significance chosen merely translates to the amount of confidence that can be placed in the conclusion that a child's Verbal and Performance IQs are really different (e.g., $p < 0.05$ means 95% confidence). The issue of significance, however, says nothing about the *frequency* with which discrepancies of various magnitudes occur within the normal population. Yet the degree to which an individual's discrepancy is common or rare, compared to others of his or her approximate ability level and background, has important interpretive significance.

Analysis of standardization data (Kaufman 1976c) revealed that the average

WISC-R discrepancy (regardless of direction) was 9.7 IQ points [standard deviation (SD) =7.6] for all children aged 6—16 years. The mean discrepancy was about 9—10 points for all age groups, with no age trends evident, and did not differ significantly by race (9.8 for whites vs. 9.1 for blacks) or sex (9.8 for males vs. 9.6 for females). Differences were fairly substantial, however, for the variables of parental occupation and Full Scale IQ. Children of unskilled laborers averaged a discrepancy of about 9 points between their Verbal and Performance IQs, as contrasted with a discrepancy of almost 11 points for children of professionals. Similarly, youngsters with Full Scale IQs below 80 obtained a mean V−P difference of 8 points compared with a discrepancy of close to 11 points for the higher-scoring children.

For most subgroups studied, significant V > P discrepancies were as common as P > V discrepancies. The only exception concerned parental occupation where children of unskilled workers tended to be more "performance minded," whereas the reverse was true for children of professionals (see p. 43). When significant P > V and V > P differences are combined, standardization data revealed that one out of two normal children had a significant ($p < 0.15$) discrepancy of 9 points, one out of three had 12-point discrepancies ($p < 0.05$), and one out of four had 15-point discrepancies ($p < 0.01$). Thus about 25% of *normal* children had V−P discrepancies of a magnitude that Wechsler (1974, p. 34) says "is important and calls for further investigation."

Verbal−Performance discrepancies on the 1949 WISC (Seashore 1951) were virtually identical to the findings for the WISC-R, and the magnitude of the discrepancies is comparable as well for both the WPPSI (Fairweather and Butterworth 1977; Sattler 1974, p. 451) and the Wechsler Adult Intelligence Scale (WAIS) (Matarazzo 1972, pp. 389—391). The WISC results were published by Seashore shortly after the test was available for clinical use, yet it seems that the findings were not internalized by very many clinicians or researchers. From personal contact, I have found numerous Wechsler examiners to be extremely surprised by the apparently large V−P discrepancies manifested by normal youngsters. The common use of a significant V−P discrepancy as an important piece of evidence for diagnosing an individual as learning disabled emphasizes the basic unawareness of test users regarding the frequency of significant V−P discrepancies within the normal population. How can a difference of 15 points, which is *normal* in the sense that one out of four youngsters displays a difference at least that large, be used to help confirm an *abnormal* diagnosis? Significant discrepancies certainly imply different functioning on the two scales and thus are valuable for helping the examiner make meaningful recommendations for the child's educational planning. But V−P differences that are fairly common in the normal population should *not* be used to diagnose abnormality.

Whether sizable V−P IQ fluctuations are even characteristic of learning-disabled children remains to be seen. In one study, learning-disabled youngsters had V−P discrepancies (regardless of direction) that were significantly larger than the average discrepancy for normal youngsters (Anderson, Kaufman, et al. 1976). However, the distributions of discrepancies for the exceptional sample overlapped greatly with the distribution for normal youngsters, and even though the study yielded differences that were *statistically* significant, the magnitude was not sufficient to be meaningful. The mean V−P discrepancy of the learning-disabled sample was only about 3 points higher than the normal discrepancy and was not large enough to be unusual in terms of its occurrence. Additional research is needed to determine whether large V−P IQ discrepancies really do characterize learning-disabled children when compared to normal children, or whether this clinical assumption was made without awareness of the fluctuations in normal profiles.

Typically, a child is administered a Wechsler test because of a suspected abnormality—whether it is emotional, behavioral, cognitive, developmental, or otherwise. Normal profiles are rarely seen or studied, and thus it is easy for a clinician or researcher to assume that observed fluctuations and patterns are in some way characteristic of the abnormal population under investigation. Primarily to help test users keep a proper perspective when interpreting the WISC-R of a child referred for evaluation, Table 2−1 is presented. This table provides a base rate of V−P discrepancies (just as do Tables 6−5 and 6−6 for subtest scatter), thereby enabling examiners to determine how unusual or abnormal any particular V−P IQ discrepancy may be. When a V−P difference is significant, examiners have a basis for making remedial suggestions; when it is both significant *and* abnormal (i.e., occuring infrequently in the normal population), they also may have a basis for interpreting this test information in the context of other test scores and clinical evidence to reach a diagnostic hypothesis.

Table 2−1 shows the percentage of children in the standardization sample who had a V−P discrepancy of a given magnitude or larger, regardless of the direction of the difference. Entering the column labeled "total sample," one reads the number 34 in the row denoting a V−P discrepancy of 12 points. This should be interpreted to mean that 34% of normal youngsters obtained V−P discrepancies of 12 points or more. Since the average discrepancy was found to be different for children from various socioeconomic categories, Table 2−1 also shows separate distributions for different parental occupations. In the article on V−P discrepancies (Kaufman 1976c), I reported separate distributions for different Full Scale IQ categories. In view of Mercer's popularization of the important concepts of pluralistic norms and sociocultural modality (Mercer 1973; Mercer and Lewis 1978), it makes more sense to me now to give separate "norms" by parental occupation. Either the separate occupational distributions or the overall distribution for the total sample may be used for any given child, depending on the examiner's preference. When parental occupation is unknown, the examiners may make their best guess at the child's socioeconomic background or else simply rely on the data for the total sample. Note that only discrepancies of 9 points and above are included in Table 2−1. Smaller discrepancies, which are not significant by any reasonable standard and thus reflect chance fluctuations, have no interpretive value; the test user who is curious about the complete frequency distribution for V−P discrepancies should consult Kaufman (1976c).

According to Table 2−1, V−P discrepancies of at least 18−19 points occur for about 15% of the normal population, with discrepancies of 21, 25, and 27−30 points occurring for approximately 10%, 5%, and 2% of the population, respectively. The decision as to how rare constitutes "abnormal" rests with the individual examiner, who also has to interpret the frequency of occurrence in the context of what the V−P discrepancy means for a given child, and whether the V−P IQ difference corresponds to a meaningful aspect of a youngster's functioning.

SIGNIFICANT FLUCTUATIONS WITHIN THE VERBAL AND PERFORMANCE SCALES

The WISC-R factor structure provides empirical support for interpreting V−P IQ differences, and it also suggests a rationale for investigating fluctuations in the scaled-score profile. Interpretation of a profile may be thought of as an experiment with $n = 1$. The null hypotheses for this experiment derive from the results of factor analysis. The robust, pervasive Verbal Comprehension factor, which closely resembles the Verbal Scale, implies that the ability underlying this factor is likely to be the major determinant of a child's performance on any Verbal subtest. The resilient Perceptual Organization or Performance factor likewise leads to the reasonable assumption that a child's score on any Performance subtest is primarily a function of his or her global nonverbal skill.

The null hypotheses used to evaluate experimentally the fluctuations in a child's WISC-R profile are as follows:

H_0: Children's global Verbal Comprehension ability determines their scores on all Verbal subtests; therefore, all fluctuations in their scaled scores are due to *chance error*.

H_0: Children's global Perceptual Organization ability determines their scores on all Performance subtests; therefore, all fluctuations in their Performance scaled scores are due to *chance error*.

Working from this experimental perspective, determining the meaningfulness of fluctuations in a child's WISC-R profile becomes an easy and straightforward clerical exercise. The examiner's task is to discover whether each Verbal scaled score differs significantly from the mean of the child's Verbal scaled scores, and whether each Performance scaled score differs significantly from his or her

Performance mean. (The mean Verbal scaled score and the mean Performance scaled score serve as convenient estimates of the child's Verbal Comprehension and Perceptual Organization ability, respectively.) Each time a significant deviation between a Verbal or Performance scaled score and the appropriate mean is obtained, a "subhypothesis" is rejected. These significant fluctuations represent relative strengths and weaknesses for the individual and serve as starting points for developing alternative hypotheses for interpreting the WISC-R profile. Two or three significantly deviating Verbal subtest scores are usually sufficient grounds for rejecting the first null hypothesis and for beginning the detective work necessary to generate new hypotheses (see Chapters 5 and 6). A similar rule of thumb applies to the Performance Scale regarding the rejection of the second null hypothesis. When only an occasional Verbal or Performance scaled score deviates significantly from its mean, the null hypotheses cannot be rejected, and the Verbal Comprehension–Perceptual Organization dichotomy serves as the primary explanation of the youngster's WISC-R profile.

The Method

Davis (1959) developed a valuable set of formulas regarding differences between averages and individual test scores. One of these formulas, which Sattler (1974) revived, is particularly useful for testing Verbal and Performance null hypotheses and has been used to construct Table 2–2. This table, based on data for the entire standardization sample, shows the magnitude of the discrepancy between a single scaled score and the average of the Verbal or Performance scaled scores required for statistical significance.

I believe that the 5% level of significance is quite adequate for investigating the WISC-R profile, although the 1% level is also provided in Table 2–2 for the interested test user. Furthermore, I would encourage examiners to use a constant difference of ±3 points from the child's Verbal or Performance mean scaled score to determine the significance of the deviation of *any* subtest. The differences required for significance converge around 3 points (range: 2.3–3.3), making ±3 a sensible choice. My main reasons for advocating the use of a constant 3-point deviation for all subtests is to reduce the examiner's dependency on a table in a book and eliminate extra clerical work. The significant discrepancy of 3 points is easily internalized by examiners and may then be applied routinely to every WISC-R profile they encounter. The steps to follow to investigate the null hypotheses, and thereby to determine significant strengths and weaknesses in the scaled-score profile, are listed as follows:

Step 1. Compute the mean scaled score of all Verbal subtests administered (five or six), and then do the same for all Performance subtests administered. Round each mean to the nearest whole number.

Table 2-2. Deviations Required for Significance When Comparing a Child's Scaled Score on One Subtest with His or Her Average Scaled Score on Related Subtests

Subtest	Deviation from Average of Six Verbal Subtests		Deviation from Average of Six Performance Subtests	
	$p < 0.05$	$p < 0.01$	$p < 0.05$	$p < 0.01$
Verbal				
Information	2.3	3.1	—	—
Similarities	2.6	3.4	—	—
Arithmetic	2.7	3.6	—	—
Vocabulary	2.3	3.0	—	—
Comprehension	2.7	3.6	—	—
Digit Span	2.8	3.7	—	—
Performance				
Picture Completion	—	—	2.8	3.7
Picture Arrangement	—	—	3.1	4.0
Block Design	—	—	2.3	3.0
Object Assembly	—	—	3.3	4.4
Coding	—	—	3.2	4.2
Mazes	—	—	3.3	4.4

Note: Values identical to those shown here for the six Verbal subtests should also be used when only five scaled scores are used to compute the average (Digit Span excluded). The same rule applies for the Performance Scale. In addition, the exact values in the table should be used to determine significant deviations from the average of all 12 subtests. [The values for 10 or 11 subtests are trivially smaller than the values shown here; see Sattler (1974, p. 560)].

Step 2. Examine the Verbal scaled scores and check off all values that are 3 or more points above the Verbal mean. These are significant *strengths* for the child and should be labeled with an "S." Then check off all values that are 3 or more points below the Verbal mean and label them "W" to signify *weaknesses*.

Step 3. Examine the Performance scaled scores and check off all values that are at least 3 points above or below the Performance mean. Label these significantly deviating scaled scores "S" and "W" to denote strengths and weaknesses, respectively.

Step 4. Treat all scaled scores that do not deviate significantly from the appropriate mean as chance fluctuations. They should not be interpreted as strengths or weaknesses per se but may be used to support hypotheses (see Chapter 6).

The method described here for WISC-R profile interpretation has several advantages to recommend it. Apart from being supported by the results of factor analysis, it permits the examiner to obtain an overview of the child's abilities. It does not depend on haphazard decisions about apparent peaks and valleys in the profile or on arbitrary comparisons of extreme scaled scores; rather, each scaled score is systematically compared to the child's own midpoint, with statistically significant differences used to determine meaningful fluctuations. Using the midpoint as the frame of reference also serves the function of assuring that strengths and weaknesses will be relative to the child's own level of ability on each scale. This type of ipsative measurement forces the examiner out of a normative mold and paves the way for making meaningful recommendations.

The fairly common practice of using the *group* mean of 10 and the *group* standard deviation of 3 as the statistical bases for determining significant strengths and weaknesses (Flynn, Vitelli, et al. 1978) is antagonistic to individualized profile interpretation. Group parameters are useful when dealing with group data; individual mean scores serve better for individual profile interpretation. The use of 10 ± 3 to determine strengths and weaknesses leads to particularly one-sided views of the abilities of high-IQ and low-IQ children, with the former individuals emerging with few weaknesses and the latter with only an occasional strength. Yet a balanced spectrum of relatively good and poor skills is especially conducive to translation of test scores to educational suggestions. A normative referent is fine for computing the scaled scores and IQs and for interpreting some aspects of the global IQs; however, an ipsative referent, which employs each child as his or her own private norm, is ordinarily preferable for analyzing subtest fluctuations.

I also find little value in methods of interpretation that depend on tables showing significant differences between pairs of subtest scores, such as the ones presented by Wechsler (1974, p. 35) and expanded by Piotrowski and Grubb (1976). Pairwise comparisons are often made between the several extreme values that are evident in a profile rather than systematically or between predetermined pairs. Selecting the extremely high and low scores takes fortuitous advantage of chance errors, thereby distorting the meaning of the values required for significance that are reported in the tables.

Apart from this statistical consideration, evaluating the significance of the difference between pairs of scaled scores fails to give the kind of crisp overview that is obtained by using the child's own mean as the yardstick of comparison. Rather, the pairwise method yields a series of separate statements about the child's abilities that are not integrated and sometimes require a competent logician to convert to a meaningful overview of the profile. Furthermore, focusing on the separate subtest scores as important entities by themselves does not take advantage of the empirical results of factor analysis that emphasize the primacy of the global verbal and nonverbal abilities in profile interpretation. Hypotheses about the unique abilities presumably measured by each subtest should be secondary to global hypotheses involving the role of Verbal Comprehension and Perceptual Organization in determining a child's scaled scores. Yet the use of the pairwise comparisons usually puts the uniqueness of each subtest in the foreground and, in effect, puts the cart before the horse. Thus, even though the computation of significant differences between various pairs of scaled scores provides an ipsative view of the child's strengths and weaknesses, this technique may not offer the most insight into a child's WISC-R profile.

Illustration—Emily B., Age 8 Years

The following profile is used to illustrate the four-step procedure described in the preceding section for determining significant fluctuations in WISC-R profiles, and serves primarily to demonstrate the mechanics of the procedure. The detective work required to make interpretive sense out of the relative strengths and weaknesses is discussed in Chapter 6.

WISC-R Profile

Verbal	Scaled Score	Performance	Scaled Score
Information	11	Picture Completion	15-S
Similarities	7	Picture Arrangement	10
Arithmetic	9	Block Design	8-W
Vocabulary	8	Object Assembly	13
Comprehension	10	Coding	10
Digit Span	8		

Verbal sum of scaled scores = 45; Verbal IQ = 94.
Performance sum of scaled scores = 56; Performance IQ = 108.
Full Scale IQ = 100.

1. The mean of the Verbal subtests is based on all six subtests administered. Adding the scaled score of Digit Span to the Verbal sum of scaled scores, a total of 53 is obtained; dividing by 6, the mean equals 8.8. Rounding to the nearest whole number yields a Verbal mean of 9.

   Since Mazes was not administered, the Performance mean equals the average of the scaled scores on the five regular tasks. Dividing the Performance sum of scaled scores by 5, a mean of 11.2 is obtained, which rounds to 11.

2. Looking at the separate scaled scores on the Verbal subtests, it is apparent that all values are ±2 points from the mean of 9. Therefore, Emily evidenced no relative strengths or weaknesses on the Verbal Scale. The

null hypothesis cannot be rejected; her Verbal Comprehension ability seems to account for her performance in all verbal areas measured, and the minor fluctuations may be attributed solely to chance error.

3. The story is different on the Performance Scale. Emily's scaled scores of 15 on Picture Completion and 8 on Block Design are significantly($\geqslant 3$ points) different from her Performance mean of 11, suggesting that the second null hypothesis should be rejected. Alternative hypotheses are needed to explain her strength on Picture Completion and weakness on Block Design.

4. Despite the fact that Emily's scaled scores on Information and Comprehension are *each* significantly greater than her scaled score on Similarities (Wechsler 1974, p. 35), these findings are treated as artifacts. Based on the technique presented here, the extreme values merely represent chance deviations from the Verbal mean; individual subtest interpretation is discouraged.

In the Performance profile, the apparent peak in Object Assembly is ignored because it does not reach statistical significance. (Actually, even if it were significant, it would be of limited meaning by itself because of insufficient subtest specificity—see pp. 111–115.) However, the score of 13 in Object Assembly offers insight into the explanation for the strength in Picture Completion. Taken together, these subtests require the Gestalt-type ability that characterizes right-brain processing, and they require extremely little verbalization by the examiner to communicate the tasks. Hence, although not a strength in itself, the Object Assembly scaled score pairs up well with the observed strength to help explain Emily's strong ability. Had she scored, say, 9 or 10 on Object Assembly, a different hypothesis for her high score in Picture Completion would have to be entertained. Chapter 6 further explicates this type of detective work.

The fact that Digit Span and Arithmetic did not deviate significantly from the Verbal mean does not necessarily mean that Emily's Verbal Comprehension ability accounted for her performance on these subtests; similarly, her Perceptual Organization skill cannot necessarily explain her Coding score. Since these subtests are primarily associated with the third WISC-R factor, it is possible that the trait measured by that factor was responsible for her performance on the three subtests. One cannot be sure which factor was more influential on her performance, but it really does not matter in view of her consistency. It is primarily when one or more of these three subtests deviates significantly from their respective means that the examiner should investigate the third factor (see pp. 74–78).

This example not only shows the mechanics of the stepwise method of determining significant strengths and weaknesses, but it also indicates the value of using separate referents for the Verbal and Performance subtests. Emily earned a significant V–P IQ discrepancy of 14 points, suggesting differential functioning in the verbal and nonverbal areas. If her Full Scale IQ had been used as the midpoint of her performance, the 8 she obtained in Block Design (which is of the same order of magnitude as her Verbal scaled scores) would have been masked as a relative weakness.

ILLUSTRATIVE CASE REPORTS

The two actual case reports that follow (both with fictitious names) were selected because they illustrate some of the points expressed in this chapter concerning interpretation of the IQs, particularly discrepancies between the Verbal and Performance IQs. David S., a white boy of about 7½, was referred to a clinic for evaluation primarily because of hyperactive behavior at home. Although the discrepancy between his Verbal and Performance IQs was not statistically significant at the 5% level, the report shows how a behavioral variable may have hidden real differences between his verbal and nonverbal intelligence. The case report for Jose B., a Chicano boy nearly 10 years of age, reveals the typical P > V profile found for many bilingual youngsters and shows one approach to interpreting such a profile. (Note that no Full Scale IQ is computed for Jose, a practice suggested on p. 33 for bilingual children from a Spanish background.) Like all of the case reports appearing throughout this book, the reports on David and Jose stress integration of background information, behavioral observations, and other test scores with the obtained WISC-R scores to properly interpret the intelligence-test data. Note that Mazes, rather than Coding, was used to compute David's Performance IQ. This decision, which was made *before* administering the battery, was based primarily on Wechsler's (1974, p. 8) suggestion that Mazes be used for children below 8 years of age because it is more reliable than Coding at the younger age levels.

David S., White Male, Age 7 Years 8 Months

WISC-R Profile

Verbal	Scaled Score	Performance	Scaled Score
Information	12	Picture Completion	14
Similarities	11	Picture Arrangement	14
Arithmetic	17-S	Block Design	14
Vocabulary	8-W	Object Assembly	12
Comprehension	12	Mazes	11
(Digit Span)	16-S	(Coding)	9-W

Verbal IQ = 112. Performance IQ = 121. Full Scale IQ = 118.

Referral and Background Information

David was referred for evaluation by his mother through the advice of his pediatrician. Both parents are actively involved in seeking help for their son and report numerous high-priority problems with him at home. Of greatest concern to them is his hyperactive behavior, where David is described as being unable to sit still or concentrate. Accompanying his arm waving and foot stomping are his demands for excessive attention, his forgetfulness, resistance to directions and structure, low frustration tolerance, and manipulative behavior.

Developmental milestones for David have occurred rather slowly, and his medical history includes hospitalization at age 2 for a bad fall on his head. At the age of 3½ his mother was hospitalized for 3 weeks for injuries suffered in a car accident, and she feels this was a traumatic event for David, who was confused and withdrawn at the time of her return.

At home with his parents, 5½ year-old sister, and 1½-year-old brother, David joins his family in daily activities. Mrs. S. works at a local factory on an assembly line. In school, David is in the second grade, and his mother describes him as curious and eager to learn new things.

Appearance and Behavioral Characteristics

Slim and tall for his 7 years 8 months, David has long blond hair that covers up his brown eyes and handsome face whenever he bends his head down. Because he wrote in this position consistently (with his head nearly touching the paper), the possibility of a visual problem needs checking. David's hands and fingernails were very dirty. Whereas he was eager to begin working with the examiner, this eagerness did not compare with the stimulated, excited emotional state he displayed whenever he was in his father's physical presence. He talked rapidly and animatedly to his father both prior to the separation for testing and on his return to his waiting father at the close of the evaluation. Here he pulled his father back to the testing room with him and grabbed the various drawings and record forms the examiner had safely tucked away. This appeared as an effort on David's part to please his father, and he showed off with special delight his portrayal of Mr. S. "drinking beer." During the actual evaluation, however, David was totally cooperative, pleasant to work with, and contributed much to the personal interaction and conversation. He responded with obvious comfort to the structure of the situation, and he worked meticulously and methodically on all tasks.

During the drawing tests David demonstrated an incredible degree of compulsive behavior, so much so that on one task he had to be stopped and ultimately asked to just draw stick figures so that the projective content rather than the motor act could be focused on. When copying abstract designs, he counted dots and circles over and over again, erased repeatedly, expressed great dissatisfaction with his every pencil line, pressed so hard with his pencil that the point broke twice, and used his finger to keep his place on the stimulus card—even when no counting was possible. In all, he evidenced his inability to meet his own high standards and took a significantly long time to complete all drawing tasks. This emotional attitude was reflected in other tests as well, where he worked slowly and gave further evidence of his compulsive tendencies. On nonverbal tasks in the WISC-R he failed some puzzles and block designs because of overattention to the exact alignment of the pieces, and he checked and rechecked his work on a highly speeded clerical test of psychomotor ability. In addition, his pressing need led him to instances of manipulative behavior. For example, when trying to define the word "alphabet," David slowly started calling off each letter. When he finally reached "P," the examiner wrote "etc." on the record form. At this David became enraged, and even when explained what "etc." means and why it was written, he insisted that his "letters" be copied to the end. David was extremely aware of the examiner's marks on the record form and revealed a high level of anxiety over his test performance. Frequently, he asked if he was right, or stated "I hope I get it right; I sure don't know if I can." It should be noted that David was fully able to read the examiner's hastily written cursive writing and watched closely to make sure all i's were dotted, and so on. He soon "caught on" that the initials "DK" stood for "don't know" and subsequently revealed his sense of humor by reciting the abbreviation "DK" when responding to items he couldn't figure out.

Some restlessness on David's part was observed, as he leaned his body over the table during verbal activities, and worked standing up on most nonverbal tasks employing concrete materials. In general he was able to think quickly but act slowly, requiring little trial-and-error learning and appearing greatly organized. He responded with keen alertness to the examiner's facial expressions and other subtle cues that affected his behavior. David demonstrated both verbal and nonverbal creativity, as there was evidence of fluency and elaboration in many of his responses. For example, he included the wrinkles in Santa Claus's brow on one detailed drawing, and when defining the word "nail," he said "it's sharp, pointed, has a flat head, you can hammer it in wood."

Tests Administered

WISC-R
Bender−Gestalt
Draw-A-Man
Kinetic Family Drawing
Sentence Completion

Test Results and Interpretation

David scored at a High Average (Bright) to Superior level of intellectual functioning on the WISC-R, obtaining a Verbal IQ of 112, Performance IQ of 121, and Full Scale IQ of 118. Scoring better than 88% of the children his age on the

Full Scale, his true IQ is likely (90% chance) to be in the 113–123 range. Although the 9-point difference in favor of David's Performance IQ is not statistically significant, it is reasonable to conclude that he expresses his intellectual ability better when manipulating concrete materials than when responding vocally to verbal items. His compulsive behavior certainly renders his Performance IQ as an underestimate of his nonverbal intelligence in view of his quick thinking and good organizational skills on the speeded Performance tasks. Conversely, his Verbal IQ may be a slight overestimate of his verbal intelligence since his elaborations and strings of responses to some items earned him extra points on the untimed verbal tasks.

Within the Verbal sphere David demonstrated remarkable skill in two tasks involving numbers. He scored at the 99th percentile in a test of his arithmetic problem-solving ability, indicating an impressive level of numerical reasoning and computational skills for a second-grade child. In addition, he achieved the 98th percentile in a task requiring him to repeat digits both forward and backward. He was exceptionally adept at repeating digits backward which is consistent with his facility with numbers. Furthermore, high performance on tests of short-term memory and oral arithmetic demand exceptional attention and concentration—attributes that he demonstrated throughout the evaluation. Ironically, one of David's main presenting symptoms was his difficulty with concentrating, his short attention span, and distractibility. In marked contrast, David surpassed only 25% of children his age on a test of his oral vocabulary. His limited word knowledge was sufficiently pervasive to be noted during tasks on which he did well, as he had a hard time understanding some of the wording in the questions he was asked. A relative deficiency in word knowledge is surprising since this test tends to correlate very highly with general intelligence. However, more information is needed about David's academic achievement and outside reading habits before any hypotheses can be generated.

Unlike the scatter that highlighted the Verbal Scale, his test scores on the Performance Scale were fairly consistent. David's excellent nonverbal functioning was evidenced in virtually all of the separate tasks, suggesting well-developed nonverbal reasoning, visual–motor coordination, and understanding of spatial relationships. He evidenced a single relative weakness (37th percentile) on a psychomotor task requiring him to rapidly copy simple figures associated with different shapes. His compulsive behavior was probably responsible for his weakness since perfectionism is particularly damaging to performance on this highly speeded clerical task.

David earned a Koppitz error score of 4 on the Bender–Gestalt. This is within the average range of performance for children his age, and it is roughly equivalent to an 8-year-old level of visual-motor development. Whereas David did much erasing and used heavy lines to redraw parts of some designs, this was not done impulsively nor with any show of aggression. Instead, it was an aspect of his already described perfectionistic attitude, and frustration over his feelings of inadequate performance.

The human figure David produced for the Draw-A-Man Test was a detailed version of Santa Claus, equipped with his complete costume, beard, mustache, pot belly, and wrinkled forehead. The figure earned a Goodenough—Harris Standard Score of 123, which is fully commensurate with his WISC-R performance. It was perfectly reasonable for David to be thinking about the coming Christmas holidays, and thus his decision to draw Santa merely reflected this.

It was on the Kinetic Family Drawing that David grew so extraordinarily compulsive, and after 15 minutes of his working on, erasing, and redrawing the head of his mother, the examiner suggested that he use stick-figure representations to free him to concentrate on the more projectively useful information of what each family member was busy doing. Beginning with his mother washing dishes, he drew his father holding a beer can, then himself holding a football, his brother holding a baby rattle, and finally his sister holding her doll. Thus arms figure prominently in this picture, perhaps taking on their importance as aids in controlling one's environment. Incidentally, although David was prevented from continuing in his nonproductive style of drawing, he still demonstrated the same superneed for structure as he made sure the examiner knew the father was drinking "Schlitz" beer, that he drew himself "without his helmet," and still lingered unhappily erasing as he commented "My foot a little longer; my sister's body a little shorter," and so on. David drew himself, his mother, and his siblings all in profile, but he made his father a front-face view. Perhaps David feels that his father is more open in his dealings with him, and is subtly representing this. There were no displays of either competition or interaction between family members.

The Sentence Completion test to which David responded revealed many of his already noted personality variables. His need for structure (for which a sentence-completion test is specifically useful) is observed by the security he derives from routines and schedules: When I go to bed "I feel cozy; I snuggle up." He also gains structural satisfaction from his school successes; he sets high goals for himself but gains stability from following the necessary academic steps to reach them. David apparently experiences a good relationship with his mother, as she figured in positive statements most frequently, even rather open-ended ones (e.g., I "love my mother."). His compliant attitude toward her indicates his internalization of her wishes for his appropriate behavior; he wants to conform to her expectations. David's desire for a gun is closely associated with his masculine identification (and especially with his father), as he sees it as an artifact of manhood. His whole view of "big boys" is one of roughness and aggressive behavior, and this is what he is shaping himself for. He verbalized with pride his own ability to fight, telling how he "gives 'em one," that he can "give 'em something to eat—my fist in their mouth." David's association of socially aggressive behavior with being grown up and manly needs diversion into more socially acceptable patterns of behavior before he painfully realizes its negative consequences.

Of immediate concern is David's poor relationship with his 5½-year-old sister. Whereas he is aware of his negative behavior toward her, he is unable to control his resentment and its subsequent release. When questioned on one of his hostile responses about her, David simply said "let's go on" and refused to talk further on this issue.

Summary and Recommendations

A 7½-year-old boy referred for evaluation due to parent-described hyperactivity and its syndrome-associated symptoms, David was amazingly able to attend without distraction for long periods of time and to sit still and cooperatively concentrate on all work tasks placed before him in the current evaluation. Virtually none of the behavioral difficulties ascribed to him were revealed during the lengthy testing session, although extreme need for structure and a compulsive desire for perfection and routine characterized his behavior. David was very anxious to do well. Whereas he was a quick thinker, he moved in a slow, methodical style, perhaps guided by caution.

David's IQ of 118 (High Average) revealed an extraordinary strength in number ability. His visual–motor development and nonverbal reasoning were better developed than his verbal comprehension skills, and projective techniques again underscored his need for structure and rigidity.

A bright and handsome boy, David certainly displayed his potential for socially acceptable behavior. The compulsiveness he demonstrated was concerning; clearly, David is attempting to regulate his behavior by carefully structuring his actions and by following rigid routine. This requires time and deliberate effort on his part, which might be put to better use. In view of his parents' description of the high-priority problems at home, David's compulsiveness may suggest the presence of underlying difficulties with impulse control. If so, he is relying too heavily on this defense. David could use more appropriate male peer models to open other pathways toward proving himself a worthy and independent person. His association of aggressive behavior as representative of the epitome of male-approved society will need guidance to engage more mature ways of dealing with one's needs and with others.

David's relationship with his family members could use exploring. He has expressed hostile feelings toward his sister, yet he is unable to explain this or to cope with it constructively. It would also be fruitful to review his family's lifestyle to search out why David is responding negatively at home, and yet possesses the potential ability to behave desirably elsewhere. Parent counseling is recommended to foster understanding by Mr. and Mrs. S. of their son's particular personality needs for structure and routines. His rigidity and inflexible adaptation to changing demands and stimuli must increase David's undesirable behavior. The examiner's brief glance at the way David relates to his father gave some insight into the family's role as catalyst in producing his "hyperstimulatable" way of interacting with them, and the energy this creates.

A visual examination is advised to determine if there are any acuity problems.

Nadeen L. Kaufman
Psychologist

Jose B., Chicano Male, Age 9 years 11 months

WISC-R Profile

Verbal	Scaled Score	Performance	Scaled Score
Information	7	Picture Completion	16-S
Similarities	5-W	Picture Arrangement	10
Arithmetic	11-S	Block Design	12
Vocabulary	6	Object Assembly	12
Comprehension	11-S	Coding	10
Digit Span	8	Mazes	13

Verbal IQ = 87.   Performance IQ = 114.

Referral and Background Information

Jose was referred for evaluation by his school because of inability to get along with his classmates and his disobedience to adults. In school, where Jose is repeating third grade, he is experiencing reading difficulties, and he stutters when tense and anxious. There are problems at home, too, where he lives with both parents (of Mexican descent), two younger sisters aged 7 and 4, and twin brothers aged 1½. He fights constantly with his sisters, especially the 7-year-old, and is described by his mother as selfish, jealous, and possessive. Although English is the predominant language spoken at home, Jose has been taught both Spanish and English throughout his childhood and speaks fluently in both languages. Family life is very structured and routinized; his father is strict and unaffectionate but is willing to spend much time with Jose. Both Jose and his father have many similarities, including a good ability to work with their hands and poor ability in academic-oriented activities. Help with his homework is forced on Jose, creating daily tension for all parties.

Appearance and Behavioral Characteristics

Just 5 days short of his 10th birthday, Jose is physically well developed and very handsome, with his black hair and large black eyes reflecting his Mexican heritage. He entered the building alone and appeared quite mature and capable, executing a quiet businessman-like manner. Throughout the testing session he evidence restricted behavior. On various drawing tests this air of tightness and compression reflected a kind of rigid self-structuring of the task. Jose apparently needs a great deal of order for him to function well, and he has learned how to provide it for himself.

Remaining silent when he didn't know an answer, Jose lacked confidence and feared failure. He found it difficult to express his pleasure when praised; although highly responsive to praise from the examiner and to seeing his own successful performances, he only allowed a restrained smile on such occasions. Going along with this emotional self-restriction was Jose's avoidance of eye contact (although it was inconsistent) and his attempt to conceal the fact that he was counting on his fingers during numerical questioning.

Jose's stuttering did not begin until the first task requiring him to respond verbally to conceptual questions. Until this time he either worked silently or replied with short phrases. However, on later tasks requiring even more verbal expression (such as when making up stories in response to picture-stimulus cards, or when verbalizing lengthy answers about practical life situations), he did not stutter. It was observed that his greatest stuttering occurred on tasks in which he was most deficient, highlighting his awareness and anxiety in these circumstances. His speech impairment took the form of prolongations of certain words, rather than the repetitive type of stuttering.

The most predominant behavioral characteristic Jose displayed was his general slowness. His reflective cognitive style impaired his performance on the intelligence test (e.g., he was able to finish difficult puzzles correctly—but after the time limits had expired). This slowness was on both verbal and motor levels and was complemented by Jose's general thoroughness in completing tasks.

Tests Administered

WISC-R
Bender–Gestalt
Draw-A-Man
Children's Apperception Test

Test Results and Interpretation

On the WISC-R, Jose earned a Performance IQ of 114 ± 7, classifying his nonverbal intelligence as High Average (Bright) and ranking him at the 82nd percentile for children his age. In great contrast was his Low Average (Dull) Verbal IQ of 87 ± 5 (20th percentile). Striking discrepancies as large as 27 points are unusual within the normal population (occurring only 3% of the time), but large discrepancies in favor of the Performance IQ are common for bilingual children from Spanish backgrounds. Low Verbal IQs are usually associated with a Spanish child's difficulties with the English language, subculture differences, or the problems inherent in learning two languages simultaneously. The latter explanation seems most likely to account for Jose's limited skills in the Verbal area because he understood and spoke English well, and performed quite adequately (63rd percentile) on a culture-saturated subtest assessing his ability to demonstrate practical information and to evaluate and use past experience in responding to socially oriented verbal questions.

Because of his bilingual background, Jose's Verbal IQ does not reflect his intellectual functioning or potential; consequently, a Full Scale IQ has not been computed for him. Nevertheless, it is revealing to examine his profile of verbal abilities. In addition to his verbal strength, Jose demonstrated a relative strength (63rd percentile) in his ability to solve oral arithmetic problems. His two strong areas suggest that Jose has well-developed reasoning skills. In contrast, he evidenced poor verbal concept formation, scoring at only the 7th percentile on tasks requiring him to define words and to point out similarities between pairs of words or concepts (e.g., elbow and knee). His weakness in this area may have been accentuated by his reading difficulties, since reading is an activity that facilitates growth of vocabulary and verbal concepts. Clearly, then, Jose does not have a global verbal problem but is below average in certain aspects of cognitive functioning. He seemed to be aware of his conceptual lack, either consciously or unconsciously, since he stuttered and appeared quite anxious during the tasks on which he performed poorly.

Jose's Performance IQ indicates that he has good intellectual ability. His IQ of 114 may even underestimate his mental functioning in view of his very slow, reflective problem-solving approach. Thus he may have Superior, rather than High Average, nonverbal intelligence since the WISC-R Performance Scale places a stress on quick responding. Jose evidenced exceptional ability (98th percentile) in a task requiring good visual perceptual skills with little emphasis on motor coordination (i.e., finding the missing part in a picture). His other specific nonverbal skills were quite consistent with his overall Performance IQ; these skills include nonverbal reasoning, psychomotor speed, spatial relations, and visual–motor coordination.

Jose's performance on the Bender–Gestalt earned him a zero error score on the Koppitz scoring system, indicating superior visual–motor development for children his age. One emotional indicator—small size of drawings—was present, suggesting anxiety, constriction, and withdrawal behavior. It was also observed that all nine of Jose's Bender drawings were produced on only a small part of the paper. Although not a valid emotional sign, this, too, is associated with anxiety.

The person Jose drew when scored by the Goodenough–Harris system received a Standard Score of 110, which was commensurate with his nonverbal performance on the WISC-R. The person was depicted holding a hammer. Interestingly, Jose's father frequently constructs things with and for his son, and this spontaneous addition is therefore probably an identification association. His style of attacking the task was uniquely methodical, beginning with the crotch and proceeding from the legs up to the head, completing the hand detail before the shoulders, and so forth. This orderliness, along with the relative smallness of the figure, was very similar to his approach on the Bender. The one valid emotional indicator, omission of feet, is considered to reflect insecurity.

On the Children's Apperception Test, Jose used the primary defense mechanisms of reaction formation, along with isolation and projection–introjection. His stories consistently portrayed the mother as punitive and withholding and the father as a source of overbearing power. Oral deprivation themes occurred, with anxiety surrounding the fear of losing his symbolic nurturance. Jose described the child-hero self as disobedient and troublesome to his parents, unlike the other "good" siblings. He apparently sees this as his role in the family constellation, as this was a repetitive theme. Jose was able to give age-appropriate solutions to story problems, demonstrating adequate ego and superego development.

Summary and Recommendations

Jose, a Chicano almost 10 years of age, was referred for evaluation because of poor relationships with peers and family members. He is experiencing difficulties in school with reading and stutters when tense. During the present testing session he revealed his self-restrictive manner of behavior and his needing and providing structure for himself as he worked slowly and reflectively on tasks. The WISC-R yielded disparate IQs for him, with a Verbal IQ of 87 (Low Average, Dull) and a Performance IQ of 114 (High Average, Bright). Jose's low Verbal IQ is probably related to his bilingual background and thus does not signify poor intellectual ability. He is able to express himself well and to reason adequately, but he has poorly developed verbal concept formation. His Performance IQ indicates good intellectual ability and may even be an underestimate because of his reflective approach to problem solving. Projective measures were consistent in describing a child who is experiencing some anxiety and conflict over the father who is seen as greatly dominant and with whom Jose identifies his own sense of masculinity.

Jose needs special attention paid to his development of verbal concepts. Perhaps a real-life setting of social situations might facilitate such learning; however, his poor vocabulary and reading skills will need much improvement. Since he has excellent visual perceptual ability, a remedial method such as Bannatyne's color program for reading skills might prove instrumental in obtaining better achievement.

The pressure placed on Jose by his parents at home needs relief, since he tends to apply this to himself as well—overloading the whole family with unnecessary tension. What he needs is more praise for even small successes. Family activities that stress cooperation rather than competition or comparison could be focused on. More affection, nurturance, and approval from both parents is vital for Jose's healthy development. Since he feels deprived, he guards whatever he does have very tightly, creating the additional possessiveness and friction at home.

Nadeen L. Kaufman
Psychologist

CHAPTER 3

Interpreting the Distractibility Factor

It may seem that the third WISC-R factor has been almost forgotten in the preceding chapter, but this is not quite true. The fact that Arithmetic, Digit Span, and Coding load together is always kept in mind when interpreting the Verbal and Performance IQs and sometimes plays a key role in understanding V−P discrepancies (see pp. 43−46). Indeed, scores on the third factor are characteristically low for reading-disabled children (McManis, Figley, et al. 1978; Robeck 1971; Rugel 1974b) and are sometimes depressed for learning-disabled children as well (Lutey 1977; Myklebust, Bannochie, et al. 1971; Smith, Coleman, et al. 1977b). Nevertheless, the distractibility factor does not always play a featured role in test interpretation; it is easily the smallest of the three factors (in terms of the percentage of variance accounted for), is occasionally not isolated in factor-analytic studies (Reschly 1978), and is the only factor that may correspond to a behavioral rather than intellective variable.

Consequently, the method of interpretation described in this book focuses on the large Verbal Comprehension and Perceptual Organization factors and operates firmly from the vantage point of Wechsler's V−P dichotomy. Factor scores for the third factor do not even have to be computed routinely for each child tested. There are, however, some children for whom the third factor holds the key to competent WISC-R interpretation, and hence it must be understood thoroughly by examiners. This chapter is devoted to an explanation of the various possible meanings of the so-called Freedom from Distractibility factor; it also discusses and illustrates when to interpret the dimension and how to make sense out of the third factor for different individuals.

The third factor was labeled Freedom from Distractibility for historical reasons involving factor analyses of the Wechsler−Bellevue, WAIS, and 1949 WISC, and also because of research (Wender 1971, pp. 88−93) showing that drug therapy with minimally brain-impaired children typically results in decreased distractibility coupled with a corresponding increase in their scores on memory and arithmetic tests (Kaufman 1975). It is easy to see how children may score very poorly on the three WISC-R subtests constituting the third factor because of distractible behavior, but it is more difficult to visualize children scoring very well on the three subtests merely or primarily because of close attention to the tasks. Thus the possibility that the third factor may reflect a cognitive ability rather than a behavioral attribute (a notion that I touched on in my 1975 article) is very real and must be considered as an active hypothesis when interpreting any child's WISC-R profile. Reschly and Reschly (in press) presented some empirical support for a relationship between the third WISC-R factor and a subjective measure of children's attention but concluded legitimately that examiners must be cautious in interpreting the distractibility factor score as a measure of attention.

A more insightful view of the meaning of all three factors, particularly the one labeled "distractibility," is obtained by considering two other methods for grouping WISC-R subtests: Guilford's SOI analysis derived from theory, and Bannatyne's categorizations of WISC subtests, derived primarily from clinical experiences.

GUILFORD'S STRUCTURE-OF-INTELLECT CLASSIFICATIONS

Guilford's (1967) three-dimensional theoretical model of intelligence has provided a convenient technique for labeling the abilities measured by various cognitive tasks. Meeker (1969, 1975b) has used Guilford's method to define SOI factors for the Stanford–Binet and Wechsler batteries and has developed a comprehensive technique for interpreting these tests. Her method involves the use of cardboard templates placed over the pages of a record form to facilitate obtaining scores on each SOI factor measured by the intelligence test. Meeker's approach is fine for a devotee of Guilford's theory, but it is generally too time-consuming for the type of flexible interpretation advocated in this book. Nevertheless, the Guilford SOI factors measured by each subtest (Meeker 1975b) are included in Table 3-1, primarily to offer new insights into the meaning of the three factors underlying the WISC-R.

By way of quick review, the three dimensions are listed as follows and the aspects of each dimension are defined:

1. *Operations—intellectual processes.*
   a. Cognition (C): Immediate awareness, recognition, or comprehension of stimuli.
   b. Memory (M): Retention of information in the same form in which it was stored.
   c. Evaluation (E): Making judgments about information in terms of a known standard.
   d. Convergent production (N): Responding to stimuli with the unique or "best" answer.

Table 3-1   Classification of WISC-R subtests by Guilford's three-dimensional model

| WISC-R Subtest | Operation | | | |
	Cognition	Memory	Evaluation	Convergent Production
Verbal Scale				
Information	CMU	MMU, MMR, MMS		NMU, NMR
Similarities	CMR, CMT			
Arithmetic	CMS	MSI		
Vocabulary	CMU			
Comprehension			EMI	
Digit Span		MSU, MSS		
Performance Scale				
Picture Completion	CFU		EFS	
Picture Arrangement			EMR	NMS
Block Design	CFR		EFR	
Object Assembly	CFS, CFT		EFR	
Coding A			EFU	NFU
Coding B			ESU	NSU, NSI
Mazes	CFI			

Note: SOI factors are listed for the Information subtest only if measured by three or more items.

    e. Divergent production (D): Responding to stimuli where the emphasis is on variety or quality of response (associated with creativity).

2. *Contents—nature of the stimuli.*

    a. Figural (F): Shapes or concrete objects.

    b. Symbolic (S): Numerals, single letters, or any coded symbol.

    c. Semantic (M): Words and ideas that convey meaning.

    d. Behavioral (B): Primarily nonverbal, involving human interactions with a stress on attitudes, needs, thoughts, and so on.

3. *Products—the way the stimuli are organized.*
A hierarchy extending from Units (U), where the stimuli are perceived singly, to the increasingly more complex Classes (C), Relations (R), Systems (S), Transformations (T), and Implications (I).

From Table 3-1 it is evident that the Verbal subtests are predominantly of semantic content with the Performance subtests composed primarily of figural content. As discussed on page 42, another distinction between the two scales is that virtually all Performance subtests involve the operation of evaluation, as opposed to only a single Verbal subtest (Comprehension). Not so readily apparent from the table is the fact that the only subtests to have symbolic content are Arithmetic, Digit Span, and Coding B—precisely the tasks that define the

Freedom from Distractibility factor. (Actually three assorted WISC-R *items* involve symbolic content—one each in the Information, Picture Completion, and Similarities subtests—but these classifications are too trivial to be included in Table 3-1.)

Thus the three WISC-R factors might easily be defined in terms of the content dimension of Guilford's model: Semantic, Figural, Symbolic. Some support for a Guilford-like interpretation of the factor analysis may be found in the pattern of factor loadings for the standardization sample (Kaufman 1975). For one thing, Coding A (with figural content) did *not* load significantly on the third factor at ages 6½ and 7½, but Coding B (symbolic content) did have significant loadings at seven of the nine age levels between 8½ and 16½. In addition, Arithmetic (symbolic *and* semantic content) not only had high loadings on the distractibility factor across the age range, but also had significant loadings on the verbal factor at a number of age levels.

If, indeed, the third factor is a measure of the child's ability to manipulate numerical symbols rather than to attend closely to the task at hand, then all three factors are in the cognitive domain. Very possibly, the third factor has different interpretations for different individuals; in any event, that is the approach that is advocated in this chapter.

BANNATYNE'S CATEGORIZATIONS

The reorganization of WISC subtests that Bannatyne (1971, pp. 591−592) found useful for diagnosing dyslexic children is also applicable to the WISC-R. His categorizations, including the slight modification he made (Bannatyne 1974), are shown in the table that follows. Note that Picture Arrangement and Mazes are excluded from his system, whereas Arithmetic and Vocabulary appear twice. Mazes was probably excluded because WISC examiners rarely administered it; logically, it belongs with the Spatial tasks. Picture Arrangement was originally classified as a Sequencing task, but Bannatyne (1974) reconsidered and replaced it with Arithmetic.

Verbal Conceptu-alization Ability	Spatial Ability	Sequencing Ability	Acquired Knowledge
Similarities	Picture Completion	Arithmetic	Information
Vocabulary	Block Design	Digit Span	Arithmetic
Comprehension	Object Assembly	Coding	Vocabulary

Bannatyne's Sequencing category is identical in composition to the Freedom from Distractibility factor and to the group of WISC-R tasks with symbolic content, thereby offering the examiner yet another logical explanation of the third factor! The Verbal Conceptualization Ability grouping bears an obvious relationship to the Verbal Comprehension factor, and Spatial Ability closely resembles Perceptual Organization. In fact, the three subtests included in Bannatyne's Spatial category had the highest loadings on the perceptual factor across the age range (Kaufman 1975). Thus Bannatyne's first three categories might easily have been used to label the WISC-R factors. Just as factor interpretations based on Guilford's model place all three factors in the cognitive domain, so do interpretations based on Bannatyne's orientation.

The same three factors identified for normal children have been found for reading-disabled children (Rugel 1974a), and these youngsters have been shown in numerous studies to have a characteristic WISC profile: they score highest on Spatial tasks, next highest on Verbal Conceptualization tasks, and lowest on Sequencing subtests (Rugel 1974b). Smith, Coleman, et al. (1977b) found this identical pattern for learning-disabled youngsters and also found that their learning-disabled sample performed as poorly on the subtests measuring Acquired Knowledge as they did in the Sequencing area. The fact that these researchers were operating out of a Bannatyne framework does not imply that reading and learning-disabled children necessarily have deficient Sequencing skills or well-developed Spatial Ability. As Smith, Coleman, et al. (1977b) indicate, the problem might be distractibility; other possible explanations, such as lack of numerical ability and anxiety, are discussed later in this chapter. Furthermore, Bannatyne's Spatial category comprises the three subtests that have been found to be closely associated with field independence (see pp. 39–42), suggesting that cognitive style may be a partial explanation of the profiles for the exceptional populations. Finally, the high Spatial/low Sequencing pattern may relate to superior simultaneous/holistic processing coupled with inadequate successive/sequential processing (see pp. 157–165).

WHEN TO INTERPRET THE THIRD FACTOR

It is evident that the third factor can have several meanings, including (but not limited to) freedom from distraction, ability to manipulate numerical symbols, and sequencing ability. However, before examining ways to determine *what* the factor measures, it is important to delineate *when* to interpret the factor for a given individual.

As a general rule, the third factor should be investigated when at least one of the three component subtests deviates significantly from its respective mean score (Verbal or Performance), using the method described on pages 54–57. When scaled scores on Arithmetic and Digit Span do not deviate significantly from the Verbal mean and are, therefore, consistent with the child's Verbal Comprehension ability, it is usually unnecessary to treat these subtests as part of a separate and distinct factor. Similar logic holds for a Coding scaled score that is not significantly divergent from the Performance mean.

If any one of the three subtest scores is significantly higher or lower than its mean, the examiner's immediate task is to find out why. The first hypothesis to be entertained should be that the significantly deviating score was due to the ability or trait underlying the third factor. To check out this hypothesis, the remaining two subtest scores should be considered. If the other two scores are fairly similar in magnitude to the one that deviated significantly from its mean, then the examiner should compute a factor score for the third WISC-R factor. For example, consider a child whose scaled score of 5 on Digit Span was significantly below his or her Verbal mean of 9. The examiner then checks the scaled scores for Arithmetic and Coding and finds that they are 8 and 7, respectively. Even though the examiner discovers that these scores do not deviate significantly from their appropriate scale mean, they are in the same general direction as the Digit Span score (on the low side) and are not inconsistent with the significant discrepancy. In this circumstance, the examiner has reason to hypothesize that the child's area of weakness is the global ability or trait measured by the third factor. Had two or perhaps all three scaled scores been significantly below the child's mean scores, the examiner would have even more evidence for inferring the importance of the third factor for the youngster and for placing greater confidence in the hypothesis. Nevertheless, one significantly deviating scaled score is sufficient for interpreting the third factor, as long as the other two scaled scores are in the same "ball park."

In the previous example, it would have been inappropriate to interpret the distractibility factor if the Arithmetic and Coding scaled scores had been, say, 8 and 12, respectively. When the three scaled scores span a considerable range, it is difficult to conceive that some unitary ability is a primary determinant of the child's performance on all three tasks. Therefore, taking the average of three diverse scaled scores has no psychological meaning and is senseless. How wide a range is necessary to preclude computing an overall score for the third factor? There is no simple answer to the question. As a general rule, when one of the three subtest scores deviates significantly from the appropriate mean, the other two scores should show deviations in the same direction—even though these deviations may not be significant. For example, if children score significantly above their Performance mean on Coding, the examiner should interpret the third factor as long as the Arithmetic and Digit Span scaled scores are both above the Verbal mean. However, this is not a rigid rule and can be bent or modified at the examiner's discretion.

The four sample profiles shown below should help clarify the preceding discussion. Relative strengths and weaknesses in these scaled-score profiles have been determined based on the ±3 method described in Chapter 2 (see pp. 54–57) and are labeled "S" and "W," respectively. The means of the Verbal and Performance scaled scores are given below each profile.

Anna A.

Verbal	Scaled Score	Performance	Scaled Score
Information	9	Picture Completion	12
Similarities	11	Picture Arrangement	16-S
Arithmetic	10	Block Design	10
Vocabulary	12	Object Assembly	9-W
Comprehension	8	Coding	13
Digit Span	9	Mazes	14

Verbal mean = 10.   Performance mean = 12.

In Anna's profile, none of the subtests associated with the distractibility factor deviated significantly from their respective means. The Arithmetic and Digit Span scaled scores were quite consistent with the Verbal Comprehension subtest scores, suggesting that Anna's overall verbal ability was primarily responsible for her scores on all six Verbal subtests. Similarly, her performance on Coding was totally in keeping with her ability on the other nonverbal subtests. It is hence inadvisable to interpret the third factor for Anna since no new information will be revealed. Wechsler's V−P dichotomy provides a more efficient means of interpreting her profile than does the three-factor approach. Whereas the third factor is not involved in the interpretation, the type of detective work described in Chapter 6 should help make sense out of Anna's relative strength and weakness on the Performance Scale.

Bill B.

Verbal	Scaled Score	Performance	Scaled Score
Information	11	Picture Completion	10
Similarities	9-W	Picture Arrangement	13
Arithmetic	12	Block Design	11
Vocabulary	11	Object Assembly	10
Comprehension	10	Coding	9
Digit Span	17-S	Mazes	15-S

Verbal mean = 12.   Performance mean = 11.

Bill's WISC-R profile reveals a significant strength in Digit Span, but not in Arithmetic or Coding. The fact that one of the three subtests deviated significantly permits the examiner to investigate the role of the third factor in understanding the profile. However, further examination indicates that Bill's distractibility scores ranged from 9 on Coding to 17 on Digit Span. This large spread of scores makes it apparent that a unitary ability was not responsible for his performance on the three subtests. Indeed, far from being a strength like Digit Span, Bill's scaled score on Coding was *below* his Performance mean. Hence the third factor should not be interpreted for this youngster, as it clearly was not responsible for his strength in Digit Span. In this instance, it is likely that an exceptional short-term memory for auditory stimuli accounted for Bill's high Digit Span score.

Cathy C.

Verbal	Scaled Score	Performance	Scaled Score
Information	7	Picture Completion	5-W
Similarities	12-S	Picture Arrangement	8
Arithmetic	5-W	Block Design	11-S
Vocabulary	11	Object Assembly	9
Comprehension	10	Coding	6
Digit Span	8	Mazes	8

Verbal mean = 9.   Performance mean = 8.

In Cathy's profile, Arithmetic represents a significant weakness on the Verbal Scale. Even though Cathy did not display weaknesses in Digit Span and Coding, her scaled scores of 8 and 6 are below their respective means and are clearly similar to the score of 5 on Arithmetic. It is thus suggested that the examiner interpret the third factor for Cathy and consider the ability or trait underlying the factor as a possible explanation for her weakness in Arithmetic. Precisely what the third factor stands for can be determined by clinically evaluating Cathy's behaviors and scrutinizing her responses to pertinent items (see the next section of this chapter).

Dennis D.

Verbal	Scaled Score	Performance	Scaled Score
Information	8	Picture Completion	11
Similarities	9	Picture Arrangement	10
Arithmetic	14-S	Block Design	8
Vocabulary	8	Object Assembly	13-S
Comprehension	7-W	Coding	12
Digit Span	13-S	Mazes	7-W

Verbal mean = 10.   Performance mean = 10.

Dennis demonstrated significant strengths in both Arithmetic and Digit Span, and his score on Coding was above his Performance mean. For him, the third factor must clearly play a crucial role in test interpretation. The Verbal Scale splits into two fragments, corresponding to the Verbal Comprehension subtests and the third-factor subtests. Interpretation of the distractibility factor will obviously yield a more meaningful picture of Bill's abilities than can be obtained from the Verbal and Performance IQs or from examination of each subtest's uniqueness (see pp. 103 and 105).

There are some instances where interpretation of the third factor is advised even when the three subtest scores do not differ markedly from scores on other subtests. For example, a child who manifested considerable anxiety, hyperactivity, or distractibility during the testing session would be expected to score poorly on one or more of the subtests constituting the third factor. When children perform adequately on these subtests despite their behavioral characteristics, it is a noteworthy occurrence and merits discussion. Similarly, children who are referred for learning problems in arithmetic and are reported to have difficulty working with numerical symbols should not perform too well on the three third-factor subtests; when their distractibility scores are comparable in magnitude to their scores on Verbal Comprehension and Perceptual Organization tasks, such a finding demands analysis and interpretation. The same type of reasoning holds for children referred for reading problems or learning problems in general, since these groups of children typically score poorly on the third factor, as indicated earlier.

Naturally, an examiner has the option of interpreting the distractibility factor for each child by routinely computing a factor score regardless of strengths and weaknesses and without paying attention to the range of the three scaled scores. I prefer to respect Wechsler's $V-P$ dichotomy and give it the benefit of the doubt over the factor-analytic trichotomy, unless analysis of the profile clearly indicates that the third factor is a *distinct* and *unitary* ability.

HOW TO INTERPRET THE THIRD FACTOR

Knowing when it makes sense to interpret the third factor does not mean that the examiner will intuitively understand its meaning for a given youngster. The issue of how to interpret this factor has two important facets: psychometric and clinical.

Psychometric Issues

The psychometric aspect concerns the method for obtaining factor scores. Originally, I suggested using Verbal and Performance IQs as the factor scores for the first two factors, with the mean of the Arithmetic, Digit Span, and Coding scaled scores serving as the factor score for the third factor (Kaufman 1975). I no longer hold to this position. The Verbal and Performance IQs are excellent factor scores when there is no need to interpret the distractibility dimension. However, when the Arithmetic and/or Coding scaled scores are discrepant with the other subtest scores in their respective scales, the IQs are less adequate as factor scores. Since these latter discrepancies trigger interpretation of the third factor, the examiner would be wise *not to use Verbal and Performance IQs as factor scores whenever all three factors are interpreted for an individual.* Instead, examiners should compute the average of the four Verbal Comprehension scaled scores and use this mean value as the factor score for the first factor; they should use the mean of the five Perceptual Organization subtests (four, if Mazes is not administered) as the factor score for the second factor and should consider the mean of the three subtests constituting the third factor as its factor score.

Apart from getting better estimates of the first and second factors than is provided by the Verbal and Performance IQs, the averaging method yields three factor scores that are nonoverlapping in terms of content. The fact that the factor scores are mutually exclusive facilitates interpretation of their differences. As a rule of thumb (not to be followed rigidly), the factor score for the third factor should differ by 3 or more scaled-score points (at least one standard deviation) from the factor score of either of the other two factors to be considered a meaningful discrepancy. In Cathy's profile the mean factor scores for the three factors were 10, 8, and 6, respectively. Thus Cathy's score on the distractibility factor was substantially lower than her score on the Verbal Comprehension but *not* on the Perceptual Organization factor. In Dennis's case the third factor score was meaningfully above *both* of the other factor scores as he obtained mean scaled scores of 8, 10, and 13. Even though a distractibility factor score of 13 may also be computed for Bill, this value is really meaningless because his range of scaled scores on the three pertinent subtests is so wide (9—17) that the third factor does not correspond to a unitary ability. Therefore, it is irrelevant and of no consequence that Bill's distractibility factor score was 3 points above his Verbal Comprehension factor score.

Sattler (1974, p. 546) and Sobotka and Black (1978) propose the use of a deviation IQ as the factor score for the third WISC-R factor, but I am opposed to that suggestion. The IQ is already the subject of so much controversy that it seems unwise to compute yet another type of IQ when it is unnecessary. Reporting an IQ analog for the third factor may mislead or confuse some readers of case reports, especially in view of the fact that the third WISC-R factor may well be in the behavioral rather than the cognitive domain. Sobotka and Black (1978) also encourage the computation of deviation IQ equivalents for the Verbal Comprehension and Perceptual Organization factors. Whereas these IQ equivalents might be computed to facilitate the examiner's behind-the-scenes interpretation of profiles (see pp. 43—46), these additional IQs should *not* be included in a case report or discussed at a staffing. Three IQs can cause enough confusion when communicating the results of a Wechsler examination. Why add to the communication barrier by throwing in a few extra IQ equivalents?

Admittedly, scaled scores do not communicate that well to people who are not intimately involved with individual testing. Therefore, converting the factor scores to percentile ranks or to deviations from the mean, depending on the psychometric sophistication of the audience, will facilitate understanding. Using Wechsler's (1974, p. 25) table, the factor scores reported for Dennis have been converted to percentile ranks and deviations from the mean.

Factor	Factor Score	SDs from the Mean	Percentile Rank
Verbal Comprehension	8	−2/3	25th
Perceptual Organization	10	0	50th
Freedom from Distractibility	13	+1	84th

There is some evidence that for mentally retarded youngsters the third factor should include Picture Arrangement in addition to Arithmetic, Digit Span, and Coding (Baumeister and Bartlett 1962a, 1962b; Van Hagen and Kaufman 1975). The examiner thus has the option of including Picture Arrangement with the third factor instead of the second factor when computing factor scores for retarded youngsters. However, it would probably be wiser to use the conventional grouping of subtests into three factors for all children, including the mentally retarded, because of limited research in this area. Baumeister and Bartlett studied the 1949 WISC, and Van Hagen and Kaufman's WISC-R study involved a group of very low-scoring retarded youngsters (average WISC-R Full Scale IQ of 51); hence generalization to other samples of retarded children requires caution.

Clinical Perspective

Once examiners have determined that it is sensible to interpret the third factor and have computed factor scores for all three factors, they still have the crucial task of deciding what the strength or weakness on the third factor means. Does it reflect distractibility, symbolic facility, sequencing ability, attention−concentration, or some other dimension? Some examiners automatically interpret low scores on the third factor as evidence of distractibility, but such an interpretation is nonsensical for a child who attended closely to all tasks and concentrated on each item presented. Inferences about the meaning of the third factor simply cannot be made without considering children's test-taking behaviors and the nature of their wrong responses to Arithmetic, Digit Span, and Coding items.

When youngsters are obviously distracted during the testing session, as evidenced by inability to focus attention on the task at hand, overattentiveness to irrelevant stimuli in the environment or loss of rapport following noises and distractions outside of the testing room, it is perfectly reasonable to infer that their relatively low score on the third factor was due to distractibility. By the same token, a low third-factor score may be attributed to anxiety if the examiner detects anxious behavior in the course of the WISC-R examination, such as rigid posture, nervous mannerisms, overconcern with the stopwatch, pressing too hard on the pencil, or overreaction to failure. According to Lutey (1977, p. 184), an "anxiety triad" composed of the three third-factor subtests has frequently been postulated in the literature, and the distractibility factor might easily be interpreted as "freedom from disruptive anxiety." Lutey (1977, p. 222) warns, however, that these subtests are sensitive to the influence of the kind of anxiety that reflects a disturbed or uneasy *state*—perhaps specific to the testing situation—rather than the chronic anxiety associated with neuropsychiatric patients. She also cites research that shows Arithmetic and Digit Span to be particularly related to measures of anxiety and suggests that Coding be used mostly as a check on an anxiety hypothesis (Lutey 1977, p. 222).

Whenever a behavioral variable like distractibility or anxiety is used as the explanation for poor performance on the third factor, the examiner should keep two things firmly in mind. First, no suggestion should be made that the child is in any way deficient in his or her numerical problem-solving ability (Arithmetic), short-term memory (Digit Span), or psychomotor speed (Coding). Such deficiencies *may* exist, but one cannot infer them from the test administration since the low scaled scores are presumed to reflect the inhibiting effect of a behavioral variable rather than a cognitive or psychomotor deficiency. Second, the child's IQs have to be considered as underestimates of his or her current intellectual functioning because of the behavioral interference. Whereas the Verbal Comprehension and Perceptual Organization factor scores may come closer than the IQs to measuring his or her mental functioning, these scores are also possibly underestimates; extreme distractibility or anxiety can easily have some impact on the child's score on any WISC-R subtest, not just the three associated with the third factor.

Clear-cut observations of distractible or anxious test behavior force an examiner to be flexible when interpreting the third factor. These behaviors may have been evident during Verbal subtests, but not during Performance tasks because of the interest value of the concrete materials. For such individuals, a behavioral explanation for poor performance on Digit Span and Arithmetic would be warranted even if they evidenced a strength on Coding. Similarly, the number of distractibility subtests may be expanded to four or more for given youngsters if they clearly evidenced performance-inhibiting behaviors during the Block Design and Comprehension subtests, for example.

The examiner would be wise to record incorrect responses for Arithmetic and

Digit Span items, rather than merely marking them pass or fail. Some answers to Arithmetic problems will reflect poor mastery of computational skills, whereas other wrong responses can be used to infer selection of the wrong mathematical processes, forgetting the precise question, sequencing difficulties, and so on. For example, a child whose wrong response is the right answer to step 1 of a two-step process may have difficulty sequencing the steps of a complex problem. In Digit Span a sequencing problem may be evidenced by a child who consistently recalls the correct numbers spoken by the examiner but recites them in the wrong order. In contrast, a child with a deficient short-term memory might omit the last digit or one or two digits in the middle of an item; a distractible child may respond with numbers that bear no relationship to the digits in the item or may give no response at all.

Behavioral observations during Coding often give great insight into the child's poor or excellent performance on this subtest. A child with an exceptional visual memory may memorize the symbol that is paired with each number and thus not have to refer back very often to the legend at the top of the Coding page. On the negative side, a child may perform poorly because of motor difficulties in copying the symbols; visual perceptual problems, resulting in several unacceptable responses; distractible behavior, leading to an inability to sustain attention to the task; sequencing deficiencies, manifested by failing to grasp the notion that the items must be done one after the other, or by searching for each symbol in the legend without awareness that each numeral occupies a predictable place in the sequence; poor problem-solving approach, as illustrated by left-handed children who do not take advantage of the second Coding sheet that is provided for them; immaturity, highlighted by being oblivious to the need to work quickly, and sometimes reflected by the asking of unimportant or irrelevant questions; and so on.

Observations during Arithmetic and Digit Span also facilitate understanding the role of different behaviors on performance. During Arithmetic items children may attempt to "write" with their fingers on the table, count on their fingers, repeat the item out loud to aid their recall of the exact wording, or ask for numerous repetitions of items (only one repetition is allowed). On Digit Span, mouthing the digits as they are spoken, auditory rehearsal, and covering up one's eyes to block out the outside world are all fairly common behaviors. Each behavioral observation tells the examiner something different about the child and aids understanding of his or her test scores.

To interpret the third factor effectively, it is apparent that subtest scores, behavioral observations, and the nature of wrong responses have to be integrated for each individual. Whether low scores on the third factor are due to sequencing, distractibility, anxiety, or a number problem can often be inferred from behaviors and wrong responses. It is also useful to weigh additional information about the child to help deduce a working hypothesis. When sequencing is suspected as the difficulty, the examiner should check the child's Picture Arrangement scaled score; one would anticipate relatively poor performance on this temporal sequencing task. In addition, a child with a sequencing problem is likely to manifest this deficiency in social situations and in academic achievement. Was one of the reasons for referral possibly associated with a sequencing lack—such as inability or refusal to follow directions? Is the child reported to have serious reading problems?

If examiners believe that a behavioral variable accounted for the low third-factor score, they should anticipate distractibility, anxiety, inability to concentrate, short attention span, and hyperactivity as likely reasons for referral. When the behaviors observed during a testing session corroborate referral problems, examiners have extra justification for reaching a conclusion regarding the meaning of low scores on the third factor. However, they should not be intimidated if an apparently distractible or anxious child has been described as extremely attentive or relaxed in school. Test behaviors are sometimes quite different from behaviors in other circumstances; the examiner's task is to interpret scores in the context of behaviors observed during the testing session. Therefore, it would be inappropriate to consider low third-factor scores as due to a behavioral variable if distractibility or anxiety was listed as a referral problem but was not at all evident during the WISC-R administration. Whenever distractibility or anxiety is believed to have contributed to depressed scores on the three subtests constituting the third factor, the examiner should also anticipate relatively low scores on any other subtests during which these behaviors were clearly observed. In addition, an anxious child may well score relatively poorly on *both* the Perceptual Organization and distractibility factors because of the vulnerability of highly speeded tasks such as Object Assembly or Block Design to the influence of anxiety.

Inadequate mastery of computational skills, compensatory behaviors such as finger counting or finger writing, the solving of oral arithmetic problems after the time limits expire, and a history of poor mathematical achievement all suggest that a child's low score on the third factor reflects an inability to handle numerical symbols. A child with this deficiency is sometimes found to have an adequate forward digit span, which involves recall but no manipulation of numbers, coupled with almost a complete lack of ability to reverse digits. In general, however, Arithmetic and Coding are the best indicators of a child's numerical facility (or lack of it), with Digit Span merely serving as a check on a number-related hypothesis (Lutey 1977, p. 222). Other important checks are the Information and Block Design subtests since a child with a severe symbolic problem may also fail most of the quantitative fact items (e.g., pennies in a nickel, days in a week) and may experience considerable difficulty in copying two-dimensional abstract designs out of blocks. As a rule, when an attentive and relaxed child with apparently normal sequencing ability performs poorly on the third-factor subtests, the examiner should suspect a symbolic difficulty even in the absence of corroborating behaviors.

The preceding sections have focused on low scores on the third factor, yet high scores are also encountered and require careful consideration. Despite the formal name given the factor, it is unlikely that a person obtains a high factor score primarily because of Freedom from Distractibility. Similarly, even though Bannatyne considers the subtest grouping to reflect Sequencing Ability, it is unlikely that children will earn high scores merely because of skill at sequencing (although a more generalized strength in successive−sequential processing is feasible—see pp. 157−165). Attention, concentration, sequencing ability, and freedom from anxiety are necessary requisites for good performance on the third-factor subtests, but they cannot usually account for the high scores. More likely these traits enable the child to exercise the skill or skills that underlie the tasks. In most instances, this skill is probably the Guilford-related ability to manipulate symbolic content and is closely associated with quantitative ability. Supporting information might come from school achievement, where the child may excel in mathematics. In addition to performing well in arithmetic achievement, an adolescent may have made a relevant vocational choice such as becoming a mathematics teacher, accountant, or computer programmer.

The suggestion that high third-factor scores usually reflect numerical ability does not mean that examiners should abandon their own creativity in the interpretation of this factor. High scores may have a particular meaning for a given child based on observations and background information that are applicable only to the child tested; the same is true for low scores. Furthermore, an examiner from a specific orientation might have an entirely different interpretation of the third factor. As indicated earlier, an examiner who is closely attuned to the distinction between successive and simultaneous processing (Das, Kirby, et al. 1975) may conceivably interpret an extreme third-factor score as a strength or weakness in *successive* processing of stimuli. Similarly, WISC-R examiners who feel comfortable with the ITPA psycholinguistic model (Kirk, McCarthy, et al. 1968) may find it appropriate to interpret the third factor in terms of level of organization. Most WISC-R subtests are at the *representational* level of organization, which involves the mediation of complex activities requiring the meaning or significance of linguistic symbols. In contrast, Coding A and B and the Digits Forward portion of Digit Span are more closely associated with the *automatic* level of organization, which controls the retention of symbol sequences and the execution of overlearned, highly organized habits. Even though Arithmetic is legitimately a representational task (Osgood and Miron 1963), the subtest also involves mastery of computational facts; when these facts are learned at an automatic rote level, performance on Arithmetic will be elevated. In Guilford's terminology, the Arithmetic subtest requires Memory of Symbolic Implications, which Meeker (1975a) defines as "Memory for well-practiced number operations." The latter skill is clearly automatic, supporting the notion that a high or low third-factor score may reflect strong or weak automatic functioning for some individuals.

One other label that has been given to the third factor by investigators of mentally retarded individuals (Baumeister and Bartlett 1962a, 1962b; Baumeister, Bartlett, et al. 1963) is Stimulus Trace. These investigators interpret the factor from the perspective of Ellis's (1963) theory and consider it to reflect a youngster's ability to maintain the neural trace of a stimulus over brief intervals of time. This interpretation, which is also consistent with Hebb's (1949) theoretical framework, may well explain a low third-factor score for some mentally retarded youngsters. The term "Stimulus Trace," as interpreted by Baumeister and his associates, is akin to short-term memory—a label that Cohen (1957) once believed was characteristic of the distractibility factor. The physiologically based Stimulus Trace or immediate memory factor, which is believed to relate to behavioral differences between normal and mentally retarded individuals, has typically included secondary loadings by Picture Arrangement and Block Design to supplement the major loadings by the three third-factor subtests. Additional research, such as the construct validity study conducted by Baumeister, Bartlett, et al. (1963), should be designed to shed more light on the "trace" interpretation of the third factor.

A final note on interpreting the third factor concerns the fact that an individual's high or low factor score may not have a unitary explanation. More than one of the various interpretations given this factor may be reflected in an extreme factor score. For example, as Lutey (1977, p. 223) aptly states: "The examiner should not over-look the possibility that [low third-factor scores] reflect *both* anxiety *and* poor numerical ability, since these logically may be related for many subjects."

ILLUSTRATIVE CASE REPORTS

The WISC-R profiles for Jamie C., Randi R., and Jennie L. (fictitious names) all require interpretation of the third factor, as demonstrated in the case reports that follow. For each child, the third factor seems to mean something quite different. Jamie, a boy of almost 9, performed poorly on the three component subtests because of his extremely distractible behavior. The low scores earned by 9½-year-old Randi, however, seemed to reflect her fairly pervasive numerical difficulties. Jennie, almost 10½, did relatively well on the three subtests, probably because of good ability on tasks demanding automatic responding. Even though both Jamie and Randi are anxious children, it was felt that their chronic anxiety did not play a primary role in their low third factor scores. This interpretation is consistent with Lutey's (1977) statement that the third factor is subject to the influences of state or test anxiety rather than more chronic anxiety.

Jamie C., White Male, Age 8 years 10 months

WISC-R Profile

Verbal	Scaled Score	Performance	Scaled Score
Information	15	Picture Completion	11
Similarities	13	Picture Arrangement	14-S
Arithmetic	11-W	Block Design	8
Vocabulary	15	Object Assembly	10
Comprehension	19-S	Coding	6-W
Digit Span	10-W		

Verbal IQ = 128.   Performance IQ = 98.   Full Scale IQ = 116.

Referral and Background Information

Jamie was referred for evaluation to check on his current intellectual functioning. The huge discrepancy found in his last intelligence test indicated a 42-point difference between his very superior verbal abilities and his average nonverbal performance; updating of this situation was requested. His emotional problems have previously been diagnosed as a psychoneurotic disorder. An only child, Jamie lives with his parents and paternal grandfather. He reportedly has a history of separation anxieties from significant others, especially his mother. He is seen by his teacher as a controlling, self-derogatory child who dislikes school and resists discipline. His mother, a gynecologist, feels that Jamie experiences difficulty in expressing his feelings and demands excessive attention. Jamie's father is an accountant.

Appearance and Behavioral Characteristics

Jamie virtually "popped" into the building, and speaking rapidly in a loud voice, dragged his unwilling father down the hall to where a remembered Coke machine stood. Jamie proceeded to efficiently purchase a soda, secure more money from his father, and ask his father not to leave the premises, all the while ignoring the examiner who was present. When his father refused to stay and wait, Jamie grew more anxious and ran out the door after him. Mr. C. demonstrated no patience with Jamie's fears of being left; finally the examiner got Jamie to come into the testing room while his father would "wait in the car."

Wearing a shirt with a large hole in it but otherwise appearing neat, Jamie's opening remark once he was alone with the examiner was "You'd like my father better if you knew him; he's got a good sense of humor." Jamie was apparently aware of the abrupt manner that his father displayed and feared that he had made a poor impression. Instead of resentment or anger, he felt protective and understanding towards him. On one task that required him to find missing parts of pictures, Jamie's responses became more rapid as he began to feel successful. He indicated great desire to please his father about this and repeated many times "Make sure to mention that to pop." When the session was over and the examiner told Mr. C. of Jamie's speedy performance, his response was "Well, we'll have to see if we can get him even faster"—as though he were training Jamie for an Olympic competition. Jamie's attention to speed on the picture task is in complete contrast to his slow, dawdling behavior on a later task of psychomotor speed requiring him to copy symbols accurately. Whereas he was distractible and had a short attention span, he also demonstrated ambivalent emotions about being pressured for time.

Jamie's distractibility surfaced in several tasks for which concentration was necessary, and he needed continual repetition of items. His high anxiety level was displayed throughout the evaluation by a steady stream of conversation. The examiner had to exert great effort to keep him quiet long enough to complete the necessary measures. This excessive talking gave insight into Jamie's great sense of humor and entertaining manner. He even tried putting on a show for the examiner's benefit by sneaking in humorous comments, such as responding to "How far is it from New York to Los Angeles?" with the remark "Well, it's not spitting distance!" While drawing pictures as part of an ice-breaking activity, Jamie couldn't resist displaying his humor and need for approval by: (a) putting an "X" on one picture and then saying "X marks the spot" and (b) writing the words "how's that?" at the end of another picture. He showed his insecurity and fear of failure most prominently on nonverbal tasks, with which he experienced great difficulty. Examples of his steady stream of self-doubting commentary are: "I'll never make it; it's impossible; I can't get it," and so on. Also, his activity level exploded during these frustrating moments, and he began kicking his feet violently in constant motion. At one point during such stress Jamie began scratching his arm hard until it bled.

Jamie's most poignant remark was simply stated: "My mother says something ridiculous to me every day. She says 'Have a good day' every morning before I leave for school."

Test Administered

WISC-R

Test Results and Interpretation

Whereas Jamie's WISC-R Full Scale IQ of 116 ±5 places him in the High Average category, this becomes meaningless when we look at his separate scores on the Verbal and Performance Scales. His Verbal IQ of 128 indicates Superior ability in his verbal comprehension and expression and ranks him at the 97th percentile. On the other hand, his Performance IQ of 98 (45th percentile) reveals only Average ability when manipulating visual stimuli. Thus we see a child who has superior intellectual potential but is unable to demonstrate his potential when operating in the visual—motor modality. In short, the 30-point discrepancy is huge, occurring in only 3% of the children of professionals, and must be dealt with when trying to understand Jamie's behavioral problems.

Relative to his own superior verbal skill, Jamie displayed a strength (99.9th percentile) in his ability to evaluate and use past experience when responding to socially relevant questions. However, he also demonstrated relative weaknesses in his ability to solve arithmetic problems presented orally (63rd percentile) and in his immediate recall of digits (50th percentile). Success on oral arithmetic and short-term memory tasks is hindered by a child's distractibility. Jamie, who required repetition of every arithmetic item, clearly had a difficult time attending to both tasks. Nevertheless, note that Jamie was still about average for his age in his weak areas of functioning.

On the Performance tasks one area of relative strength surfaced. When compared to his overall average level of nonverbal ability, Jamie did quite well on a task measuring his nonverbal reasoning capacity when dealing with social situations (91st percentile). Thus we see that his skill in comprehending social interactions is not limited to the verbal sphere, but is also evident when Jamie manipulates visual stimuli (although verbal mediation may have facilitated his performance). A clear picture emerges of a child with well-developed social understanding and interpersonal skills. This ability was also evidenced in his test behavior; as noted previously, he was talented in conducting interesting and relevant conversation with the examiner.

It is important to note that Jamie's one area of relative weakness on the Performance Scale (9th percentile) was in a task of psychomotor speed where quick response is essential for good performance. During this task, which is highly influenced by inability to attend closely to the stimuli, Jamie yawned, scratched himself, dropped his pencil, and was generally distractible. Therefore, the examiner feels that his relative weaknesses in both the Verbal and Performance Scales were primarily a function of his failure to concentrate, not deficiencies in the specific skills involved. Reinforcement for this hypothesis is provided by an examination of his profile of scores from a testing on the 1949 WISC at age 7. At that time Jamie performed considerably better on all of the "distractibility-related" tasks. His IQs at that time (Verbal IQ = 142, Performance IQ = 100, Full-Scale IQ = 125) are basically consistent with the present findings, as he showed Very Superior verbal and Average nonverbal skills. Nevertheless, the 14-point drop in his Verbal IQ from age 7 years 3 months to 8 years 10 months is worthy of comment. First of all, research has shown that the WISC-R norms are more difficult than the old WISC norms, and this would account for about half of the observed 14-point difference. Second, the distractibility that he manifested during the administration of the WISC-R may have hindered him somewhat on other tasks as well. Finally, his Verbal IQ of 142 at age 7 was so extreme that one would expect a lower IQ on retesting simply due to the statistical phenomenon of regression to the mean. Therefore, there is no basis for concluding that Jamie's lower Verbal IQ on the WISC-R than the WISC reflects any loss of verbal function.

Summary and Recommendations

Jamie is an engaging boy of almost 9 who has previously been diagnosed as psychoneurotic. Current evaluation was made to check on a reported 42-point differential between his verbal and nonverbal mental abilities. During this evaluation he was highly distractible and easily frustrated and talked excessively. Jamie displayed separation anxieties and fears of inadequacy as well as a tendency for his coping behavior to disintegrate when placed under stress. He uses his good sense of humor as a mechanism to meet the insecurity, self-doubt, and fear of failure that he encounters daily.

On a measure of intelligence, Jamie obtained a WISC-R Verbal IQ of 128 (Superior ability) compared to his Performance IQ of 98 (Average ability). His relative strengths lie in his well-developed social understanding and interpersonal skills, while his weaknesses were more a function of his extreme distractibility than deficiency in the specific areas measured.

Jamie's weak nonverbal skills can be reduced in their effect on his functioning through compensatory use of his superior verbal abilities. He demonstrated the ability to accomplish this, as seen by his relatively better performance on a visual-motor task which has the highest verbal component. Jamie also needs extensive supportive therapy to help him relieve his overwhelming anxieties and to find more satisfying means of expressing his emotional needs.

Nadeen L. Kaufman
Psychologist

Randi R., White Female, Age 9 years 6 months

WISC-R Profile

Verbal	Scaled Score	Performance	Scaled Score
Information	14	Picture Completion	16-S
Similarities	15-S	Picture Arrangement	14
Arithmetic	8-W	Block Design	13
Vocabulary	13	Object Assembly	15
Comprehension	11	Coding	8-W
Digit Span	10		

Verbal IQ = 113.   Performance IQ = 123.   Full Scale IQ = 120.

Referral and Background Information

Randi was referred for evaluation by her parents, who are concerned about her 3-year history of theft (mostly jewelry or clothing) from them and others with no apparent reason other than the fact that "she wanted to." Whereas her mother stated that Randi knows this behavior is unacceptable, she neither admits to stealing nor apologizes unless she is forced to under duress. Randi reportedly either hides the stolen materials or gives them away. The home atmosphere is described as rigid and cold, with Randi's father (a physical chemist engaged in "top-secret" research) totally immersed in his work and unwilling to respond to his children's demands on his time. Mrs. R. refers to herself as "unaffectionate." Randi is presently in the third grade, having repeated second grade because of behavioral immaturity. Whereas she has exhibited academic ability, her schoolwork is impaired by her immature behavior (e.g., doesn't finish her work, daydreams, is constantly out of seat). Her main interests are cats, hamsters, and horses (she takes weekly lessons in horseback riding), and she is studying guitar. Neither Randi nor her 13½-year-old brother is allowed to watch television on school days—all part of their strictly structured home environment. The children must earn all of their spending money by performing chores and extra duties.

Appearance and Behavioral Characteristics

Randi is small for her 9½ years, and her reddish-blond hair, freckles, and long eyelashes all contribute to her delicate good looks. She was neatly dressed and quiet as she cooperatively approached the examiner. She was somewhat anxious initially (during the drawing tasks, which were given first), performing requested activities with an unsmiling face and little spontaneous comment. As the evaluation continued she loosened up considerably but retained her reluctance to express herself verbally on open-ended questions. When Randi did speak, she spoke rapidly and revealed a slight speech immaturity in the form of an inconsistent lisp.

On the drawing tasks Randi executed a slow, reflective style, working with her chin resting on her clenched fist on the paper. Her distinctly methodical approach included much counting and studying of the models presented in a design-copying task; also, she systematically began her human-figure drawing with the feet up to the waist, then added the trunk, and then finally the head was attempted. During visually related items on the intelligence test, Randi used the compensatory behavior of cupping both her hands around her eyes to aid her in focusing her attention on the task at hand and to prolong her concentration.

Interestingly, despite her slowness on the drawing tasks, she was able to respond very quickly on timed visual items presented to her. Randi's deliberateness appears to be more involved with the visual–motor aspect of fine coordination rather than with the nonverbal reasoning process.

Tests Administered

WISC-R
Bender–Gestalt
Draw-A-Woman
Children's Apperception Test—Human Form
Kinetic Family Drawing

Test Results and Interpretation

On the WISC-R Randi obtained a Full Scale IQ of 120 which classifies her in the Superior range of intelligence and ranks her at the 91st percentile for children her age. Her true Full Scale IQ has a 90% chance of falling within the range 115–125. Although her Performance IQ of 123 and her Verbal IQ of 113 correspond to different ability levels (Superior versus High Average), the 10-point difference between them is not sufficient to be statistically significant. Thus for all practical purposes, she performed as well with manipulation of concrete materials and visual–motor activities as she did with tasks requiring verbal comprehension and expression.

The pattern of her scores on the separate subtests may be best understood by grouping the tasks in accordance with the results of factor analysis. Randi performed exceptionally well on the tasks constituting the Verbal Comprehension factor (86th percentile) and on the tasks included on the Perceptual Organization factor (93rd percentile). Her best verbal ability (95th percentile) was in logical abstractive (categorical) thinking (e.g., telling how "anger" and "joy" are alike). However, her other verbal comprehension skills such as word knowledge and general range of information were virtually as well developed. Concerning the Perceptual Organization factor, Randi did best on a task that assessed her attention to visual detail but performed about equally well in all tasks requiring both visual–motor coordination and nonverbal reasoning.

In marked contrast to Randi's superior Verbal Comprehension and Perceptual Organization abilities were her relatively weak skills in the three tasks constituting the third factor. This factor has been labeled Freedom from Distractibility, but other interpretations of this factor also abound in the literature. In Randi's case it is clear that her poor performance could not be attributed to distractibility, because of her attentiveness and effort on all tasks administered; in addition, she displayed no test anxiety during the WISC-R despite the initial anxiety that was evident in her behavior and the more generalized anxiety that surfaced in her projective responses (described in the text that follows). The tasks on which Randi did poorest (33rd percentile) all involve manipulation of numbers. Two of the tasks are on the Verbal Scale, one requiring short-term memory of digits and the other assessing school-related computational skills (oral arithmetic problems). The third task is on the Performance Scale and requires the rapid copying of abstract symbols that are paired with numbers. Therefore one may infer that Randi has a clear and consistent weakness not only in her quantitative reasoning but in all tasks involving the mental manipulation of numerals. Even on a test of general information, Randi failed some quantitative factual items (e.g., "How many things make a dozen?" "How many pounds make a ton?") despite responding correctly to many of the more difficult non-numerical items. It should be noted that Randi's problem with numbers is not just low when compared to her superior nonverbal skills; it is also below average for children her age.

Several qualitative aspects of Randi's test performance are worthy of comment. Impressively, she responded at an extremely abstract level for a child of 9½. For example, she said that a piano and a guitar are alike because "they're musical instruments," and she defined the word "bicycle" as a "vehicle with two wheels." Also underscoring her exceptional nonverbal skills was the rapidity with which she solved the problems, earning many bonus points for solving items quickly. She was unusually quick in items requiring her to arrange pictures in the correct order to tell a sensible story. Intriguingly, she passed nearly every item in this task except for an *easy* item dealing with a burglar in the act of committing a crime. Since this subtest measures social awareness, Randi may not have learned the appropriate social response in dealing with this topic. This failure may also reflect an emotional reaction to the topic that disrupted her performance. In any case, both interpretations are congruent with her presenting problem of stealing. Another indication of Randi's awareness of her disturbing behavior was her double take when asked to define the word "thief." She proceeded to answer this vocabulary item correctly, however, after a noticeable pause.

Randi's three errors on the Bender—Gestalt test placed her visual—motor coordination at the average 8½-year-old level—a year below her C.A. of 9½. Whereas this performance is within the average ability level for children her age, it is still well below her superior nonverbal abstract reasoning skills. The drawings Randi made were of small size—a characteristic associated with anxiety, withdrawal behavior, and timidity in children. Randi's Draw-a-Woman yielded a Goodenough—Harris Standard Score of 102, which is also consistent with visual—motor coordination less well developed than nonverbal reasoning. Her score is lower than one would expect based on her reported IQs, although her lowest score on the WISC-R Performance Scale was on the one paper-and-pencil task administered (which involves psychomotor and numerical abilities). Of greater interest is the presence of two valid emotional indicators in Randi's drawing. Her figure was slanting more than 15 degrees, and there was shading of the face. Slanting figures suggest general instability, and shaded faces are associated with anxiety and poor self-concept.

On the Kinetic Family Drawing, Randi drew her mother opening a large refrigerator strategically placed in the center of the page, separating both parents. Her father was drawn walking the dog, while she drew both herself and her brother watching television high above the lower parental figures. All family members were independent of each other, with no interaction or even contact. The refrigerator, which serves here as a symbolic barrier erected to avoid conflict, also is generally associated with deprivation and depressive reactions to the deprivation. Whereas the refrigerator is a source of nurturance, it is also a cold object. Thus it may possibly reflect Randi's nurturance needs and feelings of unmet dependency in relation to her mother. In her drawing Randi apparently identified with her brother, who like herself is watching the usually denied television set. He is portrayed in appropriate dimension, seated in a chair, but Randi drew herself as a tiny, infantile figure crouching on the floor and reaching toward the TV with both hands. Perhaps the TV is a kind of parent substitute that is also unavailable to her. The faces of both Randi and her brother are shaded beyond any visibility of features, revealing generalized anxiety. Certainly this drawing presents a picture of a withdrawing, insecure child with poor self-concept rather than one drawn by an acting out child who steals.

Whereas Randi's projective stories on the Children's Apperception Test—Human Form were largely unproductive and brief, two points are worthy of mention. Randi appears to view her parents as denying and withholding of their involvement with her, of interpersonal freedom, and of material pleasures. She perceives the environment as powerful and herself as defenseless; she is simply not equipped to handle the situations that arise. With such few personal resources, she feels defeated (as opposed to harmed). Thus she exerts little effort to cope with problems, and receives instead frustrations without gratification or reward. Also revealed was Randi's feeling of rejection from her father in particular, which led to her quick rejection of a specific stimulus card.

Summary and Recommendations

Randi, a small 9½-year-old girl whose parents are concerned about her stealing, lives in a strictly regimented home with parents who neither display emotional warmth nor provide adequate time to meet her nurturance needs. In school Randi's problems revolve around behavioral immaturity. During the present evaluation Randi was cooperative although somewhat anxious at first. Whereas she was slow and deliberate on drawing tasks that emphasized visual—motor fine coordination, she was unusually rapid in responding to visual perceptual items which stressed nonverbal abstract reasoning. Her Superior IQ of 120 revealed Randi's exceptional verbal comprehension and perceptual organization but uncovered a relative weakness in the mental manipulation of numbers. Randi's responses during the testing indicated her awareness of stealing as a source of concern. Projective measures combined to describe a very anxious, withdrawing girl with low self-concept. Her sense of personal defeat, parental rejection, and lack of adequate coping mechanisms leads one to suspect that her stealing is a means by which Randi seeks to infuse herself with a greater sense of personal worth. Her taking of objects more symbolic in their actual use to her than in their fulfillment of a material need reflects her internalization of parental values. Randi needs redirection to help her gain self-esteem and status in her parents' eyes by other, socially acceptable means. There does not appear to be any course of action presently available to her that would enable her to receive parental approval. Mr. and Mrs. R. would thus benefit from parent counseling to help them establish mutually satisfactory means for Randi to communicate her needs and subsequently receive appropriate gratification.

Nadeen L. Kaufman
Psychologist

Jennie L., Black Female, Age 10 years 4 months

WISC-R Profile			
Verbal	Scaled Score	Performance	Scaled Score
Information	5	Picture Completion	3
Similarities	4	Picture Arrangement	1
Arithmetic	5	Block Design	1
Vocabulary	3	Object Assembly	2
Comprehension	5	Coding	8-S
Digit Span	9-S	Mazes	4

Verbal IQ = 66.   Performance IQ = 54.   Full Scale IQ = 56.

Referral and Background Information

Jennie was referred for evaluation by her school, where she attends a fifth-grade EMR class. For the past 2 years she has demonstrated "spells" during which she is unresponsive, uncommunicative, has abnormal eye movements, and displays symptoms of petit mal epileptic seizures. These spells have been occurring more frequently now, about 1 or 2 days per week, and followed by an afternoon of sleep. During the rest of the time Jennie appears to be a normally behaved girl with none of these problems. When tested in school last month, she was seen on a "bad day" and no valid test scores were obtained.

Coming from a concerned and cooperative family, Jennie lives at home with both parents, an older sister who has a 4-year-old daughter, and three older brothers. Jennie is described as being jealous of her 4-year-old niece who has taken over her status as baby of the family. Her spells occur at home as well, where she is seen as "drifting off" and unaware of what is going on around her. Other than this high-priority problem, low-priority difficulties are seen by her parents as involving her lack of concentration, distractibility, crying spells, demands of excessive attention, and sensitivity. She does play with other children, although she is sometimes teased by them about her size.

Appearance and Behavioral Characteristics

At almost 10½ years of age, Jennie is a broad, heavy-set, but attractive black girl with her hair worn in several ponytails. When first brought by her public-school teacher, one short lapse of attention occurred during a small-talk conversation; Jennie responded appropriately to the teacher's placing her finger under Jennie's chin, however. This behavior did not recur during the evaluation.

Starting out with a good work set and cooperative attitude, Jennie occasionally looked up from her work and smiled at the examiner. Remaining quiet and soft spoken, she maintained a diligent pattern of concentration that rarely wavered. She appeared tired (and yawned more frequently as the session advanced), and her overall affect was somewhat dull. Her mouth often dropped open, and she did not react with noticeable emotion to either the test materials or exchanges with the examiner. Her verbalization "gol-lee" was her most vibrant expression.

During drawing tasks Jennie was concerned over her difficulty in managing to get down on the paper what she was thinking in her head. Her inadequacies appeared to be involved in the associative and expressive end of the visual–perceptual process, as she exclaimed her dissatisfaction with her productions. For example, when drawing her family, she kept repeating "These ain't not my family—my Mama don't really look like this." On abstract designs she said "that don't look right," and on both types of drawing tasks (concrete and abstract) she erased constantly. Similarly, on other visual–perceptual tasks, such as assembling cut-up picture puzzles, her trial-and-error attempts were grotesquely wrong. Jennie's methods of coping with this frustration alternated between laughing at her productions and wanting to give up. She was able to be encouraged to continue her efforts, however, and worked for the full time allotments. Her lack of confidence and fear of failure were realistic, therefore, and led to brief attempts to control the testing situation. Jennie wanted to play physical, gross-motor type of activities and coaxed the examiner in this behalf. At the end of the evaluation, the examiner did play ball with her, and she demonstrated both reasonably good athletic ability as well as the appropriate affective expressions of her enjoyment.

The most concerning behavior Jennie evidenced throughout the testing session was the pervasiveness of the perseveration she demonstrated. She fell into a repetitious pattern of response on several different tasks, although the examiner was eventually successful in breaking her "closed circuit" and getting her back to more careful evaluation of test items.

Tests Administered

WISC-R
Bender−Gestalt
Draw-a-Woman
Kinetic Family Drawing
Sentence Completion

Test Results and Interpretation

Jennie scored in the Mentally Deficient range of intelligence on the WISC-R, obtaining a Verbal IQ of 66, a Performance IQ of 54, and a Full Scale IQ of 56. Her true Full Scale IQ has a 90% likelihood of falling in the 51−61 range, indicating that even allowing for a reasonable band of error her mental functioning is below the first percentile for children her age. Although her Verbal IQ ranked her at only the first percentile, her verbal comprehension skills were still superior to her inadequate abilities in the nonverbal sphere (in which she surpassed only one out of 1000 children her age).

Two outstanding strengths were evidenced by Jennie—one on a short-term memory task (37th percentile) and the other on a test requiring her to rapidly match symbols with numbers (25th percentile). On the memory subtest she displayed an exceptional forward span of seven digits, although she was unable to reverse even two digits. Repeating digits forward and the rapid matching of symbols are both essentially "automatic" tasks insofar as they require the child to use overlearned operations instead of higher-level problem-solving skills. Her performance on a test of oral arithmetic was not commensurate with these two strengths, but she still displayed mastery of rote counting skills and simple addition and subtraction facts despite an inability to reason numerically. Her Low Average ability (19th percentile) on the three tasks involving automatic functioning far outstripped her verbal comprehension ability and is dramatically higher than her performance on tests requiring spatial and nonverbal reasoning. For example, Jennie was virtually unable to arrange pictures to tell a meaningful story or to copy designs out of blocks.

Jennie displayed little scatter in the various tests of verbal comprehension and expression. In other words, her verbal concept formation, logical thinking, and common sense understanding of social situations are all about equally developed and are consistent with her mentally retarded functioning.

Overall, her most pervasive cognitive deficiencies reflect possible dysfunctioning in the right hemisphere of the brain. Lending support to this hypothesis is the fact that Jennie did so poorly on the Bender–Gestalt test. Earning a Koppitz error score of 9, her performance is more than 4 SDs below the mean for children her own age, and in fact is typical of a 6-year-old's level of visual–motor development. All her errors are considered either significant or highly significant indicators of brain injury when found in the protocols of children her age. Rotations and distortions of shape comprised the majority of her errors. Two emotional indicators were evidenced in Jennie's Bender drawings: overwork or reinforced lines and second attempts at drawing figures. Both of these signs are associated with impulsiveness. As mentioned previously, she was both critical of her productions and very aware of her errors. These behaviors, with other suggestions of neurological impairment (e.g., constant counting of the dots and circles in designs), all point to compensations for her visual–motor deficit.

The woman Jennie drew on the Draw-a-Woman test received a Goodenough–Harris Standard Score of 80. Although this score is quantitatively superior to her other test scores, qualitatively speaking the human figure was quite consistent with her deficient performances. Whereas many essential body parts were represented, her ability to conceptualize the relationship between these parts is deficient, and the resulting drawing was extremely primitive. The head was huge, as large as the entire remaining figure, and the stick body extended down between the legs almost as long as a third appendage. Both hands and feet resembled chicken feet. The one valid emotional indicator, poor integration of parts of the figure, has been found most frequently on the drawings of brain-injured youngsters and is associated with neurological impairment.

By her own admission, food and eating represent very pleasurable stimuli to Jennie, so it is not surprising that for the Kinetic Family Drawing she drew family members sitting at the table for dinner. Oddly, though, she drew the food first, erasing and labeling the various dishes, and only later when questioned by the examiner about her family did she include her mother, father, one brother, and herself. The brother she drew is the sibling closest in age to herself. Jennie omitted all other family members. Both her constant erasing (and corresponding concern with the differences between her creations and reality) and perseveration (e.g., each person wore the same square hat and was identically drawn) characterized the picture. All of Jennie's drawing efforts led to the same suggestion of neurological impairment rather than emotional causation of the inadequacy and distortions displayed.

Jennie enjoyed the projective Sentence Completion test and took a long time to respond thoughtfully to each new stimulus stem. Here, too, perseveration abounded throughout the 40 items. Her responses indicated a normal relationship at home and with others, with special attachment to her parents. This closeness is even greater between Jennie and her mother, and many of her statements revolved around her wanting to please and be like Mrs. L. There is an immature dependency nature about this relationship, however. At times Jennie gave a "clang" word association instead of an appropriate response (e.g., "When I get mad *I get glad"*). In all, Jennie appears to function consistently like a child with brain dysfunction.

Summary and Recommendations

A heavy 10½-year-old black girl referred for evaluation due to "spells" described as loss of contact with her world, Jennie did not experience any such spell on the day of testing. Instead she worked with full effort, despite frustrations over her inadequate performances on many of the tasks put to her. She demonstrated various behaviors typical of a brain-injured child and scored in the Mentally Deficient range (Full Scale IQ = 56) on the intelligence test. She was greatly impaired in her visual—motor abilities, and all her test results were consistently within the mentally deficient category except for her near average functioning on tasks such as short-term memory that require "automatic" responding.

Although not viewed during the current evaluation, Jennie is apparently experiencing some type of brain seizure affecting her behavior during the described "spells." These seizures are symptomatic of the underlying brain dysfunction that has probably resulted in both her intellectual loss and behavioral abnormalities. Her most urgent need, therefore, is a thorough neurological examination, which includes a series of electroencephalograms (EEGs). Perhaps medication can be prescribed that will alleviate some of her aberrant brain activity. An appointment has already been set up with Jennie's teacher to administer the AAMD Adaptive Behavior Scale (Public School Version, 1974 revision). By examining Jennie's profile based on regular class norms, more specific information will be provided about the breadth and range of her apparently deficient functioning; the supplementary use of EMR norms will help determine the appropriateness of her current EMR placement.

Since Jennie has a strength in automatic skills, this wonderful asset should be relied on for simple association-type learning. Use of gross motor activity should be incorporated into the academic setting as much as possible; subject matter can be programmed right into a physical game. This approach can provide both a motivational device and a built-in source of success in her endeavors. Jennie will need conclusions drawn for her, since this level of reasoning probably will not come on her own during learning experiences. Special attention from both her mother (and father) at home and her teacher at school will be advantageous to watch for Jennie's perseveration tendencies; she will need to be stopped and redirected when repetitious patterns cripple her functioning.

Jennie is approaching puberty and the accompanying social pressures of adolescence; it is especially necessary at this time to watch her diet to preserve her appearance. If Jennie can develop outside interests to take the emphasis off food as provider of her major source of gratification, that will certainly benefit her in more than one area. In conjunction with this suggestion, a program designed to build up a sense of greater independence and self-direction on Jennie's part would be a valuable addition to her remediation. She has the motivation and initiative to respond to domestic activities and chores if given appropriate encouragement. Mrs. L. can easily facilitate this development at home.

Nadeen L. Kaufman
Psychologist

CHAPTER 4

Abilities Measured by the WISC-R Subtests

SHARED AND UNIQUE ABILITIES

Each WISC-R subtest measures some abilities that are shared with one or more other subtests and some abilities that are subtest specific. In this chapter the issues pertaining to the interpretation of unique abilities are treated, although the decided focus of the sections that follow is on shared abilities. Skills that transcend several subtests have already been discussed in Chapters 2 and 3 from the vantage points of factor analysis, Bannatyne's recategorizations of subtests, and Guilford's SOI model. Overlapping abilities remain in the forefront of this chapter despite the shifting of attention from the IQ scales and factor scores to the separate subtests, because I believe that the WISC-R is maximally useful when tasks are grouped and regrouped to uncover a child's strong and weak areas of functioning. Chapter 5 offers a research-oriented discussion of some of the more important shared abilities underlying the WISC-R, and Chapter 6 details the kind of detective work that is required to pinpoint which abilities, measured by two or more subtests, reflect strengths or weaknesses for a child. Whereas the detective work may lead to the ultimate conclusion that a child has a strong or weak ability only in the skill assessed by a single subtest, such a finding is always the last resort of a good detective and is usually of limited practical value.

  The present chapter is intended to serve as a source of raw materials for the generation and testing of hypotheses that characterize Chapters 5 and 6. Consequently, the reader would be wise to pay particular attention to the diversity of abilities that are each assessed by several subtests and to try to internalize an understanding of these shared abilities.

Overview of Shared Abilities

In the next section each of the 12 WISC-R subtests is analyzed in terms of the abilities it presumably assesses and the influences (e.g., richness of early environment, anxiety) to which it is believed to be vulnerable. This section serves as a road map for the subtest-by-subtest analysis that follows.

First, each subtest is classified in terms of its primary (and in some instances secondary) factor loadings based on factor analysis of the WISC-R standardization sample at ages 6½ − 16½ years (Kaufman 1975), its grouping(s) according to Bannatyne's (1971, 1974) recategorization scheme, and its mental operation(s) from the vantage point of Guilford's model (Meeker 1969, 1975b). Although only the Guilford operation dimension is featured for each subtest in the next section, the devotee of SOI theory can refer to Table 3-1 for a three-dimensional analysis of each subtest.

Following the three major, widely used classification schemes indicated here is a list of other abilities that each subtest shares with at least one other WISC-R subtest. These abilities, listed in alphabetical order for each subtest, are based primarily on the various discussions of what Wechsler's tasks measure. Sources consulted extend back to the 1940s (Rapaport, Gill, et al., 1945−1946), although the most influential references were Glasser and Zimmerman (1967), Lutey (1977), Mayman, Schafer, et al. (1951), Sattler (1974), and Wechsler (1958). Some of the abilities attributed to the WISC-R subtests in the next section are not found in the sources consulted but seem to be important from the perspective of cerebral specialization (Bever 1975; Bogen 1969; Kaufman in press a), or from the psycholinguistic models that stress the nature of the input and output rather than the item content (Myers and Hammill 1976).

The conventional abilities supposedly measured by Wechsler's subtests, which appear repeatedly in sources such as Sattler (1974) or Glasser and Zimmerman (1967), include diverse skills such as verbal concept formation, mental alertness, social judgment, synthesis, and planning ability. From the cerebral specialization literature emerges the abilities of holistic (right brain) processing versus integrated brain functioning (see pp. 157−163); and from the psycholinguistic approach come abilities focusing on the nature of the stimulus (visual perception of abstract stimuli) or the response (verbal expression). All the abilities listed for each WISC-R subtest are considered to be required for successful performance on that task, although the lists are necessarily not exhaustive. Psychologists from different orientations would compile somewhat different lists of abilities, and any given child tested on the WISC-R may succeed or fail on some subtests due to skills and variables that are unique to him or her. Consequently, the lists of abilities shared by two or more subtests should be a starting point to be used flexibly by examiners, with additional skills added to the lists based on their clinical experiences and theoretical beliefs.

Following the enumeration of shared abilities for each subtest is a list of the influences that are considered to affect an individual's performance on that task. Although these influences are basically derived from the same sources as the conventional abilities and are often not treated separately from the abilities by the various authors, they are grouped separately here. Distractibility, anxiety, cultural opportunities at home, attention span, and other factors play an important role in a person's Wechsler profile. However, it is difficult to conceive of mental tasks as being primarily a measure of concentration or attention, as Rapaport and his colleagues claim for Arithmetic and Digit Span, respectively. By keeping the abilities and influences in discrete groupings, examiners will have a constant reminder of whether their hypotheses are in the cognitive or the behavioral—background domain. As explained in Chapter 3 regarding the Freedom from Distractibility factor, hypotheses of low scores due to a behavioral or background variable (i.e., due to an "influence") do *not* imply that the child is deficient in the abilities measured by the subtests. Even more so than the lists of abilities for the subtests, the lists of influences affecting subtest scores can always be increased and modified based on the particular testing conditions, the child's unique background and approach to each new task, the examiner's clinical acumen and range of experiences, and so forth.

Finally, the unique ability or abilities probably tapped by each WISC-R subtest are indicated following the shared abilities and the influences affecting test performance. Derived from the conventional sources in the literature, these so-called unique abilities are essentially those skills that have been associated with one and only one subtest by numerous psychologists. Thus, for example, Similarities is often considered to measure verbal concept formation, degree of abstract thinking, distinguishing essential from nonessential details, and logical abstractive (categorical) thinking. The first two abilities are also assessed by Vocabulary, and distinguishing essential from nonessential details is measured as well by Picture Completion and Picture Arrangement; since these skills are shared with other subtests, they are included in the list of Similarities' shared abilities. In contrast, no other WISC-R task assesses categorical thinking, qualifying this skill as the subtest's uniqueness.

Subtest-by-subtest Analysis

This analysis presents the six Verbal subtests first, followed by the six Performance subtests.

Information

Abilities Shared with Other Subtests:

Factor analysis	—Verbal Comprehension
Bannatyne	—Acquired Knowledge
Guilford	—Memory (primarily)
Other skills	—Fund of information
	—Long-term memory

Subject to Influence of:

Cultural opportunities at home
Interests

Outside reading
Richness of early environment
School learning

Unique Ability:

Range of general factual knowledge

Similarities

Abilities Shared with Other Subtests:

Factor analysis	—Verbal Comprehension
Bannatyne	—Verbal Conceptualization
Guilford	—Cognition
Other skills	—Degree of abstract thinking
	—Distinguishing essential from nonessential details
	—Reasoning (verbal)
	—Verbal concept formation
	—Verbal expression

Subject to Influence of:

Interests

Outside reading

Unique Ability:

Logical abstractive (categorical) thinking

Arithmetic

Abilities Shared with Other Subtests:

Factor analysis	—Freedom from Distractibility (primarily)
	—Verbal Comprehension (secondarily)
Bannatyne	—Sequencing
	—Acquired Knowledge
Guilford	—Cognition
	—Memory
Other skills	—Facility with numbers
	—Mental alertness
	—Long-term memory
	—Reasoning (numerical)

Subject to Influence of:

Attention span

Anxiety

Concentration

Distractibility

School learning

Working under time pressure

Unique Ability:

Computational skill

Vocabulary

Abilities Shared with Other Subtests:

Factor analysis	—Verbal Comprehension
Bannatyne	—Verbal Conceptualization
	—Acquired Knowledge
Guilford	—Cognition
Other skills	—Degree of abstract thinking
	—Fund of information
	—Learning ability
	—Long-term memory
	—Verbal concept formation
	—Verbal expression

Subject to Influence of:

Cultural opportunities at home

Interests

Outside reading

Richness of early environment

School learning

Unique Abilities:

Language development

Word knowledge

Comprehension

Abilities Shared with Other Subtests:

Factor analysis	—Verbal Comprehension
Bannatyne	—Verbal Conceptualization
Guilford	—Evaluation
Other skills	—Common sense (cause–effect rela-
	tionships)
	—Reasoning (verbal)
	—Social judgment (social intelligence)
	—Verbal expression

Subject to Influence of:
Cultural opportunities at home
Development of conscience or moral sense

Unique Abilities:
Demonstration of practical information
Evaluation and use of past experiences

Digit Span

Abilities Shared with Other Subtests:

Factor analysis	—Freedom from Distractibility
Bannatyne	—Sequencing
Guilford	—Memory
Other skills	—Facility with numbers
	—Mental alertness

Subject to Influence of:
Attention span
Anxiety
Distractibility

Unique ability:
Short-term memory (auditory)

Picture Completion

Abilities Shared with Other Subtests:

Factor analysis	—Perceptual Organization (primarily)
	—Verbal Comprehension (secondarily)
Bannatyne	—Spatial
Guilford	—Cognition
	—Evaluation
Other skills	—Distinguishing essential from nonessential details
	—Holistic (right-brain) processing
	—Visual organization without essential motor activity
	—Visual perception of meaningful stimuli (people—things)

Subject to Influence of:
Ability to respond when uncertain
Cognitive style (field dependence—field independence)

Concentration

Working under time pressure

Unique Abilities:

Visual alertness

Visual recognition and identification (long-term visual memory)

Picture Arrangement

Abilities Shared with Other Subtests:

Factor analysis	—Perceptual Organization (primarily) —Verbal Comprehension (secondarily)
Bannatyne	—Excluded, but requires Sequencing Ability
Guilford	—Convergent production —Evaluation
Other skills	—Common sense (cause—effect relationships) —Distinguishing essential from nonessential details —Integrated brain functioning —Planning ability (comprehending and sizing up total situation) —Reasoning (nonverbal) —Social judgment (social intelligence) —Synthesis —Visual perception of meaningful stimuli (people—things) —Visual organization without essential motor activity

Subject to Influence of:

Creativity

Cultural opportunities at home

Exposure to comic strips

Working under time pressure

Unique Abilities:

Anticipation of consequences

Temporal sequencing and time concepts

Block Design

Abilities Shared with Other Subtests:

Factor analysis	—Perceptual Organization

Bannatyne	—Spatial
Guilford	—Cognition
	—Evaluation
Other skills	—Integrated brain functioning
	—Reproduction of models
	—Synthesis
	—Visual–motor coordination
	—Visual perception of abstract stimuli (designs–symbols)

Subject to Influence of:
Cognitive style (field dependence–field independence)
Working under time pressure

Unique Abilities:
Analysis of whole into component parts
Nonverbal concept formation
Spatial visualization

Object Assembly

Abilities Shared with Other Subtests:

Factor analysis	—Perceptual Organization
Bannatyne	—Spatial
Guilford	—Cognition
	—Evaluation
Other skills	—Holistic (right-brain) processing
	—Synthesis
	—Visual–motor coordination
	—Visual perception of meaningful stimuli (people–things)

Subject to Influence of:
Ability to respond when uncertain
Cognitive style (field dependence–field independence)
Experience with puzzles
Working under time pressure

Unique Abilities:
Ability to benefit from sensory–motor feedback
Anticipation of relationships among parts
Flexibility

Coding (A&B)

Abilities Shared with Other Subtests:

Factor analysis	—Freedom from Distractibility
Bannatyne	—Sequencing
Guilford	—Convergent production
	—Evaluation
Other skills	—Facility with numbers (Coding B only)
	—Integrated brain functioning
	—Learning ability
	—Paper-and-pencil skill
	—Reproduction of models
	—Visual–motor coordination
	—Visual perception of abstract stimuli (designs–symbols)

Subject to Influence of:

Anxiety

Distractibility

Working under time pressure

Unique Abilities:

Ability to follow directions

Clerical speed and accuracy

Psychomotor speed

Short-term memory (visual)

Mazes

Abilities Shared with Other Subtests:

Factor analysis	—Perceptual Organization
Bannatyne	—Excluded, but requires Spatial Ability
Guilford	—Cognition
Other skills	—Integrated brain functioning
	—Paper-and-pencil skill
	—Planning ability (comprehending and sizing up total situation)
	—Reasoning (nonverbal)
	—Visual–motor coordination

Subject to Influence of:

Ability to respond when uncertain

Experience in solving mazes
Working under time pressure

Unique Abilities:
Following a visual pattern
Foresight

PSYCHOMETRIC CONSIDERATIONS

Apart from the empirical technique of factor analysis, the previous part of this chapter has been derived from clinical, theoretical, and rational perspectives accumulating from psychologists' experiences with the Wechsler scales for more than 40 years. Proper test interpretation also depends on certain psychometric guidelines; the following sections on measures of *g* and on subtest specificity are intended to facilitate the examiner's tasks of understanding and interpreting a child's profile of abilities.

Measures of *g*   *General Intelligence*

There are several methods of determining the degree to which a subtest measures *g*, or general intelligence, including the use of second-order factor analysis (Cohen 1959), hierarchical factor analysis (Wallbrown, Blaha, et al. 1975), and the unrotated first factor in principal factor analysis (Kaufman 1975). All techniques seem to yield highly similar results, and the choice of a particular approach is arbitrary. Table 4-1 presents the loadings of each WISC-R subtest on the large unrotated first factor in the age-by-age principal factor analyses of the standardization sample (Kaufman 1975); these loadings are interpreted here as the *g* coefficients for each subtest. Overall, the 12 subtests group into three categories according to their average loadings across the age range:

Good Measures of *g*	Fair Measures of *g*	Poor Measures of *g*
Vocabulary	Arithmetic	Digit Span
Information	Picture Completion	Mazes
Similarities	Object Assembly	Coding
Block Design	Picture Arrangement	
Comprehension		

The "good" measures have average loadings of at least 0.70, the "fair" have loadings of about 0.60, and the "poor" load below 0.50. [The slight discrepancies between the average values in Table 4-1 and the averages reported by Kaufman (1975) arose from the use of means in the former vs. medians in the latter].

The mean values for the total sample represent a good approximation of the findings for each year of age between 7½ and 16½ years. At age 6½, however, certain discrepancies are evident in Table 4-1: Picture Arrangement joins Block Design as a good nonverbal measure of g; Information, Arithmetic, and Vocabulary are the only good verbal measures of g; and Digit Span and Mazes are fair measures of g. Another age trend of note occurs at 8½−9½ years, at which point both Similarities and Vocabulary improve markedly as measures of general intelligence.

One should not overvalue the notion of g or the specific psychometric information reported in Table 4-1. As expressed earlier (see pp. 5−7) and elaborated more fully elsewhere (Kaufman in press a), the WISC-R Full-Scale IQ does not adequately reflect the diversity of mental functions handled by the left-brain processing system, the right-brain processing system, and by the integration between the cognitive styles of the two hemispheres. Consequently, the notion of g must be thought of as the global ability underlying a conventional intelligence test such as the WISC-R or Stanford−Binet, but not as a theoretical construct underlying human intellect. As such, the so-called g factor still has relevance in a practical sense, but it should be stripped of the almost magical powers that are sometimes attributed to it.

Practically, knowledge of the magnitude of each subtest's loadings on the

Table 4-1   Loadings of Each Subtest on the Unrotated "General" Factor, by Age

WISC-R Subtest	6½	7½	8½	9½	10½	11½	12½	13½	14½	15½	16½	Mean
Verbal												
Information	70	76	69	75	70	82	76	78	81	72	77	75
Similarities	59	68	69	81	80	79	76	79	83	76	75	75
Arithmetic	69	65	54	65	60	67	67	70	64	60	62	64
Vocabulary	69	71	71	84	80	80	83	84	83	80	84	79
Comprehension	61	65	67	75	64	74	72	73	76	70	73	70
Digit Span	58	52	36	49	40	38	49	47	49	45	49	47
Performance												
Picture Completion	60	53	58	63	59	61	69	59	64	61	62	61
Picture Arrangement	71	63	64	62	50	54	64	56	60	50	45	58
Block Design	71	73	67	74	71	73	79	76	71	70	73	73
Object Assembly	65	68	63	67	62	63	61	52	59	52	60	61
Coding	41	34	50	41	39	42	41	46	37	42	47	42
Mazes	59	54	47	45	42	44	50	31	42	48	45	46

Note: Decimal points omitted.

unrotated general factor across the age range facilitates profile interpretation. The loadings foster an anticipation of which subtests are most likely to be deviant from a child's overall level of functioning. Digit Span, Coding, and Mazes are such poor measures of global ability on the WISC-R that significant deviations should reasonably be anticipated on any or all of these subtests. Whereas such discrepancies may lead to meaningful hypotheses about the child's strong and weak skill areas, significant fluctuations on these three subtests are simply too normal to be suggestive of an abnormality.

The good measures of g, however, are much less likely to deviate substantially from a child's overall verbal and nonverbal abilities. An examiner has reason to anticipate consistent functioning on these tasks and should treat significant deviations on one or more of the good measures of g as potentially noteworthy. When individuals score very high or low on tasks that ordinarily reflect very closely their Full Scale IQ, it is reasonable to anticipate noncognitive explanations for the discrepancies. For example, relatively poor performance on Information and Vocabulary may be a direct function of an impoverished cultural environment at home, whereas uncharacteristically high scores on the same two subtests may be indicative of an enriched home environment and perhaps a strong parental push for achievement. Unusually low scores on Similarities and Block Design may be related to a difficulty in handling abstractions, a problem sometimes considered to have neurological implications. Certainly, discrepant scores on the "high g" subtests are insufficient evidence for any noncognitive interpretation of the fluctuations unless there is strong additional background, behavioral, and test data to corroborate the hypothesis. However, knowledge of the g loadings for the WISC-R subtests can provide examiners with a sense of anticipation of what to expect in a profile, thereby enhancing their ability to lend meaningful interpretation to peaks and valleys in a scaled-score pattern.

Subtest Specificity

Highly related to the concept of a general factor, and to some extent an inverse of g, is the notion of subtest specificity. Just as a subtest has reliable variance that is shared with other subtests, so does it have a portion of its reliable variance that is unique to it. To determine the feasibility of interpreting the unique abilities or traits attributed to a subtest, one must first calculate the amount of its reliable variance that is not shared with any other WISC-R subtests. If this unique variance for a given subtest is sufficient in magnitude (arbitrarily, about 25% or more of the total variance) and if it exceeds the error variance, it is reasonable and justifiable to interpret that subtest's unique contributions to the test battery.

The statistical technique for computing a subtest's unique variance or specificity is objective and straightforward. First, an estimate of the common or shared variance for each subtest has to be obtained. The common variance is then subtracted from the subtest's reliability coefficient (which equals the total reliable variance for the subtest), yielding the reliable unique variance or subtest specificity. When the specificity is compared to the error variance for the subtest (equal to 1 minus the reliability), one can determine whether it is sensible to interpret that task's uniqueness.

Adhering to Cohen's (1959) statistical technique, I used the communalities of the subtests, derived from factor analysis, as estimates of shared variance for computing subtest specificities (Kaufman 1975). Although accepting the communality approach as valid, Silverstein (1976) has argued cogently for the preferential use of squared multiple correlations as estimates of common variance. He stresses the greater objectivity of the squared multiples, and I am convinced by his arguments. Consequently, I have used the more objective estimate of common variance to compute subtest specificities (see Table 4-2), which yields somewhat different information about uniqueness than was reported in my 1975 article.

As shown in Table 4-2, the mean proportion of specific variance exceeds the mean error variance for every WISC-R subtest except Object Assembly. Of the 11 subtests with more specific than error variance, only Vocabulary had an average amount of reliable unique variance that dipped below the arbitrary cutoff of 25%.

An age-by-age analysis of Table 4-2 reveals that the following subtests had more specific variance than error variance at nine or more of the 11 age levels: Information, Arithmetic, Digit Span, Picture Arrangement, Block Design, Coding, and Mazes. It is certainly logical to interpret the unique abilities for these seven subtests across the entire age range. With some caution it is also sensible to interpret the subtest specificity at ages 6½–16½ years for Vocabulary and Picture Completion. For Vocabulary, the specificity was greater than the error variance for eight different age groups; for Picture Completion, the proportion of specific variance was at least 0.25 at each level. In addition, for both of these subtests, the difference was typically quite small whenever the specific variance did not exceed the error variance. Note that the amount of specificity for Picture Completion is particularly impressive at ages 6½–8½.

Like Picture Completion, Similarities has an ample amount of specific variance up to age 8½, far exceeding its error variance. Unfortunately, Similarities' specificity at ages 9½ and above is inadequate. The specific variance for Comprehension exceeded 25% at most ages, although the specificity was greater than the error variance at only four age levels. Nevertheless, since the differences in favor of the error variance were typically small, Comprehension's subtest specificity may be interpreted across the age range, if caution is exercised. In contrast, Object Assembly does *not* have sufficient subtest specificity to warrant meaningful interpretation.

Table 4-2 Percent of Specific Variance for Each WISC-R Subtest, by Age

WISC-R Subtest	6½	7½	8½	9½	10½	11½	12½	13½	14½	15½	16½	Mean Specific Variance	Mean Error Variance
Verbal													
Information	19	25	*31*	22	33	21	29	23	20	*30*	27	25	16
Similarities	*52*	*37*	*30*	14	17	18	25	17	15	17	28	25	19
Arithmetic	*31*	29	*36*	*32*	*38*	*34*	*32*	29	24	*41*	29	32	23
Vocabulary	26	15	*31*	13	21	19	20	16	18	18	*19*	20	15
Comprehension	30	26	25	20	27	27	*31*	25	22	19	22	25	23
Digit Span	*41*	*55*	*59*	*41*	*43*	*49*	*40*	*44*	*48*	*47*	*42*	46	23
Performance													
Picture Completion	*47*	*49*	*49*	*32*	28	*38*	25	*31*	27	27	*32*	35	24
Picture Arrangement	*30*	*33*	27	*35*	*47*	*43*	*33*	*38*	*38*	*45*	*48*	38	27
Block Design	*31*	*28*	*39*	*23*	*32*	*29*	*26*	*24*	*26*	*28*	*30*	29	15
Object Assembly	*29*	22	19	20	19	21	22	29	25	28	22	23	30
Coding	*42*	*47*	*50*	*55*	*55*	*52*	*56*	*40*	*49*	*57*	*56*	51	27
Mazes	*42*	*43*	*53*	*46*	*39*	*50*	*35*	*41*	*46*	*38*	*29*	42	30

Note: These subtest specificities were computed using *multiple squared correlations* as the estimates of common variance. Italics are used to indicate each percent of specific variance that *exceeds* the percent of error variance for the subtest at that age. Error variance, by definition, equals 1 minus the reliability coefficient.

113

The following groupings summarize the preceding discussion:

Ample Specificity	Adequate Specificity	Inadequate Specificity
Information	Vocabulary	Similarities
Similarities	Comprehension	(ages 9½ − 16½)
(ages 6½ − 8½)	Picture Completion	Object Assembly
Arithmetic	(ages 9½ − 16½)	
Digit Span		
Picture Completion		
(ages 6½ − 8½)		
Picture Arrangement		
Block Design		
Coding		
Mazes		

The results of the subtest specificity analysis conducted here are similar to the findings reported in my 1975 article, but not identical. The use of squared multiple correlations as estimates of common variance produced slightly higher specificities than were yielded by the use of communalities in virtually every computation for all 12 subtests; some increments were as large as 0.10, although typical increases were about 0.05. The net effect is to modify some of the recommendations made in my article regarding interpretation of a child's unique abilities. Despite what was suggested in the article, the new analysis indicates that Information and Block Design each have an ample amount of specificity rather than a borderline amount; Vocabulary and Comprehension have just enough specific variance to warrant cautious interpretation, not inadequate amounts, and Mazes' unique abilities can be interpreted across the entire age range, not only for children below age 12.

How does the subtest specificity information translate to action? First, it gives examiners the right to make subtest-specific interpretations for all subtests *except* Object Assembly and (at ages 9½ and above) Similarities. The data do not, however, elevate unique interpretations of subtests into the foreground. The fact that examiners *can* make specific inferences about subtests does not mean they necessarily *should* make such inferences. For half of the regularly administered subtests, the common variance exceeded the specific variance at every age level, and for an additional three subtests the common or shared variance was higher at most age levels. Only the three poor measures of g—Digit Span, Coding, and Mazes—consistently displayed more specific than common variance across the age range. Consequently, it is more justifiable to stress the likelihood that a child's performance on most WISC-R subtests is due to abilities shared with other subtests than to focus on uniqueness.

The method for interpreting strengths and weaknesses described in Chapter 2 (see pp. 54−57), involving significant discrepancies from the child's own mean scaled scores on the Verbal and Performance Scales, is deeply rooted in the notion that shared variance is the most likely determinant of a youngster's score on any WISC-R subtest. Significant fluctuations are defined as scaled scores 3 points or more from the child's mean. *I believe that a subtest's unique abilities should be interpreted for children only when their scaled score on that subtest deviates by at least 3 points from their average scaled score on the relevant scale.* However, the mere fact of a significant fluctuation does not imply that the examiner should automatically interpret that subtest's uniqueness. To the contrary, the examiner's first line of investigation should be to conduct the thorough kind of detective work outlined in Chapter 6 to try to discover what *shared* abilities might have been responsible for the significantly deviating score. Only when all hypotheses prove fruitless should an examiner acquiesce to an interpretation of a unique and highly specific strength or weakness.

For the subtests with ample specificity, the ±3 rule is a reasonable one to follow. For Vocabulary, Comprehension, and Picture Completion (the latter subtest at ages 9½ and above only), more caution is needed. Hence, unique abilities for these tasks should only be interpreted if there is a deviation of 4 points from the Verbal or Performance mean. Similarities (at ages 9½ and above) and Object Assembly should not be given subtest-specific interpretations in usual circumstances. However, when an extraordinarily large deviation from a mean is observed (say, 6 points) for one of these subtests and all hypotheses regarding shared abilities are rejected, it is reasonable for an examiner to speculate about a unique ability.

SUPPLEMENTARY ISSUES

Three additional topics are worthy of inclusion in a chapter dealing with the abilities measured by the WISC-R subtests. Although the topics are basically independent of each other, they all contribute to the examiner's increased understanding of WISC-R interpretation and should thus enhance intelligent testing. In order, the areas treated in the following sections are: deciding whether to administer Coding or Mazes; understanding the role of speed on Performance subtests; and comparing the abilities measured by the WISC-R and its predecessor, the 1949 WISC.

Coding versus Mazes

Some WISC-R examiners routinely administer Coding as part of the regular battery, totally ignoring Mazes, and unaware that they have a legitimate choice to make regarding test administration. Unlike Digit Span, which is clearly a supplementary Verbal task, Mazes may be substituted for Coding at the whim of the examiner. According to Wechsler (1974, p. 8), Coding was included in the regular battery primarily because of its brief administration time, but Mazes has much to recommend it and may be used instead of Coding. Wechsler even states that he favors Mazes over Coding below age 8 because of its much greater reliability at the young ages (low 0.80s vs. low 0.60s).

Whenever administration time is not a compelling issue, I urge examiners to administer *both* subtests to a child regardless of his or her age. As is evident from the list of abilities measured by these subtests (pp. 108–109), Coding and Mazes assess quite different skills. They load on separate factors, are included in different Bannatyne groupings, measure different Guilford operations, share few abilities in common, and are basically subject to different nonintellective influences. In view of these discrepancies and the large amount of subtest specificity that each task possesses across the age range, it is apparent that both subtests make impressive contributions to the overall measurement of a child's ability spectrum. For similar reasons, examiners are advised to continue the common practice of routinely administering Digit Span. The latter suggestion is also supported by a wealth of research investigations attesting to the clinical and neurological importance of the Digit Span subtest (Costa 1975; Hodges and Spielberger 1969; Russell 1972; Zimmerman, Whitmyre, et al. 1970).

When Coding and Mazes are both administered, the examiner is advised to use Mazes for the computation of Performance IQ. Whereas Mazes loads substantially on the Perceptual Organization factor for virtually every age group, Coding is unrelated to this global Performance dimension (Kaufman 1975). Thus the use of Mazes in the computation of Performance IQ transforms this IQ into an ideal Perceptual Organization factor score. The Coding scaled score will then provide important information regarding the Freedom from Distractibility factor (see Chapter 3), without contaminating the Perceptual Organization score. *However, the decision to use Mazes rather than Coding to compute Performance IQ must be made prior to administering the WISC-R and adhered to regardless of the child's pattern of scaled scores.* Before making the decision for any given individual, the examiner should be well acquainted with the research findings regarding sex differences on the Performance subtests discussed on page 117.

Admittedly, practical considerations sometimes make it virtually impossible to administer all 12 subtests. In such circumstances, the examiner should not automatically yield to the temptation of giving the relatively brief Coding subtest, but should weigh carefully the points presented below before deciding on Mazes or Coding.

As a rule, Mazes should be administered in preference to Coding A to all children below 8 years of age. The substantially greater reliability of Mazes than Coding A is only one of several reasons for this recommendation. An additional justification is the emergence of Mazes as the best measure of the Perceptual Organization factor at age 6½ and as one of the best measures of this factor (along with Block Design and Object Assembly) at age 7½. At ages 8½ and above, however, Mazes consistently ranked a distant fourth or fifth as a measure of Perceptual Organization (Kaufman 1975). Also, there is little evidence that Coding A belongs on the Freedom from Distractibility factor, or on any WISC-R factor, for that matter. Its loadings of 0.20–0.25 on the distractibility factor were higher than its loadings on the other WISC-R factors but trailed by a wide margin the loadings of Coding B on the Freedom from Distractibility factor at ages 8½–16½ (mean loading = 0.40).

Ordinarily, Coding B should be administered in preference to Mazes at ages 8½ and above. Coding B has just been shown to be an integral part of the distractibility factor at these age levels, whereas Mazes is *not* one of the best measures of Perceptual Organization above age 7½. The elimination of Coding B would thus greatly hinder the measurement of a child's performance on the third factor, but the deletion of Mazes would barely be missed in assessing Perceptual Organization ability. (Block Design, Object Assembly, Picture Completion, and Picture Arrangement provide excellent measurement of the nonverbal factor at ages 8½–16½). The reliability of Mazes leaves much to be desired for most age groups in the 8½–16½-year range, dipping as low as 0.57 at age 16½ and averaging only 0.64 for children aged 12½ and above (Wechsler 1974, p. 28). In addition, the stability of Mazes over a 1-month interval was only 0.50 for 104 adolescents aged 14½–15½ years, as opposed to 0.72 for Coding B (Wechsler 1974, p. 33).

Finally, the issue of sex differences enters into the rationale for preferring Coding B to Mazes if only one can be administered. Females have traditionally outperformed males on Coding and Digit Symbol (Lutey 1977; Miele 1958), and WISC-R data lend further support to this research finding. Subtest scores for the WISC-R standardization sample were analyzed, but not reported, by Kaufman and Doppelt (1976). For the total sample, girls averaged about 1½ scaled-score points higher than boys (10.8 vs. 9.2) on Coding. On all other Performance subtests, including Mazes, boys scored somewhat higher than did girls, with differences of about ½ scaled-score point for each subtest. Thus the girls' superiority on Coding counterbalances the boys' better performance on the other nonverbal tasks, leading to approximately equal Performance IQs for both sexes (Kaufman and Doppelt 1976). Clearly, then, the use of Coding B leads to equality in the IQs of boys and girls; the use of Mazes would give boys, on the average, a clear edge in their Performance IQs, about equal to the 2½-point superiority they achieved on the Verbal Scale (Kaufman and Doppelt 1976).

The discussion of sex differences may impel examiners to challenge two suggestions made previously: the preferential administration of Mazes below age 8 and the use of Mazes' scaled score to compute Performance IQ when both Mazes and Coding are administered. Regarding the administration of Mazes for young children, I believe that the advantages of this procedure, outlined earlier, far outweigh the consequences of the sex differences. The consistent use of Mazes to obtain Performance IQ, when Coding is also administered, is more open to challenge. The advantages of having a Performance IQ that closely reflects the Perceptual Organization factor across the entire age range are obvious and will be particularly appealing to examiners who are oriented toward interpretation of the three WISC-R factors. In contrast, the lack of equality in the Performance IQs for boys and girls that will result when Mazes is used in the computations is likely to upset many examiners, especially those who are unimpressed by the statistics of factor analysis. The decision is thus left to the examiners and should be governed by their personal orientation. Some examiners may decide to use Mazes or Coding to compute Performance IQ depending on the sex of the child.

Other variables sometimes need to be considered before deciding whether to administer Coding or Mazes. Coding has the advantage of a richer clinical and research heritage. Mazes is so frequently ignored in test administrations that clinicians have not accumulated an abundance of experience with the subtest, and the "lore" surrounding Mazes is meager in comparison to other subtests. Similarly, Mazes has been conspicuously absent from many of the 1000+ studies involving the WISC or WISC-R. The exclusion of Mazes from the WAIS and Wechsler–Bellevue I batteries has further limited our clinical and research understanding of the subtest, whereas many findings with Digit Symbol are directly applicable to Coding. Several areas of research have particularly stressed the important contributions of Coding–Digit Symbol, most notably investigation of children with reading and learning disabilities (Ackerman, Dykman, et al. 1976; Rugel 1974b) and assessment of brain-damaged individuals (Klonoff 1971; Russell 1972). Hence Coding might be administered in preference to Mazes even at ages 6 and 7, if neurological impairment or a severe learning disorder is suspected.

Nevertheless, Mazes also has some clear-cut advantages over Coding. Even though both subtests have much specificity (see Table 4-2), Mazes is obviously a problem-solving task involving cognitive ability for success. Since Coding is more of a clerical than intellectual task, Mazes has more of a face validity for inclusion in an intelligence battery. This latter consideration is of special concern when evaluating a child for giftedness. Mazes is also a more appealing, interest-holding task for children and is likely to arouse or maintain the interest of a youngster who is rapidly losing motivation for success. Since both tasks are administered near the end of the testing session, Mazes may be a far better choice than Coding for a child who is tired, bored, distractible, or anxious. An administration of Mazes also permits the examiner to observe the child's paper-and-pencil coordination, providing a source of valuable clinical information about the child's perceptual–motor development, similar to the information obtained by watching a child copy designs, draw a person, or complete some of the tasks on the Developmental Test of Visual Perception (Frostig, Maslow, et al. 1964). Although they involve paper and pencil, Coding's designs are too simple to permit the same type of clinical observations. Mazes also affords the examiner opportunities to observe the child's tolerance of frustration, perseveration tendencies, rigidity, ability to play by the rules (i.e., not to keep lifting up the pencil), and method of solving problems; indeed, some youngsters openly verbalize their frustrations and their problem-solving strategies while working on the Mazes. Finally, Mazes is preferable to Coding when testing a child with a mild orthopedic handicap (see pp. 122–123).

Without question, Coding contributes a great deal to a WISC-R administration, in part because of its clerical and psychomotor nature. However, more examiners should be acquainted with the potential value of Mazes for a thorough psychodiagnostic or psychoeducational evaluation.

Speed of Performance and Chronological Age

One of the most striking findings in the various analyses of the WISC-R standardization data is the relative lack of age-related changes in the abilities measured by the WISC-R. With the 1949 WISC, changes in abilities with age were quite common, forming the basis of much speculation about the meaning of the fluctuations noted across the age groups (Cohen 1959). The WISC-R factor analysis revealed the same three dimensions across the entire age range. Although there were some mild age trends, such as the factor loadings of Coding A and Mazes or the subtest specificity of Picture Completion and Similarities, these trends were minor in the face of the remarkable age-by-age consistencies (Kaufman 1975). In other analyses there were no significant or meaningful age fluctuations in investigations of V–P IQ discrepancies (Kaufman 1976c), subtest scatter (Kaufman 1976b), or sex differences (Kaufman and Doppelt 1976).

Some WISC-R subtests seem to measure slightly different abilities across the age range when analyzed from the vantage point of their item content. The first six Comprehension items tend to tap social judgment and evaluation, whereas most of the remaining items measure abstract reasoning. Alertness to the environment is the likely source of most of the factual knowledge needed for the first half of the Information subtest, but formal schooling seems to be the primary source for the second half of this subtest. In Arithmetic as well there is an apparent shift in what is required for success on the earlier versus later items: the first seven items utilize skills that are closely aligned to counting, and the remaining items require good computational skills and arithmetic problem-solving ability. Finally, the change from figural content in Coding A to symbolic content in Coding B is an age-related distinction that has already been discussed.

In great contrast to the minor age fluctuations in factor structure, scatter, sex differences, and rational analysis of subtest items, a relationship of considerable magnitude was observed between chronological age and speed of problem solving on the WISC-R Performance Scale (Kaufman in press b); a similar relationship was observed for the WISC (Woo-Sam and Zimmerman 1972). In these studies, older children were found to be far quicker (and therefore to earn many more bonus points) than younger children in solving Picture Arrangement, Block Design, and Object Assembly items. Consequently, speed of performance plays a more important role in the Performance IQs (and hence the Full Scale IQs) earned by older children than by younger ones. Thus the meaning of the Perceptual Organization factor for both the WISC (Cohen 1959) and WISC-R (Kaufman 1975) changes across the age range, with speed of responding constituting a more integral aspect of this nonverbal dimension for adolescents than for primary-grade children.

To dramatize the decrease in performance time with increasing age, consider the following results of statistical analyses of the WISC-R standardization data (Kaufman in press b):

1. *Average performance times of children solving Picture Arrangement, Block Design, and Object Assembly items correctly decreased steadily across the 6½−16½-year range.* For example, 6½-year-olds solved Picture Arrangement item No. 8 (LASSO) correctly in an average of 28 seconds, compared to an average of 18 seconds at age 11½, and 14 seconds at age 16½. Average performance times for children solving Block Design item No. 7 correctly were 43 seconds at age 6½, 28 seconds at age 11½, and only 19 seconds at age 16½. Similarly, performance times for Object Assembly item No. 3 (CAR) decreased from 83 seconds for 6½-year-olds to 41 seconds by age 16½.

2. *Bonus points for quick perfect performance were rarely earned by children below age 8, but were plentiful for adolescents.* The average child of 6½ and 7½ earned a *total* of only 1−2 bonus points on Picture Arrangement, Block Design, and Object Assembly. By age 8½, the average child earned 4−5 bonus points, with the number of bonus points earned increasing steadily to 9 at age 10½, 18 at age 13½, and 23−24 at age 16½. Thus the average adolescent of 16½ earned over 20 raw score points due to quickness of response, obtaining about 7 bonus points on Picture Arrangement, 11−12 on Block Design, and 5 on Object Assembly.

Further analysis of data revealed that 6½ and 7½-year-olds earned 96% of their raw score points on the three subtests under investigation due to the accuracy of their solutions and only 4% of their points due to time bonuses. By age 11½, the ratio of points obtained due to accuracy: speed shifted to 85:15, and by age 16½, nearly 25% of an individual's raw scores on Picture Arrangement, Block Design, and Object Assembly were earned via time bonuses (Kaufman in press b). In addition, about 75−80% of all correct responses given by 16½-year-olds on Picture Arrangement, Block Design, and Object Assembly were quick enough to merit at least one bonus point. It was thus *unusual* for an older teenager to solve a nonverbal problem and *not* earn a bonus point! At age 11½, about 55–60% of the correct responses merited bonus points, which was substantially higher than the value of about 20–25% for 6½-year-olds (Kaufman in press b).

3. *An adolescent of 14½ and above who solves every Picture Arrangement, Block Design, and Object Assembly item correctly will not earn a scaled score above 10 on these subtests.* Incredible as it seems, older teenagers who do not fail a single item on the three subtests cannot score at an above-average level unless they earn some bonus points. A 16½-year-old who solves every problem correctly but works too slowly to be given bonus points will obtain scaled scores of 9 (37th percentile) on Picture Arrangement and Block Design and 7 (16th percentile) on Object Assembly. Even at age 9½, a slow but perfectly accurate child cannot earn a scaled score above 14 on any of the three subtests when no bonus points are achieved. These results affirm the essential part played by performance time in determining an older child's Performance IQ. The data also indicate that even though the *average* primary-grade student does not earn too many bonus points, very high scaled scores are reserved for the younger children who solve at least some problems quickly.

Apparently, the amount of *variance* in children's test scores due to speed of performance increases rapidly with age, and this supposition is borne out by data. For Picture Arrangement and Block Design, the ratio of the test score variances for accuracy vs. speed is a sizable 35:1 at age 6½, reducing to 3:1 at age 11½, and to a mere 1½:1 at age 16½. For Object Assembly, the descent is even more dramatic, plunging from 70:1 at age 6½ to 1½:1 by age 11½. At ages 13½ and above, the variance due to speed *exceeds* the variance due to accuracy for Object Assembly, with the ratio reaching 3:1 at age 16½ (Kaufman in press b). In a very real sense, Object Assembly is a measure of speed of problem-solving ability for teenagers.

The key role played by speed of responding to nonverbal problems, especially for teenagers, raises some interpretive questions. One is whether performance time belongs in the intellectual domain, or whether it fits in better with noncognitive variables. A second question concerns the applicability of the WISC-R Performance Scale for orthopedically handicapped youngsters.

Regarding the issue of speed as an intellectual variable, it is obvious that nonintellective factors can greatly influence an individual's rate of responding to a nonverbal problem. Children with a reflective cognitive style (Kagan 1966) are not likely to earn too many bonus points for speed on the WISC-R, whereas impulsive youngsters will tend to respond more quickly and make more errors. For children at both ends of the reflective–impulsive spectrum, rate of responding to certain types of problems is probably more a function of a pervasive and characteristic cognitive style than of intellect. Other youngsters may solve problems slowly for a variety of nonintellectual variables such as anxiety, perseveration, distractibility, compulsiveness, or poor motor coordination.

The basic issue, however, is not whether "irrelevant" variables may be related to a slow response time, but whether children who solve a problem quickly are brighter, in some way, than children who solve the same problem more slowly. The study cited above (Kaufman in press b) explored this question. The answer was clear-cut: children who solved Picture Arrangement, Block Design, and Object Assembly items quickly performed better on other similar problems than did those solving the items slowly. In other words, youngsters who responded correctly to a Picture Arrangement item in a brief time scored higher on other picture arrangements than did those responding correctly in a longer time, and analogous relationships were obtained for Block Design and Object Assembly items. Indeed, systematic linear relationships were obtained for most items, as individuals solving an item in $1-5$ seconds were better problem solvers in general than those solving the item in $6-10$ seconds; the youngsters getting the item right in $6-10$ seconds were better at solving similar problems than those getting it correct in $11-15$ seconds, and so forth. Evidence for the linearity came from rank-order correlations between speed of responding to an item and total score on other similar items. Median coefficients of 0.87, 0.94, and 0.89 were obtained for Picture Arrangement, Block Design, and Object Assembly items, respectively (Kaufman in press b).

The impressive relationships obtained in the study of speed of performance suggest that an individual's quickness to respond to a nonverbal problem is, at least in part, an intellectual attribute. Despite the variety of nonintellective factors that can affect speed of performance, the study provided empirical justification for Wechsler's practice of assigning bonus points for quick perfect performance, and for the contribution these points make to an individual's Performance IQ and Full Scale IQ. Had nonsignificant correlations been obtained between performance time and problem-solving ability, or if speed of responding did not decrease steadily with chronological age (Anastasi 1976, p. 152), the role of bonus points in determining a child's IQs would have been open to challenge.

The question regarding the administration of the WISC-R Performance Scale to children with orthopedic handicaps must be answered from the dual vantage points of the degree of the handicap and the child's age. All Performance subtests are timed, not just the three that allot bonus points for speed. If the orthopedic handicap is so severe that the child is unable to respond within the reasonably generous time limits, then certainly the WISC-R Performance Scale is inappropriate at any age as a measure of the youngster's nonverbal intelligence. If the handicap definitely impedes performance (making bonus points unlikely) but is not debilitating, the Performance Scale should provide a reasonable estimate of ability for young children. Certainly below age 9 Picture Arrangement, Block

Design, and Object Assembly more closely resemble power than speed tests. Accuracy of performance contributed 90% or more of the points earned on all three subtests by the average child of 6½ years, 7½ years, and 8½ years. In addition, the variances for accuracy are far greater than the variances for speed at the young ages, indicating that individual differences in test scores are more a function of accuracy than speed of problem solving for 6½–8½ year olds. The ratio in variances (accuracy:speed) averaged about 11:1 for the three subtests at age 8½; by 9½ years of age, the ratio dropped to about 6:1, and by 10½ the ratio was 4:1.

For children aged 9 and 10 with orthopedic handicaps, the administration of the Performance Scale becomes risky and requires the thoughtful clinical judgment of the examiner. The role of speed looms more important for success at these ages, and even a child with a mild orthopedic problem will be penalized, perhaps substantially. A 10-year-old who solves every nonverbal problem perfectly but earns no bonus points will only earn scaled scores of 13 on Picture Arrangement and Block Design, and 11 on Object Assembly. At ages 11 and above, the prominent role of speed renders the Performance IQ inadequate as an index of the orthopedically handicapped child's nonverbal ability; consequently, the WISC-R Performance Scale should not be administered in such cases. Woo-Sam and Zimmerman (1972) reached similar conclusions regarding the ages at which it is appropriate to administer the WISC Performance Scale to orthopedically handicapped children.

As a final note, whenever an examiner deems the WISC-R Performance Scale suitable for a child with a mild orthopedic handicap, Mazes, and not Coding, should be used to compute Performance IQ. Coding A and B are both measures of psychomotor speed and are clearly inappropriate as contributors to the IQs of orthopedically handicapped youngsters. Examiners who choose to administer Coding in these instances should do so for clinical reasons but should not use the scaled score in any computations.

Abilities Measured by the WISC versus the WISC-R

The continuity between the WISC and WISC-R represents an important avenue of study, particularly for examiners with years of clinical experience using the 1949 WISC. Even for new examiners the WISC versus WISC-R issue has relevance because they may need to interpret a child's WISC-R IQs in light of the WISC IQs he or she earned years earlier. One type of comparison between the two test batteries concerns the constructs they measure; a second type relates to the magnitude of the differences in the IQs they yield. Both of these areas of investigation are treated in the remainder of this chapter.

The continuity of the abilities or constructs assessed by the WISC and WISC-R has been demonstrated in a variety of studies. Factor analysis of the WISC-R standardization data (Kaufman 1975) yielded the three major factors identified for the WISC by Cohen (1959). The WISC-R factors were more robust than the WISC dimensions, retaining their integrity even when more than three factors were extracted and emerging virtually intact for each age group across the wide 6½−16½-year range. Nevertheless, the fact that the major WISC factors tended to fragment and differed slightly in composition from age to age should not detract from the clear similarities in the WISC and WISC-R factorial structures.

Swerdlik and Schweitzer (1978) directly compared the factorial composition of the WISC-R and WISC by analyzing data for the *same* group of 164 referrals who were tested in counterbalanced order on the two batteries. In the three-factor solutions a strikingly high coefficient of congruence of 0.98 was obtained between the WISC-R and WISC Verbal Comprehension factors, and the same value was obtained for the two Perceptual Organization factors. A coefficient of congruence of only 0.77 was obtained between the third factors—a clear distractibility dimension for the WISC-R, but primarily a Mazes−Picture Arrangement dyad for the WISC. It is unfortunate that Swerdlik and Schweitzer (1978) did not examine the four- and five-factor solutions for their WISC and WISC-R data since a Freedom from Distractibility factor may have emerged fourth, as it did for two of the 11 age groups in the WISC-R standardization sample (Kaufman 1975). Additional factoring would have permitted a comparison of the robustness of the WISC-R and WISC factors, especially the degree to which the Verbal and Performance Scales fragment into less global dimensions. One may conclude from Swerdlik and Schweitzer's investigation only that the two major abilities measured by the WISC-R are virtually identical to the two major WISC abilities. Note, however, that generalizations from their atypical sample of children referred to school psychologists must be made with caution.

The greater resilience of the WISC-R than the WISC factors for their respective standardization samples warrants further discussion. Rather than implying that the two batteries measure different abilities, the more resilient WISC-R factors may simply be a product of the modifications of the WISC in the construction of the revised instrument. WISC items were eliminated in the revision process primarily because of obsolescence, ambiguity, or unfairness to particular groups of children (Wechsler 1974, p. 10). Modification or removal of obsolete, ambiguous, and unfair items serves to eliminate a portion of error variance from the measurement procedure. Logical outcomes of the reduction of error are increases in reliability coefficients (which are evident from a comparison of the reliability tables in the WISC and WISC-R manuals) and greater stability of the factor structure. Thus, even though the Verbal Comprehension II factor found for the WAIS and WISC has occasionally been interpreted and has even been given the provisional label of "relevance" by Wechsler (1958), it is conceivable that this dimension is a statistical artifact produced by error in the correlation matrix.

The major changes from the WISC to WISC-R concerned the early items in the

Similarities and Picture Arrangement subtests. The early WISC items actually measure abilities that differ from the conventional item types in Similarities and Picture Arrangement. According to Sattler (1974, p. 178), the four WISC analogy items assess logical thinking as opposed to the verbal concept formation measured by the "cat—mouse" item type. In Guilford terminology, the analogies require evaluation, whereas the conventional Similarities items demand cognition. The WISC Picture Arrangement subtest included three early items assessing spatial relationships, akin to puzzle solving, in contrast to the temporal concepts required by the story-type items. Eliminating these different kinds of items in the WISC-R Similarities and Picture Arrangement subtests and replacing them with easy items in the conventional formats produced subtests that were more uniform than their WISC counterparts in the abilities they assess across the age range. Both the greater uniformity of the WISC-R subtests and the improved reliability of most tasks are undoubtedly related to the greater age-by-age consistency in the composition of the WISC-R than WISC factors across the 6–16-year age span.

Apart from factor analysis, other evidence exists to support a close relationship between the abilities tapped by the WISC and WISC-R. Numerous studies have presented correlations between the IQs yielded by the two batteries, and the coefficients between comparable scales have been high, typically in the 0.80s (Davis 1977; Hamm, Wheeler, et al. 1976; Larrabee and Holroyd 1976; Weiner and Kaufman, in press). Whereas high correlations are not surprising in view of the large overlap in item content that characterizes the WISC and WISC-R (Wechsler 1974, p. 11), the results of these studies nevertheless support the similarity in the abilities measured by the WISC and its successor. Consider as well the following empirical evidence, all supporting the continuity of the abilities measured by the old and the new WISCs: (a) the characteristic WISC profile identified for mentally retarded children in numerous independent studies (Silverstein 1968) correlated significantly ($\rho = 0.83$) with the WISC-R subtest profile for a sample of retarded youngsters (Kaufman and Van Hagen 1977); (b) cumulative frequency distributions of V–P discrepancies on the WISC-R (Kaufman 1976c) are remarkably similar to comparable distributions on the WISC (Seashore 1951); (c) the relationship of V–P discrepancies to occupational group of parent remained strikingly constant from the WISC to the WISC-R—for example, about 60% of the children of professionals had V > P on both test batteries (Kaufman 1976c); and (d) sex differences were virtually identical on the WISC and WISC-R, with boys scoring about 2½ points higher on Verbal IQ, ½ point higher on Performance IQ, and 1¾ points higher on Full Scale IQ on both instruments (Kaufman and Doppelt 1976).

Despite the apparent close similarity in the abilities measured by the WISC-R and its predecessor, a number of studies have shown rather conclusively that the WISC-R consistently yields lower IQs than does the WISC (Doppelt and Kaufman 1977; Swerdlik 1977). Doppelt and Kaufman (1977) identified a common core of items in the two batteries and applied regression analysis to data from the WISC and WISC-R standardization samples as a means of studying IQ differences. Their results suggested that the discrepancies between WISC-R and WISC Full Scale IQs are likely to be about 6 points below age 11, but only 2 points at ages 11 and above. Swerdlik (1976, in press) conducted a well-designed counterbalanced investigation of WISC versus WISC-R using an impressively large sample of 164 black, white, and Latino children aged 6 to nearly 16 years referred for evaluation. He did not find the interaction with age predicted by Doppelt and Kaufman (1977) but did observe the WISC-R IQs to be lower than WISC IQs by about 5 points on the Verbal Scale, 6 points on the Performance Scale, and 5½ points on the Full Scale. Discrepancies were slightly larger for blacks and Latinos than for whites.

A variety of other WISC–WISC-R investigations utilizing relatively small samples have been conducted, but the discussion here is limited primarily to the researchers who used counterbalanced designs. Studies in which the WISC was administered first each time, with the WISC-R given after many months or years (e.g., Gironda 1977), are not particularly useful for assessing comparability because of the unknown impact on the results of the time factor. Similarly, studies that have been only partially counterbalanced for order of administration (Hamm, Wheeler, et al. 1976; Larrabee and Holroyd 1976) are excluded here because of the powerful practice effects observed over short intervals for the WISC and WISC-R (see pp. 48–50). Predictably, Davis (1977) found the WISC-R to yield a Full Scale IQ only 2 points below the WISC Full Scale IQ when the WISC was given first to 27 children, in marked contrast to a discrepancy of 13½ points when the WISC-R was given first to a different sample of 27 youngsters. Swerdlik (1976, in press) also found only a 1½-point difference in Full Scale IQs when the WISC was administered first, versus a 10-point discrepancy when the order was reversed. When WISC is given first the practice effect serves to mask the real difference between the norms for the two tests, but when WISC-R is given first the practice effect joins with the "easier" WISC norms to create a huge and artificially inflated discrepancy. Careful counterbalancing effectively eliminates the contamination of practice. In Davis's (1977) study, for example, the average of the two WISC–WISC-R discrepancies (7½ points) represents the real difference between the Full Scale IQs yielded by the two batteries for his sample of Spanish- and Anglo-surnamed youngsters.

Among other well-designed WISC–WISC-R studies, Berry and Sherrets (1975) found WISC-R Full Scale IQ to be 3½ points below WISC Full Scale IQ for 28 special-education EMR students; Klinge, Rodziewics, et al. (1976) observed a 3½-point difference for 32 adolescent psychiatric patients; Tuma, Applebaum, et al. (1978) obtained an overall discrepancy of 4 points on the Full Scale for 36 children, half from high and half from low socioeconomic backgrounds; Brooks (1977) obtained a 7-point Full Scale IQ difference for 30 referrals; Schwarting (1976) uncovered a 7½-point discrepancy in the Full Scale IQs for 58 randomly selected "normal" children; Weiner and Kaufman (in press) found the WISC-R Full Scale to yield IQs 8 points below its WISC counterpart for 46 black children referred for learning or behavioral disorders; and Solly (1977) obtained WISC-R Full Scale IQs that were lower than WISC Full Scale IQs by 12½ points for 12 gifted children and by 11 points for 12 mentally retarded boys and girls. In most of the counterbalanced studies, including Swerdlik's (1976, in press) large-scale investigation, discrepancies have been slightly larger on the Performance than on the Verbal Scale. Weighted averages of the discrepancies found in a variety of counterbalanced studies that reported means for the Verbal, Performance, and Full Scale IQs (total $N = 394$) indicate that the WISC-R consistently yielded lower IQs than the WISC by about $4½-5$ points on the Verbal Scale, 6½ points on the Performance Scale, and 6 points on the Full Scale. Virtually identical discrepancies on the Verbal, Performance, and Full Scales were obtained by Catron and Catron (1977), who randomly administered the WISC ($N = 33$) or WISC-R ($N = 29$) to 62 educable mentally retarded youngsters aged $12½-14½$ years. (The groups were equivalent on sex, race, and IQs earned several years earlier.)

The conclusion by Doppelt and Kaufman (1977) that WISC–WISC-R discrepancies are likely to be smaller for older than younger children (using age 11 as the point of demarcation) was *not* supported by Swerdlik's (1976, in press) data or by the results of Catron and Catron's (1977) investigation of retarded adolescents. However, support for Doppelt and Kaufman's contention was provided by two studies involving small samples of predominantly older children (Berry and Sherrets 1975; Klinge, Rodziewicz et al., 1976). In addition, an investigation of juvenile delinquents (most of whom were above age 11) given either the WISC ($N = 180$) or WISC-R ($N = 185$) yielded relatively small WISC–WISC-R discrepancies (Solway, Fruge, et al. 1976). These researchers found the WISC-R to yield lower IQs by 2½ points on the Verbal Scale, 3½ points on the Performance Scale, and 3 points on the Full Scale for the two groups that were equated for sex, race, grade level, and age. The conflicting findings suggest that the jury is still out regarding WISC–WISC-R discrepancies for younger and older children. For the present, the best approach is probably to treat the typical discrepancies of about $5-7$ IQ points as characteristic of the entire age range.

In view of the considerable evidence that the WISC and WISC-R measure the same abilities, what do the discrepancies in their IQs mean? The IQ differences most likely reflect changes in the normative populations in the course of a generation. The WISC standardization sample was tested just after World War II, prior to the impact of television and mass media in general, and before the prominence of child-development movements stressing the importance of early stimulation for young children. The WISC-R standardization group, tested in the early 1970s, had the benefits of mass media, more enlightened and better educated parents, and hence greater cultural advantages. Not surprisingly, the children in the WISC-R sample performed better than did their WISC counterparts of an earlier generation on the types of tasks included in a Wechsler battery. The end result is a set of WISC-R norms that are steeper than the WISC norms. Thus when children of today are compared to their contemporaries (when given the WISC-R), their scores will not be as high as they will be when they are compared to their less enriched age counterparts of a generation ago (in the WISC sample). Similarly, the 1972 norms for the Stanford–Binet are not nearly as "soft" as the earlier norms. The identical performance on the Binet yields a substantially lower IQ with the new norms than with the old norms at most age levels (Terman and Merrill 1973).

The WISC–WISC-R IQ discrepancies have some important implications for test users. Examiners who have much experience with the WISC, including some who have been slow to switch to the WISC-R, have to accept the fact that the WISC norms are now out of date; they need to reorient their subjective impressions about the quality of performance that is necessary to earn IQs at various levels. The WISC norms give better "news" in the form of higher scores, but the WISC-R norms provide a more meaningful reference group for children and adolescents of today. Youngsters who formerly would have scored at the Borderline level on the WISC may conceivably score in the Mentally Deficient range on the WISC-R; children classified as Very Superior on the WISC may be classified as Superior on the WISC-R. Placement in programs for the retarded or gifted may thus be affected.

Following a similar logic, discrepancies between ability and achievement for children referred for a possible school learning disorder will tend to be *smaller* when the WISC-R is used instead of the WISC. Decisions regarding assessment of learning disabilities and educational placement may thus be quite different depending on whether examiners use the new or the old WISC. Mainstreaming decisions may also be contingent on which Wechsler battery is included in the assessment procedures (Swerdlik 1977). It is evident that the mere choice of the WISC versus the WISC-R for inclusion in a multitest battery will frequently affect diagnostic or placement decisions that are reached by multidisciplinary teams. Psychologists and special educators should internalize the practical consequences of using the WISC-R or its predecessor and recognize that *any current decision based in part on the 1949 WISC is derived from an instrument whose norms are obsolete and, for practical purposes, meaningless.*

Since children referred for clinical purposes are frequently evaluated several times in their school-age years, it will be common to find WISC scores in the case folders of children just tested on the WISC-R. By being alert to the expected differences of nearly one-half of a standard deviation between the WISC and

WISC-R IQs, examiners can make a mental adjustment to the reported WISC IQs. Lower WISC-R IQs should be anticipated, and even differences as large as one standard deviation are probably normal and should not cause concern regarding a possible loss in the child's intellectual functioning (Weiner and Kaufman in press).

CHAPTER 5

Attacking Subtest Profiles: The Foundation

Wechsler organized his subtests into a clinically useful dichotomy based on intuitive and rational considerations but recognized that "the abilities represented in the tests may also be meaningfully classified in other ways" (Wechsler 1974, p. 9). Factor analysis yields a three-way division of the WISC-R, and Bannatyne (1971, 1974) has argued for a four-category system to interpret fluctuations in children's scaled-score profiles. Another classification system of clinical value involving four groups is the categorization scheme devised by Rapaport, Gill, et al. (1945–1946): Visual Organization (Picture Completion, Picture Arrangement), where motor coordination is of minimal importance; Visual–Motor Coordination (Block Design, Object Assembly, Coding); Verbal (Information, Similarities, Vocabulary, Comprehension); and Attention and Concentration (Arithmetic, Digit Span). Meeker's (1969, 1975b) application to the WISC and WISC-R of Guilford's SOI model has produced yet another method for subdividing the subtests in novel ways. Whereas the Meeker approach actually yields a larger number of separate abilities than there are subtests in the WISC-R, these abilities may be grouped effectively by mental operation and item content. (Four operations and three types of content are measured by the WISC-R; see Table 3-1.)

The variety of ways that psychologists have reorganized Wechsler's subtests, including the interpretation of small, exotic-sounding factors such as Contemporary Affairs or Maintenance of Contact (Lutey 1977; Saunders 1960), is almost endless. Virtually every technique has something to recommend it and is thus worthy of attention, if not necessarily respect. All of the methods mentioned in the preceding paragraph contributed to the lists of shared abilities and "influences" enumerated for each subtest in Chapter 4; even one of the "exotic" factors (Freedom from Uncertainty) was included.

A comparison of the plethora of categorical systems reveals contradictions among them in the way different subtests are grouped. Picture Arrangement, for example, is included in Wechsler's Performance scale and in Rapaport's Visual Organization group, but is considered by Meeker to measure *semantic* content. Coding loads on the Freedom from Distractibility factor but is excluded from Rapaport's Attention and Concentration group. Which system is correct? Should

130

an examiner adhere to Wechsler's dichotomy, the factor-analytic trichotomy, Guilford's theory, or one of the clinically derived models? How can one examine these complex issues in a systematic and direct way?

The answer to the first question is that no system is the correct one, but neither can any system be said to be wrong. Likewise, it is inappropriate to assume that one particular method is necessarily better than any other technique. Each method has its special uniqueness and utility for different individuals. Bannatyne's Acquired Knowledge and Verbal Conceptualization categories may provide the key to the interpretation of a culturally disadvantaged child's fluctuations within the Verbal Scale, whereas the factor structure may be more useful for understanding the profile of a highly distractible child who evidenced marked weaknesses in Arithmetic, Digit Span, and Coding. Similarly, the peaks and valleys in the Performance Scale profile of a youngster with obvious motor difficulties may be understood most sensibly by utilizing Rapaport's Visual Organization and Visual—Motor Coordination groups. Poor scores on both Coding and Picture Arrangement may reflect a deficiency in Sequencing skills (Bannatyne), convergent production ability (Guilford), or in some other area such as integrated brain functioning; uncovering the correct hypothesis depends on other test scores, clinical observation of test behaviors, the nature of incorrect responses, and pertinent background information.

In response to the second question, it is intuitive that no one system should be exclusively adhered to, but that all should be learned well by examiners to permit the kind of flexibility of test interpretation that is so essential. In a sense, the examiner is trying to match the system to the individual, finding the approach that best explains the available data. Many clinicians utilize *personality* theories in this eclectic manner, selecting the one or two that best match an individual's presenting problems and personality dynamics rather than remaining unflinchingly loyal to Freud, Horney, Adler, Rogers, Miller/Dollard, or Cattell. Yet these same clinicians are sometimes unwilling to employ this flexible approach in applying cognitive theories to an intelligence test profile.

Occasionally more than one model is required to explain scaled-score fluctuations satisfactorily. In the examples cited earlier, the profile of a culturally disadvantaged child with motor problems may require utilization of both Bannatyne's and Rapaport's recategorizations to interpret peaks and valleys within the Verbal and Performance Scales, respectively. In other instances, none of the popular systems may prove satisfactory, and examiners must call upon alternative strategies to decipher the mysteries of a child's ability spectrum. These strategies may involve application of theories and research findings from areas such as developmental psychology, cognitive psychology, or neuropsychology; they may require interpretation of some of the less pervasive abilities that are shared by only two or three WISC-R subtests (e.g., planning ability, degree of abstract thinking); or they may stem from clinical analysis of the child's particular background and behaviors, thereby representing a novel and unique set of hypotheses that are not generalizable to other children.

The third question, regarding a systematic approach to profile interpretation, has already been partially answered in Chapters 2 and 3. Now that the abilities measured by WISC-R subtests have been delineated in Chapter 4, it is possible to extend the method used to interpret V−P IQ differences and the distractibility factor to analysis of the subtest profile. The philosophy and logic that underlie the kind of detective work advocated for profile interpretation are set forth in the following section. Then, in the remainder of Chapter 5, appear research and theory oriented discussions of different types of WISC-R profiles. An integrated understanding of the philosophy, research support, and theoretical relevance pertaining to subtest fluctuations forms the *foundation* of WISC-R profile attack. The *method* of attack is featured in Chapter 6, along with quantitative guidelines and illustrations and applications of the approach.

A PHILOSOPHY OF PROFILE ATTACK

A WISC-R detective strives to use ingenuity, clinical sense, and a thorough grounding in psychological theory and research to reveal the dynamics of a child's scaled-score profile. The need for detective work derives from one basic assumption: that the most valuable information about a child's mental abilities lies somewhere in between the global Full Scale IQ and the highly specific subtest scores. Whereas the overall IQ is too broad to provide insight into the child's strong and weak abilities, the separate scaled scores are far too narrow in their scope to be of much value for practical usage.

In Chapter 2, the Full Scale IQ was referred to as a target to be aimed at, and this metaphor reflects the guiding principle of a good detective. An individual who is unduly concerned with the Full Scale IQ is saying implicitly that a child's intellectual abilities can be summarized by a single score. A detective ought to protest strenuously when confronted with this common allegation. Each new WISC-R profile should represent a challenge to prove emphatically that the child's abilities defy encapsulation in a single numerical value or even in a range of values.

The first line of attack to be leveled against the Full Scale IQ comes from evaluation of V−P IQ differences (see pp. 23−53). Next comes a statistical determination of strengths and weaknesses within the Verbal and Performance Scales using the logic and method outlined in stepwise fashion earlier (pp. 53−57). The technique of using discrepancies of 3 points or more from the child's own mean to denote relative strengths and weaknesses is reasonably conservative and prevents overinterpretation of chance fluctuations. The discovery of significantly deviating scores within the two scales serves as the starting point for detective work. Scrutiny of the scaled-score profile may suggest hypotheses relating to the distractibility factor (see Chapter 3) or to the variety of abilities delineated for each subtest in Chapter 4. The goal is to uncover hypotheses regarding abilities shared by two or more subtests or concerning influences that may have affected the test scores.

Importantly, calculating scaled scores that deviate significantly is the *beginning*, not the end, of profile analysis. Too many examiners seem to fall into the rut of interpreting high and low subtest scores in isolation, reciting in their case reports cookbook prose about what each subtest purportedly measures. Mindless interpretation of this sort is a cop-out, and does not usually provide information of any practical value. Some examiners explain a strong or weak ability by listing a string of skills purportedly measured by the subtest in question. For example, a low score on Block Design may be described as a weakness in "perceptual organization, analysis and synthesis, visual–motor coordination, visual perception, and spatial visualization"—implying that the child has deficiencies in all of the named areas! Apparently undaunted by the child's average or high scores in other tasks requiring good perceptual organization and visual–motor coordination, these examiners seem to sense no contradictions in their explication of the Block Design weakness. Or an examiner may credit a child with a strength in the "ability to distinguish essential from nonessential details" because of a high score in Picture Completion, totally overlooking the child's unimpressive performance on the other subtests that demand this same skill (Picture Arrangement and Similarities).

As a final illustration, an examiner may detect weaknesses in both Similarities and Comprehension, yet make no attempt to integrate the findings. Such a child may well be described as having poor "verbal concept formation" and possessing little "common sense, judgment, and practical information." These descriptive statements, apart from being based on meager evidence and not necessarily supported by the rest of the subtest profile, do not readily translate to meaningful recommendations. In contrast, by reporting that both Comprehension and Similarities measure abstract reasoning and problem-solving skills, the examiner capitalizes on an ability that the two subtests share. Hypotheses based on two subtests are more global and reliable than subtest-specific hypotheses and are generally more valuable because the child's skill transcends the specific stimuli, item content, and response style of any one task. In this instance a significant weakness in verbal reasoning (compared with better performance on the other Verbal subtests, all of which require short-term or long-term memory—see pp. 142–146) has implications for the kind of teaching style and materials that might be most effective for the child's educational program. For example, if the hypothesized weakness in verbal reasoning ability is supported by other test data and observations, the child would probably benefit from an approach that permitted the acquisition of factual knowledge and concepts without demanding much problem solving. At the same time, the weakness in verbal reasoning should be ameliorated to the fullest extent possible by utilizing any strengths that the child may have displayed during the testing session.

Thus the goals of detective work are to detect strong and weak areas in the profile that are *consistent* with all information contained in the profile and that are measured by *two or more* subtests. Pervasive hypotheses are far more likely than unique hypotheses to translate meaningfully to classroom activities. Only when the search for a global strength or weakness proves hopeless should an examiner settle for a subtest specific hypothesis. When no Verbal or Performance subtests deviate significantly from the child's own mean scores, detectives are ordinarily not given the opportunity to exercise their interpretive skills. However, even the absence of notable peaks and valleys in the WISC-R profile should not impel the examiner to yield to the Full Scale IQ as a final statement of the child's mental abilities. Other tests should be included in the total battery and interpreted in conjunction with the WISC-R. Good detectives seek clues by integrating all tests, subtests, and informal tasks that are administered to a child. A flat WISC-R profile should be a special motivation for the examiner to administer supplementary measures of intellectual skills that are not tapped well or at all by the WISC-R. Tests of creativity, adaptive behavior, and right-brain processing all serve to enhance the assessment of intelligence and provide the kinds of samples of behavior that increase the odds of detecting strengths and weaknesses in the child's ability spectrum.

The remaining sections of this chapter are devoted to an in-depth discussion of subtest patterns that seem to occur with reasonable frequency or are otherwise important. These various subdivisions of WISC-R tasks are organized and treated separately for the Verbal and Performance Scales, although interscale patterning is integrated whenever pertinent. Examiners are encouraged to internalize the different ways the Verbal and Performance subtests commonly subdivide; anticipation of these patterns greatly facilitates the detective work required for effective WISC-R interpretation.

PATTERNS TO ANTICIPATE ON THE VERBAL SCALE

The patterns selected for discussion for the Verbal Scale stem from a variety of sources such as factor analysis, Bannatyne's category system, and even subtest specific hypotheses. These patterns are intended to illustrate, but certainly not exhaust, the diversity of important analyses that are possible when the six Verbal subtests are used as the raw materials.

Factor I versus Factor III

Not infrequently, a child's six Verbal scaled scores will clearly dichotomize according to the primary factor loading of each subtest, with Arithmetic and Digit Span differing substantially from the remaining four subtests. The profile of Dennis D. in Chapter 3 (p. 77) provided an illustration of a Factor I–Factor III split of the Verbal Scale; another sample profile appears as follows:

Verbal Subtest	Scaled Score
Information	12
Similarities	11
Arithmetic	5
Vocabulary	14
Comprehension	12
Digit Span	(6)

Verbal IQ = 105.

The Verbal IQ underestimates the verbal intelligence of the child with this profile because Arithmetic did not function as a measure of the verbal ability of this youngster. The lowered estimate of verbal intelligence is not as great as it would have been with the 1949 WISC (which included Digit Span in the computation of Verbal IQ), but it is still of concern. As discussed earlier (pp. 43–46), the V–P IQ discrepancy for this child is not very meaningful and may, in fact, be misleading. The low scores on Arithmetic and Digit Span should be compared to the Coding scaled score to see whether the distractibility factor comprises a single, discrete ability for this child. Regardless of the answer, the examiner then needs to interpret the meaning of the two low Verbal scores by evaluating observations of the child's behavior, information about his or her background, and the nature of the wrong responses (see pp. 80–85).

The child's verbal functioning is more accurately portrayed by a Verbal Comprehension factor score than by the Verbal IQ. By prorating from the four factor-related subtests, an IQ equivalent of 113 is obtained (Sobotka and Black 1978, Table 1; Wechsler 1974, Tables 20 and 22). This Verbal Comprehension factor score reflects High Average (Bright) ability and corresponds to the 80th percentile; the obtained Verbal IQ of 105 underestimates the child's verbal comprehension and expression skills by denoting Average ability and ranking him or her at only the 63rd percentile. Whereas factor scores are useful for the examiner's understanding of profiles such as the one illustrated here, these prorated IQ equivalents are best omitted from case reports (see pp. 23–24 and 79–80). Percentile ranks are easily understood and will readily communicate the fact that the obtained V IQ is an inadequate representation of the verbal intelligence of the child profiled here.

The preceding sample profile showed weaknesses in Arithmetic and Digit Span, although it is equally plausible for a child to score higher on the Factor III subtests than on the Factor I tasks (see the profile of Dennis D. on page 77). When significant Verbal strengths are noted on the two distractibility subtests, the Verbal IQ then represents an *overestimate* of the child's verbal intelligence. Again, the use of factor scores will facilitate proper interpretation of the findings.

Acquired Knowledge

Potentially the most valuable category for WISC-R interpretation in Bannatyne's (1971, 1974) scheme is Acquired Knowledge. Yet this category seems frequently to be ignored by clinicians and researchers who utilize his model (Bush and Waugh 1976, pp. 130–133; Rugel 1974b). The Acquired Knowledge grouping comprises Information, Arithmetic, and Vocabulary, all of which are school related, are subject to the influence of home environment, and involve long-term memory. When a child's scaled scores on the Acquired Knowledge subtests cluster together and deviate from scores on Similarities, Comprehension, and Digit Span, the implications for test interpretation may be vital.

Consider the sample profiles of Verbal scores shown in the following tables for Sheila and Barbara, two 11-year-olds referred for evaluation to the same school psychologist. Both children are white, although they come from quite different backgrounds: Sheila lives under severe conditions of economic deprivation and is now in her fourth foster home; Barbara has upper-middle-class parents who actively expose her to culturally enriching experiences and overtly encourage her academic success. Although the two girls achieved the same Verbal IQ of 97, their patterns of scores suggest that they differ substantially in their verbal skills and that the index provides an inadequate reflection of their respective verbal abilities.

Sheila		Barbara	
Verbal Subtest	Scaled Score	Verbal Subtest	Scaled Score
Information	5	Information	11
Similarities	16	Similarities	7
Arithmetic	6	Arithmetic	11
Vocabulary	8	Vocabulary	13
Comprehension	13	Comprehension	6
Digit Span	(14)	Digit Span	(8)
Verbal IQ = 97.		Verbal IQ = 97.	

Both profiles are interpretable from the vantage point of Bannatyne's Acquired Knowledge dimension. Sheila had an average scaled score of 6.33 on the three Acquired Knowledge subtests (percentile rank equal to 11), strikingly lower than her mean score of 14.33 (92nd percentile) on the three Verbal subtests that are less influenced by formal instruction. Sheila has remarkably intact verbal intelligence, indeed well above the average of other 11-year-olds, when faced with novel problems or tasks. She can apply this intellect equally well whether responding within a meaningful context (Comprehension) or an abstract one (Similarities, Digit Span). Her verbal ability is poor, however, when responding to problems or questions that are in large part contingent on the prior acquisition of concepts or facts. The impact of Sheila's environment is clearly prominent in her performance on the Acquired Knowledge grouping and is also reflected to some extent in her school achievement. However, her success on the remaining Verbal subtests (particularly in the context of her deprived background) reveals outstanding intellectual strengths that, if channeled properly, portend well for future academic improvement.

Sheila was not even referred for learning problems because her teacher saw no inconsistency between her cultural background and academic performance. (Sheila was referred for a suspected *behavior* disorder.) However, her Verbal scaled-score profile indicates that much more can be expected of her than would be predicted from either her environment or her overall Verbal IQ. Sheila will function very well in some verbal situations and inadequately in others; her WISC-R Verbal IQ offers no insight into this distinction and is really worthless.

Barbara performed at the 71st percentile on the Acquired Knowledge subtests, compared to the 16th percentile on the other three Verbal subtests. Although this discrepancy is not as dramatic as the difference observed for Sheila, the implications are still quite important. Barbara's home environment and parental push probably elevated her scores on the Acquired Knowledge tasks, a conclusion that is reinforced by her markedly lower performance on Similarities, Comprehension, and Digit Span. Her verbal intelligence is unimpressive whenever she cannot call upon her store of verbal facts and concepts that have been acquired over the years. Barbara's fifth-grade teacher referred her for evaluation because of below average achievement in some school subjects—learning difficulties that did not surface during the more fact-oriented primary grades. Based on cross-validation of the WISC-R Verbal profile with other test scores, clinical observations, and more objective background data, the psychologist concluded that Barbara's pattern of achievement in school subjects was entirely consistent with her varied verbal skills. Although some remedial steps were recommended, the main suggestion was counseling for both Barbara and her parents.

Which triad of Verbal subtests, those in the Acquired Knowledge grouping, or the ones that are generally less dependent on formal instruction, reflect a child's "true" verbal intelligence? For both Sheila and Barbara, the answer is neither.

These children have two types of verbal intelligence and will appear bright or dull depending on the context. Consequently, both aspects of their verbal intelligence must be understood and respected to enable examiners to make optimally meaningful recommendations. As postulated in Chapter 1, *all* WISC-R subtests measure what an individual has learned. The fact that tasks such as Information and Arithmetic reflect formal learning should not minimize the incidental learning that is necessary for competence on subtests like Similarities. One can easily realize the dynamic impact of the learning environment by imagining Sheila's Verbal IQ had she been raised in Barbara's upper-middle-class home, and vice versa.

In these examples the Verbal subtests split neatly into two discrete groupings; unfortunately, profile interpretation is not usually so easy or straightforward. Examiners cannot be rigid when using a model such as Bannatyne's but need flexibility in their approach to detective work. One type of flexibility was just demonstrated: Bannatyne's Acquired Knowledge category was used to unravel the sample profiles, but his Verbal Conceptualization category was ignored because these two verbal groupings are *not* independent of content. Other kinds of flexible interpretation might be necessary in other circumstances. For example, the interpretations given to the preceding sample profiles might have remained the same even without the clear-cut dichotomies that were observed. Sheila might easily have obtained a poor Comprehension score because this subtest, in addition to requiring social judgment and reasoning, is very influenced by cultural opportunities at home. A truly impoverished environment may make several of the questions meaningless to some children, preventing them from applying their good reasoning skills to the situations depicted in the items. Additionally, some subcultures may teach responses to some questions that are socially correct within that cultural group but are nevertheless scored zero by the WISC-R scoring system. An analysis of "wrong" Comprehension responses, coupled with an understanding of the values taught in the child's subculture, can support this hypothesis; such analyses are frequently necessary to interpret properly a black or Spanish-speaking child's Comprehension scaled score.

Barbara's Verbal scores also might easily have presented a more ambiguous picture to the examiner. Just as cultural factors could have depressed Sheila's Comprehension score, Barbara's enriched environment could have substantially improved her score on this subtest. Children who have poor reasoning skills but manage to perform adequately on Comprehension are usually easy to spot because they tend to parrot overlearned responses to numerous items without reflection or apparent understanding. Barbara might also have scored relatively low on Arithmetic—a task that is more related to school learning than to cultural opportunities at home, that is included in Bannatyne's Sequencing group as well as Acquired Knowledge, and that is subject to behavioral influences such as distractibility and anxiety. Vocabulary also might have been depressed for Barbara (or inflated for Sheila) because it is still a conceptual task that has dual placement in Bannatyne's Verbal Conceptualization and Acquired Knowledge categories. These illustrations should clarify both the need for flexibility and the necessity of integrating background information, behavioral observations, and the nature of wrong responses when attempting to interpret the Acquired Knowledge triad of subtests.

Information and Arithmetic are two subtests that seem to be characteristically depressed for a variety of populations of children with reading disorders (McManis, Figley, et al. 1978; Robeck 1971; Rugel 1974b; Sattler 1974) and with learning disorders in general (Ackerman, Dykman, et al. 1976; Bryan and Bryan 1975; Myklebust, Bannochie, et al. 1971; Smith, Coleman, et al., 1977a). Since Digit Span and Coding are also characteristically low for these groups of children with school-related problems, researchers have typically focused on a third-factor deficit, with the nature of the deficiency variously interpreted along a distractibility (Kaufman 1975) or sequencing (Rugel 1974b) dimension. However, one cannot discount the possibility that the Information/Arithmetic dyad is depressed for these youngsters at least in part because of an Acquired Knowledge deficit. In a study of 208 learning-disabled youngsters aged 6–12 years who were administered the WISC-R, Smith, Coleman, et al. (1977b) examined relative performance in the four areas posited by Bannatyne. Overall, the learning disabled sample scored significantly higher on the Verbal Conceptualization tasks than on the Sequencing or Acquired Knowledge subtests. (Spatial was the highest of all. The finding for Sequencing was tempered by the fact that Digit Span was not administered to the group.)

There is thus some statistical support to the hypothesis that, as a group, children with learning problems have a deficiency in tasks that are heavily dependent on the acquisition of knowledge. Support also comes from analysis of the subtest profiles provided by investigators who did not operate out of a Bannatyne framework. For example, computation of mean scaled scores in the four Bannatyne categories for the 41 learning-disabled children evaluated by Anderson, Kaufman, et al. (1976) reveals that the lowest value was obtained for Acquired Knowledge (mean = 6.8). Furthermore, Lutey's (1977 pp. 299–300) review of 30 WISC and seven WISC-R studies of learning-disabled populations indicates that lower Acquired Knowledge scores may be expected for these children on the WISC-R than on the WISC. She ranked the learning-disabled children's median scaled scores on 11 subtests (excluding Mazes) from high to low. On the WISC-R, Arithmetic, Vocabulary, and Information occupied three of the four bottom rankings; on the WISC, Vocabulary ranked in sixth position, or precisely in the middle of the subtest distribution.

An Acquired Knowledge weakness for learning-disabled children is certainly sensible in view of their school failure. Longitudinal research is needed to evaluate changes in learning-disabled children's Acquired Knowledge scores with increasing age. Logically, their scores should decrease with age as they fall farther behind their normal age mates in reading and other school-related skills. The overall intelligence of the reading and learning disabled populations is another variable requiring systematic investigation regarding its impact on profile patterns: Smith, Coleman, et al. (1977b) found more clear-cut patterning on the Bannatyne categories for the portion of their sample identified as High IQ (mean Full Scale IQ = 93.3) than for the portion labeled Low IQ (mean Full Scale IQ = 76.3).

Probably the most crucial type of research need is to try to determine whether poor performance in the Acquired Knowledge area is more a cause or an effect of the learning disorder. It is possible that a defect in the processes requisite for acquiring factual knowledge and concepts is responsible for the decreased Acquired Knowledge score and is related to the learning disorder as well. The processing deficiency may translate into a poor long-term memory and coexist with the defect in sequential processing observed by Bannatyne (1971) in genetic dyslexic readers. Some evidence of a long-term memory problem in learning-disabled children has been provided by Nolan and Driscoll (1978), who compared the performance of learning-disabled and normal children at ages 8½ and 11½ on a free-recall task. Despite being matched for IQ, the learning-disabled children performed 3 years below their normal controls on the multitrial memory task. Nolan and Driscoll (1978) concluded from their data that the learning-disabled youngsters had a deficit in their ability to construct sufficiently large recall units.

In contrast to a process-disorder hypothesis is the notion that depressed scores on the Acquired Knowledge subtests merely provide a direct reflection of the learning-disabled child's failure to learn in school. From that perspective, the three WISC-R subtests are no different from conventional achievement tests and reflect the consequences of the learning disability. As such, the Acquired Knowledge grouping could not be considered to measure verbal intelligence and would serve only to depress unfairly the child's Verbal IQ. Indeed, the effects of the school learning problem, rather than any limitation in verbal intelligence per se, may be responsible for the prevalent finding of higher Performance than Verbal IQs in learning-disabled populations (Anderson, Kaufman, et al. 1976; Leton 1972; Lutey 1977; Smith, Coleman, et al., 1977a), and for the discovery that substantial proportions of school-labeled learning-disabled children do not meet the common criterion of "normal" intelligence (Ames 1968; Bryan 1974; Smith, Coleman, et al. 1977a). Research in this area is urgently needed because of current diagnostic practices that stipulate a minimum IQ and a sizable discrepancy between ability and achievement for children to be classified as learning disabled. If low scores on several WISC-R subtests can reasonably be attributed to poor school achievement rather than to limited cognitive ability, the *consequences* of the suspected disorder will greatly affect identification of the disorder. Thus learning-disabled children might perform poorly in the Acquired Knowledge area *because* of their learning problem, thereby lowering their IQs and decreasing the discrepancy between their ability and achievement—both of which diminish the likelihood of their proper diagnosis!

The implications of the Acquired Knowledge category have been discussed for culturally disadvantaged, culturally advantaged, reading-disabled, and learning-disabled children. Yet the most consistent findings in the literature pertaining to the three subtests in the category come from investigations of the profiles of mentally retarded children. Silverstein (1968) summarized 10 studies involving retarded populations tested on the WISC and rank ordered the mean scaled scores from highest to lowest for each group. Overall, Information, Arithmetic, and Vocabulary ranked eighth, ninth, and tenth, respectively, out of the 10 regularly administered subtests; in addition, the consistency of these low rankings across groups was remarkable. Lutey's (1977, pp. 293–294) summary of 33 WISC studies with retarded samples revealed rankings quite similar to Silverstein's. Again, the Acquired Knowledge subtests occupied the bottom three rankings.

For a group of 80 mentally retarded children aged 6–16 (mean Full Scale IQ = 50.6) tested on the WISC-R, Arithmetic and Vocabulary were again the two most difficult subtests, with Information ranking near the bottom (Kaufman and Van Hagen 1977). In Lutey's (1977, pp. 293–294) summary of seven WISC-R studies employing retarded samples, Arithmetic, Vocabulary, and Information were among the four most difficult subtests. Clearly, mentally retarded children perform more poorly on the Acquired Knowledge subtests than in any other Bannatyne category. The deficit may reflect their inadequate school-related skills, or it may be due to problems in their long-term memory. The latter possibility would tie in closely to Ellis's (1963) Stimulus Trace theory of mental retardation; again, well-conceived research investigations are necessary.

Regardless of causative factors, low scores on the Acquired Knowledge tasks are worthy of note because they are likely to be associated with low scholastic achievement. For children from culturally impoverished environments, good performance on Similarities, Comprehension, and Digit Span, despite a low Acquired Knowledge score, promotes optimism for academic improvement. When children from disadvantaged environments perform very poorly on virtually all Verbal subtests, perhaps because the cultural deprivation had a more pervasive impact on the development of verbal intelligence, there is less call for optimism unless subsequent assessment uncovers other cognitive or noncognitive strengths. Since low Acquired Knowledge scores may be associated with limited cultural opportunities, reading disabilities, learning disabilities, or mental retardation, a deficit in this area should alert examiners to the need for considerable supplementary assessment, but it has little or no diagnostic value by itself. (See pp. 203–206 for a more thorough treatment of this issue.)

Hopefully, the Acquired Knowledge category will join the three more popular Bannatyne groupings when examiners engage in recategorization of WISC-R subtests. This same suggestion was made by Aliotti (1977) in his discussion of alternative strategies for school psychologists.

Reasoning versus Recall

Another fairly common dichotomy of Verbal subtests is tabulated as follows:

Reasoning	Recall
Similarities	Information
Arithmetic	Vocabulary
Comprehension	Digit Span

Although not tied to any particular method of categorizing WISC-R subtests and not specifically associated with the profiles of exceptional populations, the reasoning—recall split has an intuitive and theoretical meaningfulness. The reasoning subtests all require problem solving and the application of old learning to new situations, whereas the recall tasks basically require the retrieval of stored information. These processes are quite different and relate to Thorndike's (1926) distinction between the higher abilities of abstraction and relational thinking versus the lower associative skills, as well as to Jensen's (1969) Level I—Level II dichotomy. From Hebb's (1949) theoretical perspective, neuroanatomical and biochemical factors affect the rate of forming and consolidating memory traces known as *phase sequences* (i.e., concepts, akin to Piaget's schemas). Long-term memory involves the activation of existing phase sequences and depends on linkups between the sensory and association areas of the brain. Short-term memory is contingent on an individual's ability to sustain a newly formed neural trace over a brief interval. In contrast to the related set of skills required for short-term and long-term memory, the reasoning process entails "hooking up" existing phase sequences in novel ways. The mental activity accompanying insightful problem solving occurs primarily within the association cortex and differs qualitatively from the processes involved in the recall of stored information. Not surprisingly, some individuals with exceptional stores of knowledge are not very good at insightful thinking, whereas others with relatively poor memories or limited experiences can solve quite difficult or subtle problems. Other theories besides Hebb's neuropsychological approach can explain the reasoning—recall distinction; the essential point to realize is that theoretical support exists for the WISC-R Verbal distinction under discussion.

A dichotomy between the reasoning and recall tasks in the WISC-R is evident in the WISC-R Verbal profiles of numerous children who possess different levels of ability in these two skill areas. However, each of the reasoning and recall subtests has sufficient unique properties to prevent a simple two-way split of the Verbal Scale for some youngsters who still show marked recall – reasoning differences. Similarities and Comprehension demand verbal reasoning, whereas Arithmetic requires the more specialized ability of reasoning with numerical symbols. Even the two measures of verbal reasoning assess problem solving under different conditions. Similarities involves application of reasoning skills to a task that is not very meaningful, that is, discovering the common properties or abstract categories that unite two different concepts. In contrast, Comprehension requires a more practical and meaningful skill, the ability to interpret or explain real-life problem situations. Whereas some children may have considerable difficulty with Comprehension items because of limited exposure to given situations, the concepts used in Similarities items are familiar to virtually all children. Even the concepts that must be related in the more difficult Similarities items, such as salt, water, first, and last, are known and used by young children. (The use of familiar words was not entirely true for the 1949 WISC Similarities subtest because of the inclusion of some less common concepts such as plum and violin.)

Arithmetic, like Comprehension, assesses reasoning in socially meaningful situations. However, the Arithmetic items do not provide an adequate measure of reasoning for children who have failed to master the essential computational skills. Consequently, Arithmetic may shift from a reasoning to a recall task for youngsters who have not overlearned, by rote memory, the basic number facts. A low Arithmetic scaled score can sometimes be attributed to a poor long-term memory or to inadequate numerical reasoning by studying the pattern of wrong responses. For example, a memory problem is suggested if a child subtracts 5 from 12 and concludes that the boy sold eight newspapers; a reasoning difficulty is implied if the child adds 5 to 12 and replies that 17 newspapers were sold.

The dual nature of Arithmetic is evident from its Guilford SOI factors: cognition of a semantic system *and* memory of symbolic implications. When operating out of a Guilford framework, only three WISC-R subtests measure the memory process, and all are on the Verbal Scale. In addition to Arithmetic, Meeker (1975b) classifies Information and Digit Span as memory tasks. Whereas Information items measure a variety of SOI operations, the fact that 22 of the 30 items require memory (Meeker 1975b) makes it primarily a memory subtest. Vocabulary, despite its apparent memory component, is classified only as a measure of semantic cognition. Thus a child who performs consistently high or low on Information, Arithmetic, and Digit Span may be evidencing a strength or weakness in memory as defined by Guilford. Scores on the remaining three subtests may cluster together, or they may divide according to their SOI operation: cognition (Similarities, Vocabulary) and evaluation (Comprehension). If Comprehension splits apart from the other Verbal subtests and is consistent in magnitude to most Performance scaled scores, the child likely has a strong or weak ability to evaluate and make judgments in terms of a known standard (see p. 42). Examiners should be alert for those instances in which only a SOI approach can unite the loose ends of an otherwise incomprehensible WISC-R profile—even if they do not ascribe to Guilford's theory or to Meeker's (1969, 1975b) comprehensive application of his theory to the profile interpretation of a wide variety of intelligence tests.

Returning to the armchair dichotomy of recall–reasoning, Digit Span is the only recall task that measures short-term memory and that is extremely subject to the influences of distractibility and poor attention span. A discrepancy between Digit Span and the long-term memory tasks is hence not surprising for some children who otherwise show a discrepancy in their reasoning–recall skills. Vocabulary may also diverge from the other recall subtests. Unlike Information and Digit Span, Vocabulary demands good conceptualization and verbal expression, which may account for Vocabulary's "switching over" to the reasoning triad for some children. (Guilford's classification of Vocabulary as solely a measure of cognition provides another feasible explanation.) The Digit Span and Information subtests are also united by their presumed susceptibility to anxiety (Mayman, Schafer, et al. 1951; Oros, Johnson, et al. 1972), although the overall research evidence for this supposition is far greater for Digit Span than for Information (Lutey 1977). Worthy of mention as well is the belief that Information is especially subject to the influence of inhibition, causing children to respond incorrectly to items that they may ordinarily know quite well (Sattler 1974, p. 175). Hence some individuals with superior memories may earn poor scores on Information (and/or on Digit Span) because of emotional rather than cognitive factors.

Information and Vocabulary are dependent on both cultural opportunities at home and on school-related learning, as was discussed at length in the previous section. Whereas the most basic principal determinant of performance on tasks like the Vocabulary subtest "must be the long-term memory structures established by previous experience with the words in question (Estes 1974, p. 746)," other determinants have to be considered as well. As Estes (1974) explains, a disadvantaged environment may hinder test performance in ways that are more subtle than mere limited exposure to facts and concepts. Children growing up in circumstances that fail to promote appropriate verbal interaction with adults may have inadequate conceptions of the characteristics of acceptable answers and fail items because their responses are meaningful only within their own frames of reference. Discerning the cause of poor Information and Vocabulary scores is no less complicated for children with learning disorders than for disadvantaged youngsters. Learning-disabled children may perform poorly because their failure to learn in school is directly mirrored in the Acquired Knowledge subtests, or they may have a long-term memory deficit, as suggested by Nolan and Driscoll's (1978) recent research findings (see p. 140). However, even a hypothesis of an inadequate long-term memory is far too global for practical purposes (Estes

1974; Rumelhart, Lindsay, et al. 1972; Tulving 1972). For example, the ability to recall a word in memory is related to its values with respect to a set of attributes (Anglin 1970), its accessibility as determined by the presence of retrieval cues (Tulving 1968), and the availability of the cues, which is a function of both the recency and frequency of usage (Allen, Mahler, et al. 1969).

Examiners need to exercise considerable clinical acumen to speculate whether poor performance on Information and Vocabulary is due to the failure of the memory structures to be established or to the inability to employ an appropriate strategy for retrieving stored knowledge. In the former instance, where learning has not taken place, it is inappropriate to suggest a deficiency in long-term memory; in the latter case, knowledge of learning theory and application of contemporary research findings are greatly beneficial to the examiner's attempts at understanding the child's memory problem. Unfortunately, the state of the art in learning theory is not sufficiently advanced to suggest specific supplementary assessment techniques to pinpoint the process deficit (Estes 1974). Yet competent clinicians should be able to integrate their knowledge of the research findings in learning theory with a child's test scores, nature of wrong responses, method of responding to the memory items, overall behaviors, and cultural background to generate pertinent working hypotheses.

As indicated earlier, the recall and reasoning categories are each fairly heterogeneous. Consequently, attempts to track down a possible global discrepancy in a child's recall—reasoning ability on Verbal tasks may lead to fairly specific hypotheses. For example, investigation of a child's profile may uncover a strength in verbal (but not numerical) reasoning and a weakness in long-term memory. These are important findings because each hypothesis is based on more than one subtest, and the discrepancy between the abilities has practical implications. But the hypotheses are not as powerful as discovery of a complete split within the Verbal Scale along the reasoning—recall dichotomy, and even a complete split becomes much more practically meaningful if additional support is provided by fluctuations within the Performance Scale and by data from sources other than the WISC-R. The greater the amount of evidence that can be martialed in support of a hypothesis, the more reliable the hypothesis and the greater the likelihood that the strength or weakness will generalize beyond a specific content or item style. When children perform relatively well or poorly on reasoning tasks in the Verbal Scale, the examiners should immediately investigate as to whether the same level of ability was displayed on nonverbal problem solving tasks, most notably Picture Arrangement and Mazes. Strong or weak performance on the verbal memory subtests demands consideration of success or failure on the nonverbal imitative subtests (Block Design and Coding) and on the Performance subtests involving long-term or short-term visual memory (Picture Completion and Coding, respectively). The reasoning—imitative distinction within the Performance Scale is discussed more fully on pages 165–166.

Children with good reasoning skills but poor recall are likely to function best in a learning environment that allows for acquisition of facts and concepts through discovery, promotes intrinsic understanding of the subject matter to be learned, and deemphasizes rote memory. The reverse pattern of good recall and poor reasoning implies the need for an educational setting that shapes children's ability to figure things out, while actually providing the youngsters with frequent explanations of various facts and concepts, and that encourages rote learning techniques as a means of acquiring new information. Examiners who are able to translate the recall–reasoning dichotomy into its educational implications should be able to make important suggestions regarding the selection of appropriate educational materials and teaching techniques and perhaps even the choice of the specific teacher or teachers whose styles are most likely to lead to the child's greatest chance for academic improvement.

Nature of the Stimulus and Response

Wechsler's subtests have traditionally been interpreted by researchers and clinicians in terms of the content of their items and the processes they are believed to assess. Picture Arrangement measures nonverbal reasoning and planning ability (processes) with regard to interpersonal situations (content), Arithmetic assesses reasoning as applied to numerical problems, and so on, in clinical text after text. Usually forgotten in these rational analyses is consideration of the nature of the input and output, apart from the specific content of the items. Does the individual have to respond to a long question or to a simple phrase? Does a correct response require much spontaneous verbalization, or will a single word suffice? Emphasis in the 1960s and 1970s on a psycholinguistic interpretation of cognitive tasks (Kirk and Kirk 1971), albeit not without controversy (Newcomer and Hammill 1976), has alerted psychologists and special educators to the impact of language disorders on test performance. Psycholinguistic learning models espoused by Wepman, Jones, et al. (1960), Osgood (1953), Kirk, McCarthy, et al. (1968), and Myers and Hammill (1976) all attribute a featured role to the nature of the input to be processed and the mode of communicating the response.

In a global sense, Wechsler's division of the 12 WISC-R subtests into the Verbal and Performance Scales addresses this issue, as the former group of subtests operates primarily within the auditory–vocal channel of communication and the latter within the visual–motor modality (see pp. 30–31). However, it is necessary to differentiate among the input–output characteristics of the Verbal subtests as a means of facilitating WISC-R interpretation; an analogous discussion for the Performance Scale appears on pages 166–169. The key notion in this type of analysis is that some aspect of the properties of the stimulus or the response may affect children's performance on certain subtests *apart from the specific content or processes inherent in the tasks*. The problem may be related to a deficiency in auditory reception or some other psycholinguistic process, although it may also pertain to factors such as memory, discrimination, and sequencing. The goal of the approach presented here is *not* to treat the WISC-R subtests as purely psycholinguistic tasks to be used as a basis for diagnosing or treating language difficulties. Problems abound in these areas and controversy reigns, even when tests developed specifically for assessment of psycholinguistic functioning are utilized for decision making (Hammill and Larsen 1978; Lund, Foster, et al. 1978; Newcomer and Hammill 1976). Rather, the aim is to generate hypotheses to explain fluctuations in WISC-R profiles from a different vantage point, one that may be especially valuable when the more conventional cognitive approaches lead to dead ends.

Stimuli for the Verbal subtests partition into two groupings, as follows:

Long Stimuli	Brief Stimuli
Information	Similarities
Arithmetic	Vocabulary
Comprehension	Digit Span

Each item in the three tasks with long stimuli requires the child to respond to a lengthy question. In contrast, Digit Span has very brief stimuli, and Vocabulary and Similarities have one- and two-word stimuli, respectively, once children clearly understand the tasks. Even before children grasp the intent of the subtests, the Vocabulary and Similarities items include simple, repetitive questions unlike the more complex and varied questions included in the Information, Arithmetic, and Comprehension subtests. Children with an auditory reception deficit, who have difficulty in deriving meaning from spoken language, may experience more problems in understanding the long questions than the telegraphic stimuli of Similarities, Vocabulary, and Digit Span. Such individuals are also likely to have difficulty following the lengthy verbal directions to several Performance subtests, most notably Coding and Picture Arrangement.

Memory may play a dominant role in a child's success on the subtests with long questions. A youngster with a poor memory may recall lengthy stimuli incorrectly and respond to questions that are different from the ones actually asked by the examiner. Errors of this sort are difficult to distinguish from conventional wrong answers, especially for clinicians with limited experience. Examiners who sense that a child is remembering questions incorrectly should obviously repeat the items, even if they are not asked to do so by the child. (For Arithmetic only one, and for Digit Span no, repetition is permissible.) When children obtain low scores on Information, Arithmetic, and Comprehension because of a presumed inadequate short-term auditory memory, this hypothesized deficit requires much cross-validation, such as by a low scaled score in Digit Span, the need for much repetition of the instructions to some Performance subtests, and low scores on supplementary measures of immediate recall of auditory stimuli.

The Verbal subtests with long versus brief stimuli differ in the degree to which context clues affect understanding of the items. Children with auditory discrimination deficiencies may be able to make sense out of the long questions by relying on the considerable context clues but have much difficulty with Similarities, Vocabulary, and Digit Span. The stimuli for the latter three subtests are not presented in a meaningful context, making the tasks potentially very difficult to comprehend for a youngster with a discrimination problem or with a mild hearing impairment.

More prevalent than a dichotomy in a child's ability to perform effectively with different kinds of stimuli is a division of the Verbal subtests in terms of the amount of vocal expression required for successful performance. Whereas some tasks require short (essentially one-word) responses, others demand a considerable degree of verbal expression skills. A division of the Verbal subtests along this output dimension is tabulated as follows:

Much Expression Required	Little Expression Required
Similarities	Information
Vocabulary	Arithmetic
Comprehension	Digit Span

Similarities merits inclusion with the two tasks that place a strong emphasis on spontaneous verbal expression, although it may occasionally group with the other triad. Some youngsters with poor expressive but excellent conceptual skills can achieve much success on Similarities by responding with a single well-chosen word on each item. On Vocabulary and Comprehension, however, it is difficult to compensate for deficient expressive ability, particularly in view of the large number of partially correct or incorrect responses that have to be queried by the examiner.

Before concluding that low scores on Vocabulary, Comprehension, and possibly Similarities are due to inadequate verbal expression, examiners need to review the child's responses and spontaneous verbalizations during the session. Verbal responses should consistently be terse, queries by the examiner should rarely lead to improved performance, and spontaneous comments are likely to be minimal and sparse of content. However, regardless of the amount of evidence that examiners can garner to support the hypothesis that low scores on some Verbal subtests reflect the children's inability to *communicate* their knowledge (rather than the *absence* of the relevant knowledge), causality is difficult to infer. The problem may be a language disorder, such as a defect in the psycholinguistic process of expression within the auditory−vocal modality. Other plausible explanations are an expressive speech problem, extreme shyness, or fearfulness (where the limited expression represents withdrawal from an unpleasant situation). In addition, bilingual children may be unable to express themselves very well when English is their second language, and black youngsters may be penalized because their slang words or jargon may not be understood by white examiners. Inexperienced examiners have to be alert to Wechsler's (1974, p. 61) firm warning that improper grammar or poor pronunciation should never lower a child's score on a Verbal item. Failure to heed this basic scoring rule will certainly artificially depress some children's scores on the three subtests demanding good expressive abilities.

Discovery of a potential speech or language disorder should yield a recommendation of a subsequent thorough evaluation by qualified professionals in these areas. When clinical observations suggest that shyness or fearfulness was responsible for depressed scores on the verbal expressive subtests, retesting on the Verbal Scale is advised under more favorable and relaxed conditions. (As indicated on pp. 48−50, practice effects are minimal for Verbal subtests.) Retesting in a different language and/or by an examiner whose cultural background matches the child's background is similarly advised when bilingualism or Black Dialect seems responsible for depressed scores on some subtests. In no case should the Verbal IQ be considered a good estimate of a child's verbal intelligence when an inability to respond effectively leads to poor performance on the cognitive tasks requiring considerable verbal expression. A similar conclusion regarding Verbal IQ is usually warranted when the properties of the stimulus, rather than the content or process of the task, seem to materially affect a child's performance on several subtests.

The discussion of stimuli and responses in this section is intended to broaden the scope of examiners' detective work and alert them to an alternate approach for interpreting fluctuations in WISC-R profiles. The same type of flexibility is needed when evaluating strengths and weaknesses on psycholinguistic test batteries. On the ITPA the Visual Reception subtest (sample items: "Do sausages frown?" "Do barometers congratulate?"), for example, can also be considered as an intellectual task that measures word knowledge, fund of information, and verbal concept formation and is subject to the influences of cultural opportunities at home, school learning, ability to respond when uncertain, and the Piaget notion of animism.

Digit Span

Not infrequently, a child's scaled scores on the five regular Verbal subtests cluster together at a level that is highly discrepant with the Digit Span score. Very high or low scaled scores on Digit Span are to be expected and ordinarily should not cause undue concern, because this subtest loads heavily on the distractibility factor and does not even have a secondary loading on Verbal Comprehension, is a poor measure of g (see Table 4−1), has an impressive amount of subtest specificity across the age range (see Table 4−2), and correlates only 0.45 with the Verbal Scale (Wechsler 1974, p. 47).

Before concluding that a highly discrepant Digit Span score reflects a unique strength or weakness, other possibilities should be explored, especially if significant fluctuations are observed within the Performance Scale. Since Coding is also on the distractibility factor and requires short-term memory to some extent (see pp. 170−171), a significant deviation on this Performance subtest may be related meaningfully to the high or low Digit Span score. In addition, Wechsler (1974, p. 7) notes that a pattern of low scores on Digit Span, Coding, and Block Design may be related to organic brain syndrome. If brief exploration of the Performance Scale does not help explain a highly discrepant Digit Span score, the examiner should readily accept a unique explanation for the strength or weakness. In the absence of distractible or anxious behavior, low scores should usually be interpreted as a deficit in short-term auditory memory; high scores invariably suggest an excellent short-term memory despite unimpressive verbal comprehension and expression skills. However, all specific hypotheses must be verified with additional test results to remain viable.

Understanding of learning-theory research is important not only for interpreting Vocabulary and Information scores, but also for evaluating a presumed short-term memory strength or weakness reflected in performance on Digit Span and related tasks. Like Vocabulary on the Binet or Wechsler scales, tasks akin to Digit Span have been the subject of numerous experimental psychology investigations (Estes 1974). Various studies have shown that the procedure of grouping or chunking of digits plays a vital role in what is remembered in short-term memory tasks by normal children and adults and by mentally retarded or brain-damaged children (Bower and Winzenz 1969; Estes 1974; Spitz 1966). It is thus essential for examiners to avoid grouping the digits subconsciously when presenting the longer sequences in Digit Span. Nevertheless, children are able to chunk digits spontaneously as a means of organizing the stimuli (Estes 1974), so extreme scores on Digit Span may reflect a superior or deficient ability to group the digits relative to children of a comparable age. The ability to code the chunks and to maintain only the memory of the set of codes also seems to be dynamically involved in the short-term memory process (Estes 1972, 1974; Johnson 1970). Consequently, the cause for poor Digit Span performance may reside not in the ability to form subgroupings of the digits, but to code the chunks adequately. Estes (1974) also notes that low scores on Digit Span may reflect insufficient familiarity with the sequential aspect of ordinal numbers (which relates to the sequencing interpretation of the distractibility factor—see Chapter 3) or the inability to exert the selective inhibition needed to order the output appropriately. He states further that insight into learning theory and research findings can enable examiners to localize the source of a child's failure under standardized conditions and thus to make better remedial suggestions.

Sometimes examiners have reason to compare an individual's forward and backward spans to determine if marked differences exist. In Chapter 3 it was mentioned that children with a deficiency in manipulating symbols are likely to have an adequate forward span coupled with poor ability to reverse digits (see p. 83). Unlike repeating digits forward, reversing the digits requires reorganization and remanipulation of the stimuli (Sattler 1974, p. 181), both higher level processes. Whereas individuals who perform much better on the forward than backward series may manifest mental disturbance (Kitzinger and Blumberg 1951) cognitive processing hypotheses are probably more likely explanations of the discrepancy for most examinees. Similarly, better performance on the backward than forward series has been associated with negativism or compulsive trends (Kitzinger and Blumberg 1951), although a psycholinguistic explanation is also plausible. The forward series requires skill at the automatic level of organization in contrast to the representational level ability needed for the backward series. Some individuals with poor automatic skills may have a short forward span but display a good backward span since the demands of the more difficult task virtually force them to call upon their representational level skill.

Empirical evidence is available to support the notion that Digits Forward and Digits Backward measure a different set of skills (Costa 1975; Jensen and Figueroa 1976). But how does one systematically determine whether a child performs differentially on the two portions of Digit Span? The first step requires understanding of the typical differences in the forward and backward spans of normal children. From unpublished standardization data of the spans of boys and girls aged 6½ to 16½, it was observed that for each age group *the forward span was an average of two digits longer than the backward span.* (Note that this difference refers to the length of the longest *spans* repeated by the child, not the raw scores earned on the two parts of the Digit Span subtest.) Consequently, forward spans that are about 2 digits longer than backward spans are normal and are to be expected.

The second step in evaluating discrepancies between spans is awareness of the relative unreliability of the separate forward and backward series. By treating the two portions of Digit Span as "half tests" and applying the Spearman–Brown formula to reliability data provided in the WISC-R manual (Wechsler 1974, p. 28), the forward and backward series are each found to have an average reliability coefficient of only 0.64 across the age range. In view of the typical discrepancies in spans found for normal children and the limited reliability of the separate forward and backward series, the following rules of thumb seem sufficiently conservative: (a) the forward span should be larger than the backward span by at least five or six digits before hypothesizing a relative deficiency in reversing digits, and (b) the backward span should be larger than the forward span by at least two digits before hypothesizing a relative deficit in simple rote recall.

PATTERNS TO ANTICIPATE ON THE PERFORMANCE SCALE

Like the Verbal Scale, the Performance Scale also subdivides in many predictable ways. Some of the more common clusters of nonverbal subtests are described and analyzed in the remainder of this chapter. These various groupings are each derived from one or more of the following sources: Bannatyne's categories, Guilford's SOI model, Rapaport's groups, research on cerebral specialization, psycholinguistic approaches to test interpretation, and data from analyses of factor structure and subtest specificity.

Spatial Ability

Bannatyne's Picture Completion, Block Design, and Object Assembly triad represents one of the most useful and practical subgroupings of Wechsler's subtests. Whereas Mazes is clearly a logical adjunct to the Spatial Ability grouping, this subtest is excluded from the present discussion for two reasons. First, the wealth of research involving Picture Completion, Block Design, and Object Assembly (whether from a Bannatyne orientation or from a field dependent–field independent cognitive style approach) has typically *not* included Mazes in the analyses. Second, although Mazes certainly has a spatial component, the task differs from the Spatial triad in some basic ways: for instance, Mazes may involve successive rather than simultaneous processing (Das, Kirby, et al. 1975; see pp. 163–165), and it assesses the Guilford operation of cognition rather than a combination of cognition and evaluation (Meeker 1975b; see Table 3-1). Consequently, one cannot tacitly assume that Mazes would have grouped with the three Spatial subtests had this frequently ignored task been included in the bulk of research investigations.

The practicality of Bannatyne's Spatial category comes from a large body of research showing that the three component subtests tend to cluster together for numerous groups of children, regardless of their performance on Picture Arrangement and Coding. Relatively low scores on the Spatial subtests are associated with a field dependent cognitive style (Goodenough and Karp 1961). High Spatial scores, relative to children's own overall performance, are typically earned by children classified as reading disabled (Rugel 1974b), mentally retarded (Kaufman and Van Hagen 1977; Keogh and Hall 1974; Lutey 1977, pp. 293–294; Silverstein, 1968), and field independent (Goodenough and Karp 1961).

Despite the difficulties associated with defining learning disabilities, several

WISC-R studies have shown groups of learning-disabled children to perform relatively well on the Spatial subtests (Anderson, Kaufman, et al. 1976; Smith, Coleman, et al. 1977b; Vance, Gaynor, et al. 1976; Zingale and Smith 1978). However, the high Spatial scores may be an artifact since the mean scaled score on WISC-R Block Design has typically been considerably lower than the mean scaled scores on the Object Assembly—Picture Completion dyad (Lutey 1977, pp. 299—300; Smith, Coleman, et al. 1977a; Zingale and Smith 1978). Unexplainably, this split in the Spatial grouping did not occur for learning-disabled samples tested on the 1949 WISC (Lutey 1977, pp. 299—300). Nevertheless, with the WISC-R, it is conceivable that the apparent strength for groups of children with learning disabilities is more related to right-brain processing (see pp. 157—163) or to the meaningfulness of the stimuli (see pp. 166—167) than to understanding of spatial relations.

Examiners need to be alert for a possible clustering of the Spatial subtests within the Performance profile of all children tested. The triad may be higher than the other two or three nonverbal subtests, lower, or somewhere in between. Regardless of the patterning, the cohesiveness of children's Spatial subtest scores, in the face of divergent performance on other nonverbal tasks, indicates that the Performance IQ does not reflect a unitary trait and may give a misleading picture of their nonverbal intelligence. Verbal—Performance IQ discrepancies will be affected. For example, a group of mentally retarded children scored significantly higher on the Spatial than on the Verbal Conceptualization category, yet they failed to show a significant P > V differential (Keogh and Hall 1974).

Importantly, the Spatial subtests may provide the fairest assessment of the so-called true intellectual ability of children from disadvantaged environments and of youngsters with reading or learning disabilities. Of all the WISC-R subtests, Picture Completion, Block Design, and Object Assembly tend to be among the least dependent on specific cultural and educational opportunities. In contrast, most Verbal subtests reflect crystallized abilities, Picture Arrangement is dependent on cultural background and interpersonal experience, and Coding is more of a psychomotor than a mental task. However, the Spatial subtests would undoubtedly provide a poor estimate of intellectual functioning for individuals shown by comprehensive evaluation to have a field-dependent cognitive style, for learning-disabled children with diagnosed visual—perceptual problems, or for brain-damaged youngsters known to have a lesion in the right cerebral hemisphere.

The well-documented association of a Spatial strength with mental retardation and reading disabilities, along with its possible relationship to learning disabilities, makes high scores in this area of little value for differential diagnosis when considered in isolation. However, integration of a Spatial strength with other pertinent test and clinical information may provide vital evidence for formulating diagnostic hypotheses (see pp. 203−206). Furthermore, just knowing that high Spatial scores in relation to other abilities is so prevalent in the profiles of a variety of exceptional populations should elevate to immediate importance the occurrence of this finding. Examiners who note the "high Spatial" trend in a child's WISC-R profile should be alerted to the possibility of some type of learning problem and should be impelled to administer pertinent supplementary measures to corroborate the suspicion, provided that the reasons for referral are consistent with such procedures. Regardless of etiology, the global strength in Picture Completion, Block Design, and Object Assembly provides an integrity to be incorporated and utilized in the child's remedial program.

Strong or weak performance in Bannatyne's Spatial category may reflect the ability denoted by the label or may be indicative of other skills. As a measure of spatial ability, that is, the understanding of spatial relationships, this grouping of subtests assesses a set of skills that was studied by Thurstone (1938) and included among his seven primary mental abilities under the name spatial relations; featured in Vernon's (1960) hierarchical theory of intelligence as one aspect of the major group factor that he termed Practical−Mechanical−Spatial; defined by Guilford (1967) as requiring the joint processes of figural cognition and figural evaluation; and investigated by Piaget and Inhelder (1967) in infants and children as a developmental progression from topological to projective to Euclidean space.

When children perform poorly or well on the three subtests in Bannatyne's Spatial group because of a strength or weakness in their understanding of spatial relationships and ability to visualize, examiners should anticipate a comparable level of skill on Mazes. Repeating digits backward may also follow suit since research has shown that the backward series (but *not* the forward series) of Digit Span is significantly related to the visual−spatial ability of brain-damaged patients (Costa 1975; Weinberg, Diller, et al. 1972). Consequently, better performance on the backward than the forward series (see pp. 151−152) may reflect good spatial ability for a child who does well on the nonverbal visual−spatial tasks; substantially worse performance in repeating digits backward may be a manifestation of poor spatial ability for a youngster with depressed scores on the pertinent Performance subtests. When the *entire* Digit Span subtest is quite consistent with a child's level of functioning on the Spatial subtests, including Mazes, examiners should consider the possibility of a global strength or weakness in fluid intelligence (see pp. 28−30).

Depending on the pattern of scores on other Wechsler subtests and on supplementary instruments, strong or weak performance on the trilogy of Spatial subtests may be indicative not only of a discrepancy between fluid and crystallized intelligence, but also between children's modes of processing information. Differential processing modes may be viewed from the perspective of right-brain−left-brain functioning (as discussed on pp. 5−7) or from the related notion of simultaneous versus successive syntheses (Das, Kirby, et al. 1975); both of these topics are treated in detail in the next section.

Finally, peaks or valleys in Bannatyne's Spatial category may be suggestive of field-independent or field-dependent cognitive styles (Witkin, Moore, et al. 1977) with high- and low-scoring individuals manifesting the opposing characteristic styles of approaching problems and situations (see pp. 39–42). This style is sometimes treated as an ability, namely, analytic field approach, by researchers in this area. Regardless of whether cognitive style is interpreted from a conative or an intellectual framework, this orientation toward WISC-R interpretation is of special interest because of the accumulating body of research relating cognitive styles to both school achievement (Denney 1974; Kagan 1965) and to the assessment of Mexican–American children (Buriel 1975; Ramirez and Price-Williams 1974). Inferred relationships between Witkin's cognitive style and school achievement have been based on both rational and empirical considerations. Logically, the analytic requirements for learning to read and to compute are quite similar to the requisite skills for success on the field-independence tasks (Cohen 1969). As Buriel (1978) explains, children who are beginning readers must identify vowels and syllables within the context of a more complex word, and analytic procedures are needed as well to carry out computations in mathematics. According to Cohen (1969), the amount of field independence and analytic thinking required for successful achievement in verbal and quantitative areas actually becomes greater with increasing grade level. Empirically, various measures of Witkin's cognitive style have been shown to correlate significantly with school achievement in reading and mathematics, with field-independent children outperforming field-dependent students (Canavan 1969; Kagan and Zahn 1975; Watson 1969).

Numerous investigators have obtained data supporting the contention that Anglo–American children are more field independent than Mexican–Americans (Ramirez and Price-Williams, 1974; Sanders, Scholz, et al., 1976). The fact that Anglo–Americans tend to score higher than Chicanos on tests of reading and mathematics achievement has also been amply documented (Coleman, Campbell, et al. 1966; Kagan and Zahn 1975). Furthermore, evidence exists to support the notion that groups that emphasize respect for family and group identification (e.g., Mexican–Americans) are more likely to be field dependent than groups that foster individuality and the challenging of conventions (Ramirez and Price-Williams 1974). These separate findings have been woven together by some researchers to infer that Mexican–American children have a culturally induced field-dependent cognitive style that may be related to their level of school achievement. For example, Knight, Kagan et al. (1978) interpreted both the greater field independence and better school achievement of third generation than second generation Mexican–American children in their sample as reflecting the effects of acculturation to Anglo–American norms. Ramirez (1972) boldly asserted that the relative school failure of Mexican–American students can be explained by their field-dependent cognitive style.

Should these claims regarding the interdependence of cultural background, cognitive style, and school achievement be upheld by systematic investigation, the practical meaningfulness of high or low Spatial scores would be greatly enhanced. This value would not necessarily be limited to Chicanos, since field independence and school achievement have been shown to correlate significantly for Anglo–Americans as well as Mexican–Americans (Kagan and Zahn 1975), and blacks were found to be much more field dependent than whites (Ramirez and Price-Williams 1974). However, some recent studies suggest that the presumed relationships for Mexican–American children are not so clear cut. Sanders, Scholz, et al. (1976) found no support for the contention that field dependence is associated with a high need for affiliation, as measures of these constructs correlated negligibly for a group of fifth- and sixth-grade students. Similarly, field independence did not correlate significantly with competitiveness (Kagan, Zahn, et al. 1977) despite predictions to the contrary by Ramirez and Castaneda (1974). Even the relationship between cognitive style and school achievement is more complicated than formerly believed. Kagan, Zahn, et al. (1977) found the significance of the correlations to be a function of grade in school, and Buriel (1978) found the relationship to be dependent on the instrument used to measure field independence and on the type of achievement (coefficients were generally significant for mathematics, but not for reading). Indeed, Buriel (1978) interpreted his data as a challenge to the well-accepted notion that Mexican–Americans are more field dependent than Anglo-Americans; he also speculated that the field-dependence construct may be different for the two cultural groups he studied.

Additional research is needed to pursue the relationships among culture, cognitive style, and school achievement. Of particular value to WISC-R users would be studies that incorporate all three WISC-R Spatial subtests rather than just Block Design or measures of field independence such as the Children's Embedded Figures Test and the Portable Rod-and-frame Test. The recent negative findings should be kept in perspective and used as a springboard to investigations that show how high or low scores on instruments used to measure the cognitive style (including Picture Completion, Block Design, and Object Assembly) can be used to improve the assessment and educational recommendations for children, especially minority youngsters. Systematic evaluation of the efficacy for Chicano children of the educational applications of the field independent–field dependent cognitive style proposed by Witkin, Moore, et al. (1977) would be extremely valuable. High on the priority list to be investigated are the implications of Witkin's cognitive style for the learning of social material, the effects of reinforcement, the effectiveness of different styles of teaching, and the nature of the teacher–student interaction (Witkin, Moore, et al. 1977).

Mode of Processing Information

Research and theoretical speculation about cerebral specialization was discussed in Chapter 1 as a criticism of current intelligence tests (pp. 5−7) and in Chapter 2 in the context of interpreting V−P IQ discrepancies (pp. 27−28). The topic is also pertinent for assessing the meaning of fluctuations within the Performance Scale because of the different processing demands of the nonverbal tasks. As described earlier, the left hemisphere is specialized for a sequential, analytic, and logical mode of processing information, whereas the right hemisphere features a Gestalt-like, holistic processing mode (Bogen 1969, 1975; Gazzaniga 1975). In view of these different cognitive styles of the two hemispheres, the left brain is especially adept at processing linguistic and numerical stimuli, and the right brain handles nonverbal information with relative ease, including both visual−spatial and musical stimuli.

The verbal and mathematical subtests in the Verbal Scale are predominantly in the domain of the left hemisphere. Certainly the right cerebral hemisphere contributes to success on some Verbal tasks since visualization is beneficial for repeating digits backward (Costa 1975) and for solving some items such as the ones on the Information subtest regarding the direction of the setting sun and the countries bordering the United States. By and large, however, a child's Verbal IQ reflects left-hemisphere processing. In contrast, the Performance Scale dichotomizes into tasks that seem to require right-brain functioning and those that are primarily dependent on a dynamic integration of the cognitive styles of the two hemispheres. The division of the Performance subtests from this perspective is tabulated as follows:

Right-brain Processing	Integrated Functioning
Picture Completion	Picture Arrangement
Object Assembly	Block Design
	Coding
	Mazes

The integrated subtests have two features that distinguish them from the right-brain tasks: (a) they require analytic or sequential processing, characteristic of the left hemisphere, in addition to the visual−spatial and nonverbal components that are more associated with the right hemisphere, and (b) they require considerable verbiage by the examiner during their administration. In contrast, Picture Completion and Object Assembly seem to require almost exclusively the holistic, synthetic right-brain cognitive style and are communicated simply by the examiner via a minimal amount of verbalization. Success on the integrated tasks seems, therefore, to depend on the right hemisphere for interpreting the visual–spatial stimuli and performing the necessary Gestalt-like syntheses, *and* on the left hemisphere for comprehending the examiner's instructions and applying sequential or analytic processing, where appropriate. The right hemisphere seems capable of coping with the demands of the Picture Completion and Object Assembly subtests without much facilitation from its counterpart.

As a group, learning-disabled children may have a strength in right-brain processing as evidenced by their WISC-R profiles. Based on Lutey's (1977, pp. 299–300) summary of seven studies involving the administration of the WISC-R to learning-disabled samples, and on two additional studies not included in her review (Smith, Coleman, et al. 1977a; Zingale and Smith 1978), a consistent finding emerged: the groups performed best on Object Assembly and Picture Completion. Block Design only ranked sixth in Lutey's summary and a distant fourth in Smith, Coleman, et al.'s (1977a) and Zingale and Smith's (1978) investigations, suggesting that the strong area of functioning is right-hemisphere processing rather than Bannatyne's Spatial Ability or Das's simultaneous processing (see pp. 163–165). However, the fact that WISC-R Picture Arrangement consistently ranked as the third easiest task for groups of learning-disabled children raises the possibility that the strength involves the ability to manipulate meaningful visual stimuli, a topic that is treated on pages 166–167. The most likely explanation of the group data is that some learning-disabled children excel in right-brain processing, whereas other individuals are especially adept at simultaneous processing, manipulation of meaningful stimuli, understanding spatial relations, or Perceptual Organization.

The role of the left hemisphere for some Performance subtests is not intended to minimize the importance of the right half of the brain for these tasks. Indeed, Reitan (1974, p. 45) believes that "Block Design is especially sensitive to posterior right hemisphere involvement and especially to right parietal and occipital damage whereas Picture Arrangement is more sensitive to anterior right temporal lesions." Nevertheless, Block Design requires analysis, a decidedly left-brain function, in addition to the subsequent holistic synthesis that is needed to assemble the blocks correctly. Picture Arrangement requires children to size up a total situation (right hemisphere) but also demands good temporal or time-oriented sequencing skills (left hemisphere) for success. Coding is unquestionably a sequencing task, and Mazes depends on the ability to analyze and sequence the appropriate movements within a spatial context.

The fact that Block Design is not merely a right-hemisphere test, but depends heavily on the analytic left-brain processing style, is evident from Matarazzo's (1972, p. 212) statement: "Oddly enough, individuals who do best on the test are not necessarily those who see, or at least follow, the pattern as a whole, but more often those who are able to break it up into small portions." Furthermore, the need for integrated functioning on Block Design is evident in Lezak's (1976, pp. 44–45) description of the test performance of one patient with known damage to the right hemisphere and of another patient with damage to the visual-association area of the left hemisphere. The first patient had considerable difficulty with the items but had some success on the easier four-block designs by overtly instructing himself on what to do and by verbalizing the relationships among the blocks. The second patient performed quite well on Block Design until he stumbled over a nine-block item that is especially conducive to verbal analysis. Similar clinical evidence of the need for hemispheric integration in spatial tasks comes from observation of the left-handed and right-handed reproductions of a cross and a cube by split-brain patients (Ornstein 1978).

There is also research evidence to support the integrated nature of nonverbal tasks that are similar to Wechsler's Performance subtests. Zaidel and Sperry (1973) concluded from data obtained on split-brain patients and from observations of their problem-solving style that performance on Raven's Coloured Progressive Matrices Test demands much interhemispheric integration for normal individuals. Hunt (1974) points out further that the Matrices can be solved by *either* an analytic or holistic processing style. In addition, the Embedded Figures Test requires a right-hemisphere skill (structuring a complex display) followed by a left-brain ability (extracting the target figure from its surrounding) according to Kinsbourne and Smith (1974, p. 279)—a contention that has some empirical support (Zaidel 1973). It is thus apparent that a variety of Wechsler and Wechsler-like nonverbal tasks demand integrated cerebral functioning rather than simple right-brain processing.

Each cerebral hemisphere operates with its own information-processing rules, with the net effect that we possess two different kinds of intelligence that can function independently or in concert (Bogen 1975). Discrepancies between children's scores on the right-brain and integrated groupings of Performance subtests may well reflect a difference in their two types of intelligence. When scores on the integrated tasks are comparable in magnitude to scores on the Verbal subtests but different from scores on the right-brain tasks, it is reasonable to hypothesize a discrepancy between the analytic−sequential and holistic−synthetic modes of processing information. In contrast, children may perform consistently on the right hemisphere (Picture Completion, Object Assembly) and left hemisphere (Verbal Scale) tasks but obtain either much higher or lower scores on the subtests requiring integrated functioning. In such instances the individuals would seem to have equally developed processing styles but a decided strength or weakness in the ability to integrate the two processes.

Integration demands a mutualism between the hemispheres. Stimuli need to be delegated to the appropriate system since handling stimuli via the inappropriate processing mode is not only inefficient but may interfere with processing in the preferred cognitive system. Sometimes one hemisphere must remain dormant to permit the other hemisphere to do what it does best. In addition, shifts from one mode to the other have to occur, often just to solve a single problem, depending on the specific demands of the task (Galin 1976; Galin and Ornstein 1974;

Gazzaniga 1975; Ornstein 1972). Individual differences in hemispheric integration are to be anticipated and are likely to be evidenced in tasks such as Picture Arrangement or Mazes, which depend to some extent on both processing systems for maximally efficient performance.

Block Design is probably the Performance subtest that is most likely to join the two right-brain tasks for any given individual. Unlike Picture Arrangement and Coding, which are primarily sequencing tasks, Block Design is heavily dependent on holistic processing for successful performance. Whereas the left-brain function of analysis is required to break up the designs into their component parts, the synthesis needed to construct the final products is quite similar to the requisite set of skills for Picture Completion and Object Assembly. When Block Design switches over to the right-brain processing group, the subtest triad is identical to Bannatyne's Spatial category. Hence, good or poor performance on the Spatial tasks may reflect a more generalized strength or weakness in the cognitive style that characterizes the right-cerebral hemisphere.

Support for any hypothesis of an integrity or deficiency in right-brain processing can only be mustered by administering supplementary measures in view of the underrepresentation of right-hemisphere tasks in the WISC-R (see pp. 6-7). Additional visual–spatial tests might be given, such as the Gestalt Completion Test (Street 1931), along with measures of other abilities that are believed to be in the domain of the right hemisphere. Suitable supplements include selected subtests from the Torrance Tests of Creative Thinking (Torrance 1974) and the Seashore Measures of Musical Talents (Seashore, Lewis, et al. 1960). The Torrance tests offer measurement of an aspect of intelligence that is conspicuously missing from conventional intelligence tests; the Seashore tasks permit assessment of nonverbal auditory perception, a right-hemispheric skill (Lezak 1976) that is almost always ignored in favor of verbal measures of auditory perception.

The accumulation of diverse pieces of evidence to suggest that blacks, as a group, have many strengths in the right hemisphere has already been documented in Chapter 1 (see p. 7). The existence of a possible right-brain leaning within the black community may render the limited coverage of right-hemisphere processing by the WISC-R especially penalizing to black children. Indeed, a relative dependency on the right hemisphere may characterize not only blacks but most "urban poor" groups as well (Cohen 1969; Galin 1976). Feasible explanations of the well-developed right-brain functioning of disadvantaged groups, which have been discussed in detail elsewhere (Kaufman in press a), are summarized as follows because of their potential importance for unbiased assessment.

The right hemisphere seems to be more mature than the left at birth, both physiologically and functionally, and is also a more pervasive force in the very early stages of life (Bever 1975; Carmon and Nachson 1973; Seth 1973). An infant perceives and learns nonverbally, sensorily, and spatially to a large extent during the first year of life (Hebb 1949), styles of learning that are congruent with the processing mode of the right cerebral hemisphere. Although less mature than the right brain, the left brain is more adaptable at birth and has the capacity of subsuming complex and analytic functions (Bever 1975). The greater adaptability of the left hemisphere may conceivably render it unusually vulnerable to the impact of cultural deprivation. Hence disadvantaged children may have a right-brain leaning, at least in part, because of the resilience of the right hemisphere in the face of deprived environmental conditions.

Indirect support for the right-brain resilience hypothesis comes from Kagan and Klein's (1973) dramatic report of the cognitive development of the infants and children within two Indian cultures in Guatemala. Although the infants are startlingly deprived of stimulation during the first 15 months of life and seem to have the affect of Spitz and Wolf's (1946) orphans, by 11 years of age the children of these Indian cultures appear normal in every way. Incredibly, they even perform quite adequately on tests of "basic cognitive competencies," all of which are predominantly right-brain in orientation, such as recall memory for familiar objects, recognition memory for pictures of objects and faces, perceptual analysis (embedded figures), and perceptual inference (Gestalt closure).

When children perform especially well on the WISC-R right-brain subtests and the results of subsequent assessment offer supportive evidence of a global strength in the holistic and nonverbal processing style of the right hemisphere, their Verbal subtest responses should be scrutinized carefully. A right-brain cognitive style can actually be penalizing to a child on the Verbal Scale. According to some researchers (Kimura 1966; Nebes 1974), the key distinction between the two hemispheres concerns the organization of data on the principle of *conceptual* (left-brain) vs. *structural* (right-brain) similarity. A cat and a mouse are alike to the left hemisphere because they are both animals (2-point response), but to the right hemisphere they both have four legs, fur, whiskers, and tails (1-point responses). Conceptual responses typically earn 2 points, whereas structural responses are more likely to be assigned no more than partial credit. Since the degree of abstractness in children's responses is rewarded for Vocabulary and some Comprehension items as well as for Similarities items, it is evident that a right-brain processing style can substantially depress Verbal IQs. A left-hemisphere processing mode, in contrast, can have a negative effect on the Performance IQs, especially on the subtest scores that reflect the understanding of spatial relations. As Galin (1976, p. 18) states, "the tendency for the left hemisphere to note details in a form suitable for expression in words seems to interfere with the perception of the overall patterns."

The potential inhibiting effect of a particular processing mode on tasks best suited to the opposite mode bears again on the importance of integrated functioning. Individuals who perform relatively well on the nonverbal tasks that demand an integration of analytic and holistic processing may possess a very special and high-level intellectual strength. Artists, mathematicians, and scientists, in discussing their own creative gifts, stress the integration of both processing modes as a key ingredient in their success (Galin 1976). Low scores on the integrated functioning tasks may also have interpretive significance. Denckla (1974) has speculated that developmental dyslexics may have faulty interhemispheric integration, and Witelson (1976, 1977) has obtained data that suggest the value of integration for effective functioning in school-related areas. The presence of a right-hemisphere component in traditional left-brain reading-related skills was shown empirically by Faglioni, Scotti, et al. (1969). These investigators found that the perceptual functions of the right cerebral hemisphere of brain-damaged patients contribute both to letter recognition and to the processing of verbal information. Several other groups of researchers have independently provided evidence that the right hemisphere excels the left hemisphere in processing the visual–spatial properties of text (Brooks 1973; Bryden and Allard 1976); Gibson, Dimond, et al. 1972).

Beginning reading seems particularly sensitive to the integration of the two hemispheres, a mutual dependency that is explicated by Gibson's (1965) model of the reading process. Based in part on his own research study (Pirozzolo & Rayner 1977), but also on Gibson's theory and neuropsychological research, Pirozzolo (1978, p. 264) states, "The right hemisphere may be indispensible in beginning reading when children are learning to recognize letters and words as gestalts. The left hemisphere meanwhile may convert these symbols into phonological units and into meaning."

The preceding discussions of left-brain processing, right-brain processing, and integrated functioning clearly relate to the cerebral cortex; furthermore, the theory stems largely from neuropsychological research and from psychometric evaluation of brain-damaged children and adults. Indeed, the generative force behind the notion of cerebral specialization was the bulk of research conducted on split-brain patients (Gazzaniga and Sperry 1967; Sperry 1968), the individuals who underwent surgery to sever the bundle of nerve fibers that connects the two hemispheres, known as the *corpus callosum*. Nevertheless, examiners must realize that low scores on left hemisphere, right hemisphere, or integrated WISC-R tasks do *not* imply any type of neurological impairment or brain dysfunction. Such a diagnosis *may* be reached after the administration of a thorough neuropsychological battery and a neurological examination, but no inferences should be drawn in isolation from peaks and valleys in a WISC-R profile. Rather, relative performance on the right-brain, left-brain, and integrated tasks should give the examiner insight into children's modes of processing information and into the type of remedial approach that might be most effective. Much has been written on the educational applications of cerebral specialization (Bogen 1975; Galin 1976; Lesser 1971; Samples 1975), with most writers stressing that we live in a left-brain environment, typified by traditional school curricula. Education is usually highly verbal, governed by the application of rules to solve problems in sequential, logical fashion. Children who excel in right-brain or integrated activities need academic approaches that allow for holistic and creative problem solving, such as the programs that are currently in the domain of the gifted (Stanley, George, et al. 1977). Curriculums such as Montessori's and the ones based on Piaget's theory and tasks, which encourage discovery by active independent interaction with the environment, are also well suited to youngsters who are not cut from a left-brain mold.

Some implications of brain specialization extend beyond education and should be of special interest to WISC-R examiners who are more clinical in orientation. Galin (1974), in his provocative paper relating specialization to psychiatry, suggests that: right hemisphere functioning is congruent with the mode of cognition termed primary process; lack of communication between the hemispheres can lead to dissociative thinking and emotional problems; the corpus callosum represents a neurophysiological mechanism for repression; the right hemisphere (with its nonverbal, spatial, non-time-oriented characteristics) provides an anatomical locus for unconscious mental content and for dreams; and depression, coping strategies, and psychosomatic ailments may be related closely to interactions between the hemispheres.

Despite the bandwagon effect that has accompanied the popularization of right versus left hemisphere functioning, a small group of researchers has approached the processing-mode issue from a vantage point that Biggs (1978) describes as a 90-degree rotation in the skull. Das and his colleagues (Das 1972, 1973a,b; Das, Kirby, et al. 1975; Das and Molloy, 1975; Kirby and Das 1977, 1978) have staunchly supported a distinction between two modes of processing—successive and simultaneous—rooted in Luria's (1966) research findings with patients manifesting *left* hemisphere damage. Whereas these modes bear an obvious relationship to left- and right-brain processing, respectively, there are also differences. Successive processing, a mode featuring serial and temporal handling of information, is presumably disrupted by damage to the fronto-temporal area of the cortex; simultaneous processing is believed to be impeded by occipito-parietal damage. According to the Das—Kirby model, the type of stimulus is independent of process; verbal stimuli are not necessarily associated with successive processing, and visual—spatial stimuli do not automatically demand simultaneous processing. Consequently, WISC-R Similarities (often considered a prototype of a left-brain task by split-brain researchers) qualifies as a simultaneous task and Mazes as a successive task, despite their respective content (Das, Kirby, et al. 1975).

From the perspective of this alternative neurological model of information processing, the following division of Wechsler's Performance Scale emerges:

Simultaneous	Successive
Picture Completion	Picture Arrangement
Block Design	Coding
Object Assembly	Mazes

The "simultaneous" grouping is identical to Bannatyne's Spatial category and closely resembles the right-brain processing subgroup; the subtests labeled "successive" all involve integrated functioning from the vantage point of the cerebral specialization model.

The empirical technique of factor analysis has been used by Das and his coworkers to support their processing model. They have identified factors that they label successive and simultaneous for groups differing in intelligence level (Das 1972), grade in school (Molloy 1973), socioeconomic status (Molloy 1973), and cultural background (Das 1973a). The two factors have been isolated in studies using only the test battery assembled by Das (Das, Kirby, et al. 1975), and also when a variety of other tasks are analyzed as well (Cummins 1973; Kirby and Das 1978). Both the successive and simultaneous modes of processing correlate significantly with verbal and nonverbal intelligence and with measures of school achievement (Kirby and Das 1977).

One problem with the successive—simultaneous approach for WISC-R interpretation is the failure of the Das—Kirby team to include traditional verbal tasks in virtually all of their studies. Verbal comprehension has been variously claimed to be primarily dependent on successive processing (Das, Kirby, et al. 1975, pp. 98—99) and as totally overlapping the two processing modes (Das, Kirby, et al. 1975, pp. 100—101). The exclusion of most Wechsler or Wechsler-like Verbal subtests from the factor-analytic investigations prevents a deep understanding of the processing components of the WISC-R Verbal Scale from Das's model. In addition, even though the successive—simultaneous dichotomy is considered to be an alternative to Jensen's (1969) Level I—II (associative memory vs. reasoning) division of intelligence (Biggs 1978; Das, Kirby, et al. 1975), there is insufficient evidence to support the claim that simultaneous processing is distinct from either spatial ability or Jensen-type Level II reasoning (Kirby and Das 1978). Furthermore, Das, Kirby, et al. (1975) have incorrectly dismissed the hemispheric specialization researchers as being content oriented (verbal vs. nonverbal) even though most of them are decidedly process oriented. There is basically nothing in the research of Das and his colleagues that precludes interpretation of their two main factors as left-brain and right-brain, rather than as successive (fronto-temporal) and simultaneous (occipito-parietal).

Nevertheless, there is much in the successive—simultaneous model that is thought provoking and compelling. A strength or weakness on the Spatial subtests may reflect an integrity or deficiency in simultaneous processing, a hypothesis that would be given considerable support if the Similarities scaled score was consistent in magnitude to the Spatial scores. High or low scores on the Sequencing grouping of Arithmetic, Digit Span, and Coding, along with comparable performance on Picture Arrangement and Mazes, may reasonably be interpreted as a strong or weak successive processing mode, as opposed to an interpretation from a Bannatyne or cerebral specialization standpoint.

Regardless of whether the neurological distinction is ultimately found to be more in tune with Luria's observations or with the Bogen—Sperry—Gazzaniga right—left distinction, the emphasis on processing is making its mark in both assessment and educational practice. The teaching of Spanish, for example, was accomplished more effectively by a logical, rule-governed method for left-brained individuals and by a more holistic approach for right-brained students (Krashen, Seliga, et al. 1973). Biggs (1978) cites similar educational applications of the successive—simultaneous approach. For example, students categorized as "serialists" on a classification task performed strikingly better when taught new material by serial rather than holistic methods; in contrast, "holists" learned better when taught by a holistic procedure (Pask and Scott 1972). Inferences for educational applications of WISC-R profiles are apparent. Following a Cronbach and Snow (1977) aptitude—treatment interaction approach, children with the same presenting problem will need different recommended remedial procedures depending on their preferred mode of processing information. Naturally, the application of cerebral specialization and successive—simultaneous research and theory is only feasible if analysis of children's WISC-R profiles, along with supplementary testing, strongly suggests differences in processing modes. Detecting such a distinction is contingent on examiners' awareness of the existing research data in this area and their conscious attempts to put psychology into action when interpreting the WISC-R.

Imitation versus Problem Solving

Block Design and Coding both require children to imitate or reproduce models and in that respect are different from the other four Performance subtests. Even though Block Design is legitimately a test of concept formation (Sattler 1974) and Coding a measure of learning ability (Kitzinger and Blumberg 1951), both are still basically copying tasks. In contrast, the remaining nonverbal subtests demand problem solving, ranging from the relatively simple thought processes required to find the missing part of a Picture Completion drawing to the complex abstract reasoning skills needed to arrange several pictures in a unique order to tell a logical story in Picture Arrangement.

The imitative aspect of Block Design and Coding is also inherent in the numerous design copying tasks such as the Bender—Gestalt (Bender 1946), WPPSI Geometric Design (Wechsler 1967), McCarthy (1972) Draw-a-design, Gesell Copy Forms (Ilg and Ames 1972), or Benton (1963) Revised Visual Retention Test. Administration of a supplementary drawing test is especially advised for children who perform well or poorly on the nonverbal WISC-R imitative tasks as one means of exploring the generalizability of the hypothesized strength or weakness. However, an equally plausible alternative explanation for extreme scores in Block Design, Coding, and drawing tests exists: the ability to manipulate abstract stimuli (see next section).

Distinguishing between the two competing hypotheses is sometimes facilitated by studying the children's WISC-R Verbal subtest scores. Youngsters who have a true discrepancy in their imitative versus problem-solving abilities are likely to experience a similar dichotomy on the Verbal Scale. For example, a child who evidences poor problem-solving and good imitative ability on the Performance Scale may conceivably show a comparable pattern on the Verbal Scale: poor reasoning coupled with excellent memory (see pp. 142−146). For such children, an ability model such as Jensen's (1969) Level I−Level II hierarchy may provide a more harmonious solution to WISC-R profile fluctuations than either a neurologically based processing model or the content-oriented distinction between the global Verbal and Performance Scales. Even if one accepts the arguments that simultaneous−successive processing is preferable to Jensen's ability approach for explaining much of the *group* data that are available (Biggs 1978), Jensen's distinction between memory and reasoning skills may provide a more accurate picture for any given *individual*.

Nature of the Stimulus and Response

The stimuli used for the Performance subtests may be divided into the following categories:

Meaningful Stimuli	Abstract Stimuli
Picture Completion	Block Design
Picture Arrangement	Coding
Object Assembly	

The tasks with meaningful stimuli all involve manipulation of people or things, whereas Block Design and Coding require children to work with symbols and designs. Mazes is excluded because its stimuli do not fit easily into either grouping.

High scores on Block Design and Coding have been found to be significant correlates of reading *improvement* (Hunter and Lewis 1973; Swade 1971). The inability to handle abstract stimuli has been related to brain damage, most notably by Kurt Goldstein (1948), who introduced the concept of the "abstract approach." Naturally, however, no inference of brain dysfunction is implied by uncharacteristically low scores on Block Design and Coding without considerable corroborating evidence. In addition, very low or high scores on the two subtests with abstract stimuli may be related to children's ability to copy a model, rather than to the nature of the stimuli, as discussed in the previous section.

It is difficult to distinguish between the hypotheses of abstract stimuli versus imitation, although examination of the Verbal profile can facilitate the detective work (as was mentioned above). The Verbal tasks of Digit Span and Arithmetic involve symbolic stimuli; individuals who perform at an extreme level on

Block Design and Coding may well obtain scores of a similar magnitude on these two Verbal subtests if the abstractness of the stimuli is indeed at the root of their strength or weakness. (This pattern was already discussed on pp. 83–84 of Chapter 3 regarding one possible interpretation of the distractibility factor.) If Digit Span but *not* Arithmetic is consistent with extreme scores on Block Design and Coding, the imitative hypothesis is given support because Digit Span involves copying the numbers spoken by the examiner. Low scores on this triad of subtests are particularly worthy of note because they "may indicate an organic brain syndrome" (Wechsler 1974, p. 7).

Picture Completion and Object Assembly are spatial, right-brained, simultaneous tasks, whereas Picture Arrangement is a temporal, successive subtest that requires integrated brain functioning from the vantage point of the cerebral specialization model. Yet they all undeniably include meaningful and concrete (as opposed to abstract) stimuli, which may account for their frequent clustering in many of the WISC-R profiles I have looked at. As mentioned earlier (p. 158), learning-disabled children, as a group, tend to score highest on the WISC-R Object Assembly and Picture Completion subtests. Holding down the third rank in the seven studies summarized by Lutey (1977, pp. 299–300) and in two WISC-R investigations not included in Lutey's review (Smith, Coleman, et al. 1977a; Zingale and Smith 1978), is Picture Arrangement. Although purely speculative, and without a sound theoretical or neurological base, the key to the strength displayed by an accumulating number of learning-disabled populations on the WISC-R may be the ability to work with meaningful or relevant nonverbal stimuli. Since such a strength has obvious remedial implications, this hypothesis merits systematic investigation by clinical or psychometric researchers.

The type of response required by the various Performance subtests has also been used to partition the scale. Rapaport, Gill, et al. (1945–1946) distinguished between nonverbal subtests demanding no essential motor coordination (Visual Organization group) and those heavily dependent on coordination (Visual–Motor Coordination group). This dichotomy, augmented slightly by Lutey (1977, p. 170), is tabulated as follows:

Visual Organization	Visual–Motor Coordination
Picture Completion	Block Design
Picture Arrangement	Object Assembly
	Coding
	Mazes

The motor component of each Performance subtest was already discussed in the context of interpreting V–P IQ discrepancies (see pp. 35–37) and needs no elaboration. When examiners detect a clustering of children's Performance scaled scores into the two subdivisions in the preceding table, they must explore several possibilities before inferring any hypotheses. Identical patterns may also relate to a child's verbal development, since Picture Completion and Picture Arrangement both have secondary loadings on the Verbal Comprehension factor. Hence high scores on the Visual Organization dyad may reflect verbal compensation for a performance deficit (see pp. 46−48); relatively low scores may imply an inability to apply an age-appropriate amount of verbal mediation to nonverbal tasks. If the Object Assembly scaled score fails to cluster with the Visual−Motor Coordination grouping and instead approaches the magnitude of the Visual Organization pair, the underlying skill may then be related to properties of the *stimulus* (i.e., meaningful vs. abstract) rather than the response. In addition, it is feasible for Mazes to switch over to the Visual Organization subgroup for some uncoordinated children because its scoring system is lenient regarding coordination errors. Such children are likely to finish each maze just under the time limit, and an examination of their responses should reveal cut corners, wavy lines that do not always stay within the path, or other instances of poor coordination that are not generally penalized by the scoring rules.

Clinical observations of children's motor coordination, evaluation of their responses, and consideration of their verbal ability and visual−perceptual skill are all essential activities for interpreting a discrepancy between Visual Organization and Visual−Motor Coordination scores. Supplementary administration of additional perceptual and motor tasks, both cognitive and noncognitive, is also especially important for a child who obtains depressed scores on the WISC-R visual−motor subtests. Drawing tests and selected tasks from a battery such as Roach and Kephart's (1966) Purdue Perceptual−Motor Survey are useful for this purpose. One key distinction to make is whether a youngster's problem is more in the cognitive domain (visual−motor integration) or in the motor domain (fine-motor coordination). As indicated on pages 35−37, confirmation of the latter hypothesis would render the Performance IQ inadequate as an estimate of the poorly coordinated child's nonverbal intelligence, thereby necessitating the administration of appropriate supplementary measures.

In the discussion of the stimulus and response properties of Verbal subtests (pp. 146−149), psycholinguistic models were credited with providing the impetus for the various subgroupings that were presented. This orientation is also pertinent for the Performance Scale. Examiners with a psycholinguistic bent will recognize that all of the WISC-R nonverbal subtests are within the visual−motor channel of communication and all but Coding are at the representational level of organization. It is thus possible to speculate about children's psycholinguistic processes within the visual−motor modality by studying their Performance profile.

Picture Completion is a reasonably good measure of *visual reception*. The incomplete pictures require children to derive meaning from visual stimuli while demanding a minimal amount of reasoning (association ability) and little or no motoric response (expression). Picture Arrangement qualifies as an estimate of *visual association*. The story-telling items demand understanding of the relationships among visual stimuli. The high-level abstract reasoning ability that is necessary for arranging the pictures in a proper time sequence highlights the preeminence of association skills for success on Picture Arrangement. Whereas good visual and auditory receptive abilities are important for Picture Arrangement, these skills are also needed for the ITPA Visual Association subtest. The limited role of manual expression for success on Picture Arrangement is consistent with Rapaport's classification of this subtest in the Visual Organization group. As indicated on page 36, the pictures need only be arranged in the right order; the neatness of the alignment is irrelevant. As a group, the Visual—Motor Coordination subtests can be thought of as a measure of children's *manual expression* since the component subtests assess the ability to express ideas manually. Since Mazes places a high premium on association ability and has a scoring system that deemphasizes coordination, this subtest should probably be deleted from any psycholinguistic analysis.

Interpretation of the Performance Scale from a psycholinguistic framework is intended as a means of generating hypotheses that may be accepted or rejected on the basis of supplementary testing with tasks that were specifically designed to measure psycholinguistic functioning or language development. Without these additional tests, any psycholinguistic hypotheses are mere speculations. However, it is possible that a child with high Picture Completion and low Picture Arrangement has a strength in visual reception coupled with a weakness in visual association. Examiners who are unwilling or unable to operate from nontraditional approaches to WISC-R profile interpretation will not be able to generate potentially valuable hypotheses such as these.

Guilford's Structure-of-intellect Model

Virtually every Performance subtest assesses the Guilford operation of evaluation (see Table 3-1). However, each nonverbal subtest is also a measure of either cognition or convergent production, offering yet another plausible basis for subdividing the Performance Scale, as follows:

Cognition	Convergent Production
Picture Completion	Picture Arrangement
Block Design	Coding
Object Assembly	
Mazes	

The cognition group, all of which measure figural cognition, are also the subtests that assess understanding of spatial relationships. Picture Arrangement and Coding, the convergent production dyad, are united as well in their assessment of sequencing ability and successive processing. Although both subtests require convergent production, Picture Arrangement is considered to have semantic content, Coding A figural content, and Coding B symbolic content.

To determine whether a split of the Performance Scale into the components shown in the preceding table corresponds to a cognition—convergent production distinction, it is useful to examine the Verbal profile. Similarities and Vocabulary are categorized as pure measures of cognition by Meeker (1975b); scores on both of these subtests should be consistent in magnitude (whether high or low) with the nonverbal measures of cognition. Arithmetic may also join the cognition cluster since it assesses the dual operations of memory and cognition. When the Verbal profile does not support a Guilford interpretation of a split in the Performance Scale, all but dyed-in-the-wool Meeker analysts will probably find an alternative approach (e.g., Bannatyne's Spatial—Sequencing categories or Das's simultaneous—successive processing) more fruitful in a practical sense. Nevertheless, examiners should become acquainted with the considerable work Meeker has done in attempting to relate SOI profiles to specific individualized curricula and to educational programming in general (Meeker 1973; Meeker and Shadduck 1973).

Some investigators have identified deficits in both Picture Arrangement and Coding (or Digit Symbol) for well-defined exceptional groups. For example, McDonald and Crookes (1967) discovered that psychiatric patients performed significantly worse on these two subtests than on other Performance tasks. In addition, intellectually gifted children have tended to score lowest on the WISC Picture Arrangement and Coding subtests in several studies summarized by Lutey (1977, p. 288). Convergent production may be the key to the apparent weakness, although numerous alternative explanations are feasible. For the gifted groups, the scores on the two subtests may be low for different reasons. Coding may be depressed because it is the least related to overall intelligence, whereas Picture Arrangement scores are sometimes deflated for children who exercise a little creativity in their responses.

Coding

In a sense. Coding is a Performance analog of Digit Span. Like the Verbal short-term memory subtest, Coding loads substantially on the distractibility factor and virtually not at all on the factor that defines its scale, is a poor measure of *g* (see Table 4-1), has considerable subtest specificity for all age groups (see Table 4-2), and correlates poorly (0.33) with its own scale (Wechsler 1974, p. 47). Consequently, as is true for Digit Span (see pp. 149—152), examiners should expect children to earn Coding scaled scores that deviate significantly from their other Performance scores. When such differences occur, global hypotheses should first be sought (e.g., by investigating the distractibility factor), but examiners should readily accept a subtest-specific interpretation if alternate explanations are not readily apparent.

The specificity of Coding may be considered as psychomotor speed, ability to follow directions, clerical speed and accuracy, or visual short-term memory (see p. 108), but other interpretations are possible. Lutey (1977, p. 211) tentatively interprets the unique ability as "speed of nonverbal learning" and Royer (1971), in an excellent study of the WAIS Digit Symbol subtest, provided empirical evidence that the task measures information-processing capacity. Since Coding correlated only 0.38 with Full Scale score across the age range (Wechsler 1974, p. 47), thereby accounting for less than 15% of the variance in overall IQ, a specific interpretation should probably stress noncognitive rather than cognitive dimensions. Hence an interpretation of the ability as psychomotor speed is probably preferable to speed of nonverbal learning in most instances, even though the task is a measure of learning ability in the experimental psychology usage of the term.

The short-term memory aspect of Coding is of interest. Certainly individuals have to "code the information distinguishing the symbol found, and carry this information in short-term memory long enough to reproduce the symbol in the proper answer box" (Estes 1974, p. 745). There is some evidence that the ability to code the information in the symbols, probably by verbal mediation, is an important factor in success on Coding−Digit Symbol tasks (Estes 1974; Royer 1971). As such, a child's *strategy* is most likely a valuable determinant of performance. But how much of the variability in children's Coding scores is likely to be due to short-term memory? In view of the limited memory demands of the task, the answer is undoubtedly "very little."

Nevertheless, memory may be a crucial variable for some children. Those with excellent memories learn several of the matched pairs during the early part of the subtest and subsequently are observed to refer back to the table only occasionally. Youngsters with extremely deficient memories may need to refer back to the table more than once per item and/or copy incorrect reproductions of the symbols in several boxes. When these behavioral observations are clear-cut, examiners certainly have a good rationale for hypothesizing visual short-term memory as the primary determinant of a high or low Coding score. Without behavioral justification, examiners are advised *not* to consider Coding as a memory task. Even the behaviors indicative of a poor memory do not necessarily imply such a hypothesis. Competing explanations such as insecurity or visual−perceptual problems must first be ruled out before inferring that a low Coding score reflects an inadequate short-term memory.

CHAPTER 6

Attacking Subtest Profiles: Illustrations and Applications

There can be little doubt that the 10−12 WISC-R subtests can be grouped and regrouped in myriad meaningful ways and that Wechsler's Verbal−Performance division represents but one of these useful categorization systems. Wechsler facilitates the comparison of a child's ability to handle verbal and nonverbal item content by offering separate Verbal and Performance IQs, along with statistical rules for comparing these scores. Factor scores reflecting a youngster's relative functioning on the three WISC-R dimensions can also be computed with minimal effort (Kaufman 1975; Sobotka and Black 1978), as can scores on a wide variety of subgroupings of Wechsler subtests (Lutey 1977). However, the computation of empirical values for a diversity of subtest groupings turns profile interpretation into a *statistical* exercise. It is not. Effective detective work is a *logical* exercise that can become rigid, unimaginative, and confusing when operating out of a framework that demands computation and comparison of scaled-score means on overlapping clusters of subtests or that depends on prorated IQ equivalents for interpretation of the factors underlying the battery.

However, this is not to imply that statistics are to go by the wayside when investigating WISC-R profiles. One must heed the results of the statistical attacks levied at WISC-R profiles (see the ±3 method to determine significant strengths or weaknesses that is described on pp. 54−57) or risk interpreting mere chance fluctuations. Thus the first step in interpreting any WISC-R profile is to apply a simple statistical rule to the Verbal subtests and then to the Performance subtests, to decide whether the child has any area at all that is relatively strong or weak. If the answer is "no," profile interpretation at the subtest level ordinarily stops immediately, and the child's Verbal Comprehension and Perceptual Organization skills should be focused on since these global abilities are likely to account for any fluctuations in his or her WISC-R profile. If, however, there is at least one (but preferably several) significantly high or low scaled score, then examiners are given their license to carry out detective work.

When a child is found to have a single strength on the WISC-R, the examiner's task is to find out what ability led to the significantly high Verbal or Performance subtest score. Surely the youngster is not strong on all abilities that are associated with each separate subtest (see Chapter 4). Similarly, children who score significantly low on a WISC-R subtest cannot conceivably be weak in all of the abilities presumably measured by that subtest. In both instances, examiners have to track down the specific area of strength or weakness by using the logical step-by-step approach of a detective.

When children have at least two strengths (or weaknesses) on the WISC-R, the examiner's challenge is to identify, if possible, the ability that is shared by the two or more significantly deviating subtests. Again, systematic detective work is necessary to isolate the child's integrity or deficiency. When many subtest scores deviate by 3 or more points from the youngster's Verbal and Performance means, it is evident that the V–P dichotomy provides a wholly unsatisfactory description of his or her abilities. The examiner's task, therefore, is to find a different model or category system that adequately and efficiently explains the obtained profile data.

The detective work necessary to explain the abilities underlying one, two, or several strengths and weaknesses in the WISC-R profile depends on: (a) *internalization* of the shared and unique abilities, as well as the noncognitive influences that can markedly affect test performance, characterizing each of the 12 WISC-R subtests (see pp. 102–109 in Chapter 4 for a subtest-by-subtest analysis), (b) *anticipation* of the common patterns and groupings of subtests both within and across the Verbal and Performance Scales, accompanied by understanding of the educational, psychological, and clinical ramifications of these patterns (see Chapter 5), and (c) *integration* of observed patterns of scores with background information about the child, clinical observation of his or her behaviors during the testing session, analysis of right and especially wrong responses to WISC-R items, and with any additional test data available on the child.

To facilitate the examiner's job as detective, Tables 6-1–6-4 have been prepared. These tables represent a summative (although necessarily incomplete) overview of the material included in Chapters 4 and 5; they provide a thumbnail review of the abilities and noncognitive influences *shared* by at least two WISC-R subtests, and offer a graphic display of many combinations and groupings of these diverse tasks. (Unique abilities measured by each subtest and influences that affect performance primarily on a single WISC-R task are excluded from these tables.) In Tables 6-1 and 6-2 the abilities underlying test performance are segregated by scale, with Table 6-1 comprising verbal abilities and Table 6-2 devoted exclusively to nonverbal performance skills. Table 6-3 includes abilities that specifically cut across the Verbal and Performance Scales, and Table 6-4 is restricted to the noncognitive influences that come into play, and sometimes loom quite large, for certain WISC-R subtests.

Tables 6-1–6-4 are not intended to be exhaustive, just as Chapters 4 and 5 are

Table 6-1 Abilities Shared by Two or More *Verbal* Subtests

Ability	Information (I)	Similarities (S)	Arithmetic (A)	Vocabulary (V)	Comprehension (C)	Digit Span (DS)
				Verbal Subtests		
Verbal Comprehension (factor analysis)[a]	I	S		V	C	
Verbal Conceptualization (Bannatyne)		S		V	C	
Acquired Knowledge (Bannatyne)	I		A	V		
Memory (Guilford)	I		A			DS
Degree of abstract thinking		S		V		
Fund of information	I			V		
Long-term memory	I		A	V		
Mental alertness			A			DS
Verbal concept formation		S		V		
Verbal expression		S		V	C	

[a] Subtests with secondary loadings on the Verbal Comprehension factor are Arithmetic, Picture Completion, and Picture Arrangement.

Table 6-2   Abilities Shared by Two or More *Performance* Subtests

Ability	Picture Completion (PC)	Picture Arrangement (PA)	Block Design (BD)	Object Assembly (OA)	Coding (Cd)	Mazes (M)
				Performance Subtests		
Perceptual Organization (factor analysis)	PC	PA	BD	OA		M
Spatial (Bannatyne)	PC		BD	OA		(M)
Convergent production (Guilford)		PA			Cd	
Holistic (right brain) processing	PC			OA		
Integrated brain functioning		PA	BD		Cd	M
Paper-and-pencil skill					Cd	M
Planning ability		PA				M
Reproduction of a model			BD		Cd	
Synthesis		PA	BD	OA		
Visual memory	PC				Cd	
Visual–motor coordination			BD	OA	Cd	M
Visual organization (without essential motor activity)	PC	PA				
Visual perception of *abstract* stimuli			BD		Cd	
Visual perception of *meaningful* stimuli	PC	PA		OA		

meant to illustrate the underlying abilities and prevalent subtest patterns, but not to exhaust the possibilities. Indeed, examiners who treat the preceding two chapters and the accompanying tables as finite and comprehensive will frequently find themselves stultified and frustrated when attempting to decode a child's profile. To serve best, the information presented here on subtest interpretation should constitute a set of guidelines or parameters that define a framework from which to operate. However, the framework has to be an open one that permits limitless expansion both to accommodate the areas of expertise of each examiner and the individuality of each child tested and to promote the flexibility that is requisite for good detective work. Even the development of Tables 6-1 – 6-4 was subjective. For example, Freedom from Distractibility is included as an *ability* in Table 6-3 because of its emergence as a consistent dimension via the empirical technique of factor analysis, but "distractibility" is also listed as an

Table 6-3 Abilities Shared by Two or More *Verbal or Performance* Subtests

Ability	Verbal Subtests						Performance Subtests					
	I	S	A	V	C	DS	PC	PA	BD	OA	Cd	M
Freedom from Distractibility (factor analysis)			A			DS					Cd	
Sequencing (Bannatyne)			A			DS		(PA)			Cd	
Cognition (Guilford)		S	A	V			PC		BD	OA		M
Evaluation (Guilford)					C		PC	PA	BD	OA	Cd	
Common sense					C			PA				
Distinguishing essential from nonessential details		S					PC	PA				
Facility with numbers			A			DS					Cd	
Learning ability				V							Cd	
Reasoning		S	A		C			PA				M
Social judgment					C			PA				

influence affecting test performance in Table 6-4. In addition, cognitive style (field dependence−field independence) is classified here as an "influence" in Table 6-4, even though Witkin and his associates often refer to "analytic ability" and some researchers (Keogh and Hall 1974) emphasize the importance of a skill called "analytic field approach." It is thus quite difficult to distinguish between cognitive abilities and noncognitive influences, much less present a complete and unambiguous method of profile interpretation.

With these limitations in mind, let us proceed to a suggested stepwise technique for attacking subtest profiles.

A STEP-BY-STEP METHOD FOR INTERPRETING SUBTEST FLUCTUATIONS

The technique described in this section is intended to generate *hypotheses* about children's functioning to better understand their strong and weak areas. To the

Table 6-4 *Influences* Likely to Affect Children's Scores on Two or More Verbal or Performance Subtests

Influence	Verbal Subtests						Performance Subtests					
	I	S	A	V	C	DS	PC	PA	BD	OA	Cd	M
Ability to respond when uncertain							PC			OA		M
Anxiety			A			DS					Cd	
Attention span			A			DS						
Cognitive style (field dependence−field independence)							PC		BD	OA		
Concentration			A				PC					
Cultural opportunities at home	I			V	C			PA				
Distractibility			A			DS					Cd	
Extent of outside reading	I	S		V								
Interests	I	S		V								
Richness of early environment	I			V								
School learning	I		A	V								
Working under time pressure			A				PC	PA	BD	OA	Cd	M

degree that ample evidence can be martialed in support of a given hypothesis, examiners will be increasingly able to utilize the information to facilitate comprehension of the nature of a youngster's presenting problem and selection of any educational or psychological intervention that may be necessary. At no time, however, should examiners lose sight of the fact that the hypotheses, which are obtained by a post hoc analysis of profile data, are not facts and may indeed prove to be artifacts. When profile interpretation leads to new insights about children, perhaps explaining why low scores do not reflect limited mental ability or showing that different educational materials or techniques are advisable, the recategorization of WISC-R subtests serves a useful function. When analysis of subtest fluctuations is used as a primary means of classifying, labeling, or placing children, or for other potentially harmful purposes, the practice should be immediately abandoned.

Examination of Tables 6-1−6-4 indicates that identical groupings of subtests can reflect different interpretations depending on the child's level of performance on other pertinent subtests. The steps outlined as follows, accompanied by examples, should help examiners distinguish among competing hypotheses. (In these steps, no mention is made of the IQs in order to focus directly on subtest analysis. Naturally, however, interpretation of the Full Scale IQ and V−P IQ discrepancies would *precede* the steps that follow.)

Step 1. Determine significant strengths and weaknesses on the Verbal and Performance Scales.

Example. Following is the WISC-R profile of Sylvia S., age 14 years 3 months. Using the ± 3 method described on pages 54−57, three strengths and one weakness were identified after first computing her Verbal mean scaled score of 8 and her Performance mean of 10.

Verbal	Scaled Score	Performance	Scaled Score
Information	6	Picture Completion	6-W
Similarities	12-S	Picture Arrangement	13-S
Arithmetic	11-S	Block Design	11
Vocabulary	6	Object Assembly	8
Comprehension	9	Coding	9
Digit Span	6	Mazes	11

Step 2. Select a significant strength, and locate this subtest in Tables 6-1 to 6-4. Write down all shared abilities (and influences affecting performance) that involve this subtest.

Example: Continuing with Sylvia's profile, let us start with *Similarities*, the highest of the two Verbal strengths. From Tables 6-1, 6-3, and 6-4, all abilities or influences involving Similarities are listed (along with the other subtests associated with each skill):

Verbal Comprehension—I S V C
Verbal Conceptualization—S V C
Degree of abstract thinking—S V
Verbal concept formation—S V
Verbal expression—S V C
Cognition—S A V PC BD OA M
Distinguishing essential from nonessential details S PC PA
Reasoning S A C PA M
Extent of outside reading I S V
Interests I S V

Step 3. One by one, consider each ability or influence affecting test performance and weigh the merits of each one by comparing scores on other pertinent subtests to the child's Verbal or Performance means.

When determining the significance of a strength, scaled scores must exceed the child's mean score by 3 points or more. However, when tracking down hypotheses to explain the strength, less stringent criteria have to be applied. It is unreasonable to expect children to score significantly above the mean on *every* subtest that measures a particular ability. (For example, seven different subtests assess the Guilford operation of cognition.) *It is reasonable to consider a shared ability as a strength if children score above their own mean scores on all pertinent subtests, with at least one discrepancy reaching statistical significance.* This rule, which should be interpreted as a guideline or rule of thumb rather than as a rigid principle, applies as well to weaknesses (i.e., for a weakness to be noteworthy, a child has to score *below* his or her mean scores on relevant subtests, with at least *one* discrepancy reaching significance).

Example: Each ability (or influence affecting test performance) listed here for Similarities should be systematically evaluated. The first ability on the list, Verbal Comprehension, is rejected as a possible area of strength because Sylvia's scores on Information and Vocabulary are below her Verbal mean and thus are not consistent with her good score on Similarities. Her low Vocabulary score is a sufficient reason to reject each of the next five hypotheses on the list as well: Verbal Conceptualization, degree of abstract thinking, verbal concept formation, verbal expression, and cognition. The next ability on the list (distinguishing essential from nonessential details) looks promising since both Similarities *and* Picture Arrangement were significant strengths for Sylvia. However, she scored well below her Performance mean on Picture Completion, thereby rejecting this ability as a possible strength.

In contrast, there is considerable support in the profile to suggest a strength in the next ability on the list—*reasoning.* Of the five subtests that measure this skill, Sylvia had significant strengths on three (Similarities, Arithmetic, Picture Arrangement); furthermore, she scored above her Verbal mean on Comprehension and above her Performance mean on Mazes. We thus have ample evidence to *hypothesize* that this 14-year-old girl has a strength in her reasoning ability, accounting for her significantly high score not only in Similarities, but in Arithmetic and Picture Arrangement as well.

The two remaining traits on the list (both of which are influences affecting test performance) can quickly be rejected because she scored below her Verbal mean on both Information and Vocabulary.

Step 4. Repeat Steps 2 and 3 for every other significant strength that has not been accounted for. Then follow analogous procedures for all significant weaknesses.

Example: Regarding strengths, all three of Sylvia's significant strong areas were accounted for by the hypothesis of well-developed reasoning skills. Turning to weaknesses, only one subtest was significantly below her Verbal or Performance mean—Picture Completion. A list of abilities (and influences affecting performance), taken from Tables 6-2–6-4, is listed as follows for Picture Completion:

X	Perceptual Organization—PC PA BD OA M
	Spatial—PC BD OA (M)
	Holistic (right-brain) processing—PC OA
	Visual memory—PC Cd
X	Visual organization—PC PA
X	Visual perception of meaningful stimuli—PC PA OA
X	Cognition—S A V PC BD OA M
X	Evaluation—C PC PA BD OA Cd
X	Distinguishing essential from nonessential details—S PC PA
	Ability to respond when uncertain—PC OA M
	Cognitive style—PC BD OA
X	Concentration—A PC
X	Working under time pressure—A PC PA BD OA Cd M

An "X" has been placed to the left of each ability or influence involving any of Sylvia's *strengths* (Similarities, Arithmetic, Picture Arrangement), indicating immediate rejection of these areas as possible *weaknesses*. Of the remaining hypotheses, Spatial Ability can be rejected as a possible weakness because both Block Design and Mazes are *above* Sylvia's Performance mean. Holistic (right-brain) processing may conceivably be her area of weakness since her Object Assembly score is below her Performance mean, or visual memory may be her weak ability in view of her performance on Coding. In addition, the possibility that her low score on Picture Completion was due to a field-dependent cognitive style or to her inability to respond when uncertain cannot be immediately rejected merely because one subtest score was slightly above her Performance mean. More information is needed to clarify her low score on Picture Completion, which brings us directly to the next step in the procedure for performing detective work.

Step 5. Integrate any apparent strengths or weaknesses in children's profiles with information about their backgrounds, observations of their test behaviors, and scores on other tests.

Inferences about strong and weak areas of functioning, or about noncognitive influences that may have affected test performance, cannot be made out of context. For example, knowledge of children's home environments, school achievement, and interest patterns is essential before concluding that one of these factors accounted for peaks or valleys in their profiles. Observations of children's eye-hand coordination, method of holding a pencil, and technique of assembling blocks or puzzles must corroborate any assertion of a weakness or strength in visual—motor coordination. Analysis of children's spontaneous verbalizations, responses to WISC-R Verbal items, and performance on other verbal tasks is essential before accepting a hypothesis of well-developed or poorly developed verbal expression skills; etcetera, and so forth.

Example: Sylvia has been presumed to possess good reasoning ability. Despite the apparent clear-cut nature of this hypothesized strength, observational evidence is highly desirable. Her thinking processes may have been revealed by any spontaneous verbalizations during Picture Arrangement, her problem-solving approach during Object Assembly and Block Design, or the quality of her responses to Comprehension items. Hopefully, these observations would have been congruent with a hypothesis of strong reasoning ability; if not, different hypotheses may need to be entertained, perhaps some that were not even included on the original list. For example, Steps 2 and 3 could be repeated using lists of abilities associated with Picture Arrangement and Arithmetic (both significant strengths) if a hypothesis of good reasoning ability is unsupported by supplementary observations and data.

Behavioral observations are especially important to determine the meaning of Sylvia's low Picture Completion score. Did she evidence a hesitancy to respond when she was unsure of herself? During Coding, did she display any behaviors suggestive of a poor visual memory (see p. 171)? Does she seem to possess any of the personality characteristics associated with a field-dependent cognitive style (see p. 40)? Did she give any evidence of deficient skills in areas associated with the holistic processing style of the right hemisphere? (Does she have little success in school in music and art? Were her responses and behaviors during the testing session stereotyped and distinctly noncreative? Did she make little use of gestural and other nonverbal cues and have difficulty interpreting the examiner's nonverbal communication?)

Whereas the answers to these questions may help narrow the likely explanation of her low Picture Completion score, behavioral observations and background information do not usually suffice. Hypotheses generated from only two or three subtests are indeed tentative at best, particularly when only one subtest is significantly low. Additional testing is needed. If behaviors imply a potentially weak visual memory, Benton's (1963) Revised Visual Retention Test might be administered; the ITPA Visual Sequential Memory subtest is also useful for younger children. If holistic (right-brain) processing is suspect, Torrance's (1974) creative tasks could be given along with selected subtests from the Seashore Measures of Musical Talents (Seashore, Lewis, et al. 1960) and additional tests of closure such as Street's (1931) Gestalt Completion Test. The Embedded Figures Test and even Rorschach's ink blots would be suitable adjunct instruments to pursue a hypothesis of a field-dependent cognitive style (see Witkin, Moore, et al. 1977).

What about the fact that Sylvia obtained scaled scores of 6 on three subtests—Information, Vocabulary, and Digit Span? Can these scores be interpreted as weaknesses even though none is significantly below the Verbal mean of 8? The answer is ''no'' if there is no external support for a weakness, such as background information or clinical observations. The answer is also negative if the scores are interpreted separately as opposed to two at a time, or all three at a time. However, the answer is a cautious yes if the examiner can integrate behaviors and/or information pertaining to the child's background with the trio of relatively low scores. The particular subtests in question all involve recall, and the examiner may have supplementary information suggestive of a deficient memory (e.g., the parent or teacher may have checked ''forgetful'' or ''does not retain'' as a primary presenting problem). As stated before, Sylvia's low score on Picture Completion may be indicative of a weak visual memory. If evidence is found to supplement the hypothesis of a deficient visual memory, the examiner might want to explore the possibility that Sylvia has a pervasive deficit in memory, extending to verbal short-term and long-term memory tasks as well. External support for a poorly developed memory, coupled with her below-average performance in a wide variety of WISC-R tasks demanding good recall ability (Picture Completion, Information, Vocabulary, Digit Span, Coding), would be enough to sustain a global-memory hypothesis. The fairly common pattern of good reasoning—poor memory (or vice versa) was discussed in Chapter 5 (pp. 142–146). Pending additional information about Sylvia, this dichotomy might hold the key to the fluctuations in the present profile. However, supplementary facts and data are essential. Information and Vocabulary are both very subject to the influences of early environment; the examiner may know that the teenage girl in the illustration was raised in an impoverished environment.

All hypotheses generated from fluctuations in WISC-R profiles depend on external verification to remain truly viable. Such verification is especially crucial when the hypotheses are developed in the absence of at least one scaled score that deviates significantly from the Verbal or Performance mean. The administration of pertinent supplementary tests or subtests is almost a necessity in these instances. Testing the limits is also an effective way to clarify the nature of ambiguous strengths and weaknesses (see pp. 39 and 47). This technique, also known as *extension testing*, should ordinarily be conducted after the entire battery has been administered under standardized conditions. Then examiners improvise and administer the subtests under altered conditions to try to decipher the specific cause of poor (or occasionally good) performance. Children may be asked to identify the picture of a word they could not define, arrange pictures to tell a story when less formal language is used than that required by the directions for administration, select a block design that matches a model that they were unable to construct, explain how they solved an arithmetic problem, and so on. Whereas children's responses during a testing-the-limits session cannot alter their obtained scores, examiners can gain insight into the dynamics of their integrities and deficits. Limit testing is one method of securing less biased assessment of minority-group youngsters (Aliotti 1978); clinicians may wish to consult some of the sources dealing with this topic (Glasser and Zimmerman 1967; Kaufman and Kaufman 1977; Sattler 1974; Taylor, 1959; Volle 1957).

Step 6. If detective work fails to uncover hypotheses which "link" two or more subtests together, then interpret the unique abilities that are presumably measured by significantly high or low subtests.

Every effort should be made to explain significant discrepancies from the child's Verbal and Performance mean scores in terms of shared hypotheses that unite several subtests and are corroborated by behavioral observations. When examiners fail to uncover reasonable hypothesized strengths and weaknesses after a flexible and eclectic analysis of profile fluctuations, they may resort to subtest-specific interpretations. These unique interpretations are listed in Chapter 4 for each subtest and may reflect either cognitive abilities or influences affecting test performance. For example, depending on other knowledge about a child, a low Comprehension score may indicate an inability to demonstrate practical information or a failure to develop a conscience; a high score on Mazes may denote good foresight or merely reflect much experience in solving mazes.

One limiting factor in interpreting unique abilities or influences is the amount of specificity for each subtest (see Table 4-2). The division of WISC-R subtests into groupings based on their specificities (ample, adequate, inadequate, see p. 114) should be respected. Most subtests have ample specificity across the age range, permitting unique interpretations of their abilities when they deviate significantly (±3 points) from the relevant mean. However, the subtests with *adequate* specificity (Picture Completion at ages 9½ – 16½, Vocabulary, and Comprehension) should be interpreted uniquely only when their scaled scores are ±4 from the mean, as suggested on page 115. Furthermore, tasks with *inadequate* specificity (Similarities at ages 9½ – 16½, Object Assembly) should not be given unique interpretations unless they differ dramatically from their respective mean scores.

Example: In the sample profile we have been studying, all three significant strengths were united by the hypothesis of good reasoning ability. Consequently, no specific or unique interpretations should be given to any of the three tasks; her elevated scores on all of these subtests are presumed to be a direct result of her well-developed reasoning skills. Had it been impossible to find one or more hypotheses to explain the three high subtest scores, unique interpretations could have been used to account for the good performance on Arithmetic and Picture Arrangement, but *not* Similarities. Sylvia is 14 years of age, and Similarities has *inadequate* specificity above age 8½. Consequently, it is fine to interpret a *shared* hypothesis that includes Similarities, but it would be inadvisable to interpret the apparently high Similarities score in isolation.

Picture Completion is the only subtest score that is significantly below the girl's Performance mean. Several hypotheses were raised (e.g., holistic processing, visual memory) that might subsequently be found to explain the deficit in Picture Completion. Should none of these fairly global explanations be given external support, it would be feasible to interpret Picture Completion's unique abilities—but just barely. At age 14, Picture Completion has adequate (but not ample) specificity and thus requires a deviation of 4 points from the Performance mean to merit specific interpretation. In this example the scaled score for Picture Completion is exactly 4 points below the Performance mean of 10. Had the deficit been only 3 points, no unique interpretation would have been advised despite the statistical significance.

Illustration—Betsy B., White Female, Age 12 years 7 months

Although an example was incorporated into the stepwise procedure for attacking WISC-R subtest profiles, an additional illustration will further clarify the approach.

Betsy was tested on the WISC-R as a part of a battery that was administered to determine her eligibility for a seventh grade gifted program. Betsy's language arts teacher recommended her for the enrichment program because of her "exceptional scholastic achievement in reading and science, her keen interest in learning, and her wonderfully creative personality." Betsy comes from an upper-middle-class home that was described by her professional parents as providing much cultural and intellectual stimulation and fostering a love for learning. During the WISC-R evaluation the examiner described Betsy as "a mature, attentive, alert, relaxed young lady with a realistic grasp of what she can and cannot do well." Also noted in the report were Betsy's "well coordinated motor activity" and her "display of much creativity, particularly original thinking, in both her responses to test items and her spontaneous verbalizations." Betsy described herself as an avid reader. Her WISC-R scaled-score profile is tabulated as follows:

WISC-R Profile

Verbal	Scaled Score	Performance	Scaled Score
Information	18-S	Picture Completion	14
Similarities	16	Picture Arrangement	12
Arithmetic	14	Block Design	15
Vocabulary	16	Object Assembly	16
Comprehension	17	Coding	17-S
Digit Span	10-W	Mazes	10-W

Verbal IQ = 140; Verbal mean = 15.   Performance IQ = 133; Performance mean = 14.   Full Scale IQ = 141.

Betsy's two strengths and two weaknesses are indicated on the profile. The various hypotheses that might explain her high score on *Information*, obtained from Tables 6-1 and 6-4, are listed as follows:

Verbal Comprehension—I S V C
Acquired Knowledge—I A V
Memory—I A DS
Fund of information—I V
Long-term memory—I A V
Cultural opportunities at home—I V C PA
Extent of outside reading—I S V
Interests—I S V
Richness of early environment—I V
School learning—I A V

Support is given for the very first hypothesis, Verbal Comprehension ability, because Betsy's significant strength in Information is joined by scaled scores on Similarities, Vocabulary, and Comprehension that all exceed her Verbal mean. Even though "fund of information" is also given clear-cut support by Betsy's profile of scores (based on the Information–Vocabulary dyad), examiners should always try to deduce the most *global* area of strength or weakness. Verbal

Comprehension is unquestionably the most pervasive ability measured by the Verbal Scale and hence is selected as Betsy's strength. Whereas some examiners may have focused on a unique interpretation of Information and lauded Betsy's exceptional range of general information, the single area of strength seems trivial in view of her consistently high performance (scaled scores of 16–18) on all of the major subtests that compose the Verbal Comprehension factor.

In view of our knowledge of Betsy and her home environment, several of the influences affecting test performance probably account, at least in part, for her strong Verbal Comprehension ability. Consequently, the extent of her outside reading, the richness of her early environment, and her interests (in reading and in learning in general) are undoubtedly related to Betsy's outstanding verbal ability. In addition, her high level of school achievement and the intellectual environment provided by her parents suggest that her Verbal Comprehension strength is also a function of Betsy's cultural opportunities at home and her school learning. We can accept these latter hypotheses, even though there is incomplete support for them (Picture Arrangement and Arithmetic are both below their respective mean scores), because of the considerable external evidence of their validity.

Although typically it is sensible to interpret strengths before attacking weaknesses, the order of investigating significant discrepancies is really irrelevant. In this instance the significant weakness in Digit Span is treated next, to complete the Verbal Scale before analyzing the Performance subtests. The various hypotheses involving *Digit Span*, listed in Tables 6-1, 6-3 and 6-4, are presented as follows:

Memory—I A DS
Mental alertness—A DS
Freedom from Distractibility—A DS Cd
Sequencing—A DS (PA) Cd
Facility with numbers—A DS Cd
Anxiety—A DS Cd
Attention span—A DS
Distractibility—A DS Cd

In view of Betsy's high score on Information, the first hypothesis of memory (from Guilford's perspective) can be rejected. The second hypothesis of mental alertness can also quickly be dismissed as an area of weakness even though Betsy scored below the Verbal mean on both Arithmetic and Digit Span; as indicated by the examiner, this young lady was alert, aware, and totally in tune with her environment. The next three hypotheses are rejected as weaknesses because of Betsy's significant strength in Coding, and the final three cannot even be considered because she was decidedly *not* anxious, inattentive, or distractible during the evaluation. One additional hypothesis is suggested by Betsy's significant weakness in Mazes—the possibility that fatigue or boredom led to her depressed scores. (Digit Span and Mazes were the last two WISC-R subtests administered.) However, the examiner reported that Betsy was still eager, energetic, and highly interested in doing well at the end of the WISC-R session. The only reasonable conclusion is that Betsy has a weakness in the unique ability measured by Digit Span—auditory short-term memory. Whether this apparent weakness generalizes to meaningful content and to visual stimuli might be checked out with supplementary measures.

Since fatigue cannot explain the significantly low score on Mazes, it is of interest to try to track down an explanation for this deviation. Hypotheses pertaining to *Mazes* appear as follows:

Perceptual Organization—PC PA BD OA M
Spatial—PC BD OA (M)
Integrated brain functioning—PA BD Cd M
Paper-and-pencil skill—Cd M
Planning ability—PA M
Visual—motor coordination—BD OA Cd M
Cognition—S A V PC BD OA M
Reasoning—S A C PA M
Ability to respond when uncertain—PC OA M
Working under time-pressure—A PC PA BD OA Cd M

The first four hypotheses listed for Mazes can be rejected as weaknesses because of Betsy's above-average scores on most other nonverbal subtests. However, planning ability is given support because her significant weakness in Mazes is joined by a below-average 12 in Picture Arrangement. Even though all other hypotheses on the list can be rejected, there are two additional considerations. First, reasoning is a global ability that can be broken down further. Even though Betsy's verbal reasoning is quite well developed, she performed relatively poorly on the two tests of *nonverbal* reasoning (Picture Arrangement and Mazes), and even scored below her Verbal mean on the one test of numerical reasoning (Arithmetic). Examiners have to be alert to the possible necessity of fragmenting global abilities such as reasoning or the Guilford mental operations since the key to understanding a child's profile may lie therein.

The second consideration concerns Betsy's creativity, which was reported by her language-arts teacher, observed by the examiner, and also given empirical support by her high scores on the Torrance Tests of Creative Thinking (one of the instruments included in the battery administered to determine eligibility for the gifted program). Creativity can lower a child's score on a convergent task such as Picture Arrangement that rewards the one "best" story for each item. If Betsy's below average (for her) performance on Picture Arrangement was due to the interference of her creative mind, it would be inappropriate to suggest that she has a relative weakness in nonverbal reasoning or planning ability; her weak area would simply be in the unique ability measured by Mazes. Aware of this possibility, the examiner tested the limits on Picture Arrangement after the entire WISC-R was completed. One by one, Betsy's wrong arrangements were placed before her and she was asked to tell each story. Rather than revealing novel or defensible stories in her wrong arrangements, Betsy's verbalizations served to illustrate her difficulty in reasoning with nonverbal stimuli and her relatively weak planning ability. Consequently, her creativity did not seem to impede her performance on Picture Arrangement.

Turning to Betsy's significantly high score on *Coding*, a list of hypotheses involving this subtest is shown as follows:

Convergent production—PA Cd
Integrated brain functioning—PA BD Cd M
Paper-and-pencil skill—Cd M
Reproduction of a model—BD Cd
Visual memory—PC Cd
Visual–motor coordination—BD OA Cd M
Visual perception of abstract stimuli—BD Cd
Freedom from Distractibility—A DS Cd
Sequencing—A DS (PA) Cd
Evaluation—C PC PA BD OA Cd
Facility with numbers—A DS Cd
Learning ability—V Cd
Anxiety—A DS Cd
Distractibility—A DS Cd
Working under time pressure—A PC PA BD OA Cd M

Betsy's low scores on Mazes and Picture Arrangement lead to elimination of most of the hypothesized abilities. Empirical support is given to the hypotheses regarding reproduction of a model and visual perception of abstract stimuli. However, Betsy's good ability an Object Assembly (scaled score = 16) indicates that she does not require a visual model for success and that she has good perception of meaningful as well as abstract stimuli. These hypothesized strengths are thus *not* accepted. Her good performance on the Vocabulary–Coding dyad suggests that "learning ability" may be Betsy's strength. Yet observations during the psychomotor subtest seemed more supportive of a different hypothesized strength. She understood the task immediately and did not memorize any of the symbols; her most noteworthy behavior was the exceptionally quick and agile eye–hand coordination that she sustained for the duration of the subtest. The examiner noted in the case report that Betsy was observed to have well-coordinated motor activity, and this ability was evident on *all* manipulative tasks. It is, therefore, sensible to hypothesize that Betsy's significant strength on Coding, along with above-average scaled scores on Object Assembly and Block Design, reflects well-developed visual–motor coordination. Does the significant weakness in Mazes (which is included in the visual–motor quartet of subtests) detract from this hypothesized area of strength? Not at all. Betsy is believed to have relatively weak planning ability and nonverbal reasoning. It is unreasonable to expect excellent visual–motor coordination to compensate for her relative deficiencies.

Overall, Betsy has superior verbal and nonverbal intelligence; not surprisingly, she was selected for the gifted program. She has outstanding Verbal Comprehension ability (99th percentile, based on the average of her scaled scores on the component subtests) and exceptional visual–motor coordination (98th percentile, based on Coding, Object Assembly, and Block Design scaled scores). In contrast, she was relatively weak in her planning ability and nonverbal reasoning (63rd percentile) and in her auditory short-term memory (50th percentile). These interpretations of Betsy's profile fluctuations are far more informative and meaningful and take into account more of her subtest scores than interpretations focusing only on the unique abilities presumably measured by the specific subtests. How valuable would it be to know that Betsy is strong in her range of general information and psychomotor speed and weak in auditory short-term memory and following a visual pattern?

Is the Method for Attacking Profiles Defensible?

The procedure outlined previously (pp. 176–189) for investigating WISC-R profiles follows the same logic as procedures I have developed with colleagues for interpreting both the McCarthy Scales (Kaufman and Kaufman 1977) and the Stanford–Binet (Kaufman and Waterstreet 1978). Are these techniques justifiable? Some clinicians and researchers would certainly say ''no,'' including those who consider profile interpretation of Wechsler's subtest profile to be inadvisable (Conger and Conger 1975) or even ''a continuing malpractice'' (Hirshoren and Kavale 1976), and others who place a strong stress on a statistical and empirical approach to interpretation (Lutey 1977). The ''malpractice'' group dwells on the relative unreliability of the subtests for most age groups and the resultant large standard errors of measurement for the separate tasks. Their ultimate conclusion is to focus on the global IQs and abandon the evaluation of subtest fluctuations. The statistical purists, in contrast, engage actively in profile interpretation but prefer to use precise values for computations rather than rounded estimates (± 3 is too gross); to treat each of the 11 age groups from 6½ to 16½ years separately rather than use average values for the total sample; and, generally, to compute a wide variety of factor scores and category scores as a means of tracking down strong and weak abilities.

I respect advocates of both of these diverse positions and have a special fondness, deep down, for the theoretical soundness of the ardent empiricists, but

I disagree with both camps for practical reasons. If we adhere to the tenets of those who consider subtest analysis as virtually criminal, we are almost forced to abandon the expertise we possess as clinicians and psychologists that permits us to go beyond the IQs, and that elevates us above psychometric clerks. In Chapter 2 it was shown that the same V−P discrepancy may have almost as many explanations as there are individuals obtaining the discrepancy. Yet how can we attempt even to interpret a significant global V−P difference if we are not permitted to enter the hallowed ground of subtest fluctuations? In contrast, the approach of the statistical purists, which encourages accuracy to the nearest decimal place, fosters a superscientific attitude that places too much credence in the precision of the obtained profile of scores. The image that may be presented to the outside world is one of examiners being more enthralled with the numbers (each one bound neatly with a precise band of error), than with the underlying dynamics and personal qualities of the children tested. Overreliance on statistical comparisons and on long lists of empirical do's and don'ts can force examiners, especially novices, to focus off target and forget the real purposes of psychological assessment.

In response to individuals who are opposed to any type of subtest analysis, it should be noted that most sensible methods of profile interpretation (including the ±3 technique described in Chapter 2) take fully into account the standard errors of measurement of the Wechsler subtests. Furthermore the internal consistency and test−retest reliability coefficients of the WISC-R subtests are not so unimpressive. Verbal subtests averaged about 0.80 and Performance subtests about 0.75 (Wechsler 1974, Tables 9 and 11). Using data provided by Wechsler (1974, Table 15), the average intercorrelations of the Performance subtests were found to be substantially lower than the average interrelationships among Verbal subtests (0.35−0.40 vs. 0.50). From the vantage point of profile interpretation, the lower intercorrelations for the Performance subtests counterbalance their lower reliability coefficients; in other words, the reliability of the difference between subtest scores increases with both high reliability and low intercorrelations. Psychometrically, it is thus perfectly feasible to interpret profile fluctuations within both the Verbal and Performance Scales, if proper caution is exercised. The method advocated in this book has several built-in cautions: the use of a ±3 point criterion to permit entry into the scaled-score profile, the strong emphasis placed on deriving hypotheses from two or more subtests rather than relying on subtest specific interpretations, the necessity of trying to support hypotheses with facts about children's home and school environments and with clinical inferences based on test behaviors, and the advisability of checking out the generalizability of WISC-R derived hypotheses by administering a wide variety of supplementary tests and subtests.

Concerning the psychometric rigor of statistical purists, there are some compelling practical reasons for assuming a less-than-perfectionistic stance when analyzing profile data. There is considerable subjectivity in scoring several Verbal subtests, which can substantially affect the magnitude of Verbal scaled scores and Verbal IQ; similarly, determining bonus points for Performance items is often dependent on an examiner's subjective decision regarding the precise moment that a child has completed his or her response. The dramatic impact of examiners' differential scoring of ambiguous responses to Verbal items has been given clear-cut support (Massey 1965; Sattler and Winget 1970). Even apart from the legitimate scoring ambiguities that demand subjective judgment by the examiner, there is a mounting body of evidence (Miller and Chansky 1972; Miller, Chansky, et al. 1970) showing that qualified examiners make a considerable number of scoring and mechanical errors. For example, 64 psychologists who independently scored the same WISC protocol obtained Full Scale IQs ranging from 78 to 95 (Miller and Chansky 1972)! Such clerical errors are absolutely not to be condoned, and trainers of individual test administrators must strive to greatly reduce the carelessness and lack of mechanical precision that exist. Nevertheless, we must be aware that many examiners are likely to make at least a couple of errors that affect an individual's scaled scores and IQs. An overemphasis on statistical precision (e.g., stipulating that a precise difference of 2.6 points be required to determine a significant discrepancy between a Similarities scaled score and the child's Verbal mean) seems incompatible with this practical reality. In addition, rounding Verbal and Performance means to the nearest whole number, and using a constant ± 3 discrepancy, eliminates examiners' dependency on specific tables and demands very simple mathematical computations, thereby reducing the likelihood of extra clerical errors.

The very different IQs that may be obtained depending on the precise day a child is tested also argue against the application of rigid statistical criteria for analyzing profiles. Suppose a boy is tested on the WISC-R at the age of 6 years 3 months and obtains (for argument's sake) a raw score of 5 on each of the 10 regular subtests; he will obtain a Verbal IQ of 90, a Performance IQ of 78, and a Full Scale IQ of 83. If he had been tested at the age of 6 years 4 months (which may be only a day or a week later) and obtained the *identical* raw scores on each subtest, his IQs would have decreased by $8-10$ points(!): Verbal IQ $= 80$, Performance IQ $= 70$, Full Scale IQ $= 73$. At the age of 6 years 4 months he would be perceived as having Borderline intelligence, a nonsignificant V$-$P discrepancy, and an overall percentile rank of 4. The same performance, at the age of 6 years 3 months, produces IQs in the Low Average range (overall percentile rank of 13) along with a significant ($p < 0.05$) V$-$P difference. The changes in IQ as a function of the exact testing date are less dramatic at the older ages, when development is not so rapid. Nevertheless, it should be clear that we must not be deluded or overly impressed by the apparent precision of obtained test scores, even when these scores have high reliabilities and small bands of error (Full Scale IQ has a reliability of 0.96 and standard error of measurement of 3 points).

Readers may ponder why we bother to use any statistical criteria at all. One reason is to impose some order on a potentially chaotic situation, namely the interpretation of three IQs and 10−12 scaled scores. A second is to impose restraint on examiners who may be tempted to interpret slight peaks or valleys as meaningful fluctuations when all that these deviations may reflect is expected chance error. But first and foremost, the statistical criteria are established to serve as guidelines and parameters to support and abet the logical detective work that is the real crux of profile interpretation. Sometimes the empirical criteria can even be ignored or sidestepped, as long as examiners do so out of logic and external support for hypotheses, rather than out of ignorance or lack of respect for the data.

A final point merits attention. Why do I consistently use average values for the total sample in preference to separate age-related data? This decision was not made arbitrarily or even for simplicity of interpretation. Basically I have more confidence in data obtained on the entire standardization sample ($N = 2200$) than in the data for each of the 11 age groups ($N = 200$ per group). The combination of all age levels for determining statistical rules is completely justifiable in view of the striking lack of developmental trends in factor structure, sex differences, V−P discrepancies, and subtest scatter (Kaufman 1975, 1976b,c; Kaufman and Doppelt 1976). Although fluctuations are evident in the reliability of the subtests across the age range (Wechsler 1974), most of these changes seem arbitrary and unsystematic rather than developmental in nature. When age-related findings have been observed, as in the subtest specificity of Picture Completion and Similarities, these developmental trends have been respected. For the most part, however, data based on the entire sample seem more stable than age-specific data. In fact, in some cases it is difficult to know which age group is most pertinent for a given child. The children constituting the standardization sample were all tested within 6 weeks of their half-birthdays, so the normative group contains 6½-year-olds, 7½-year-olds, and so on, but no 6-, 7-, or 8-year olds. Should a child who is near his or her eleventh birthday, for example, be compared to the norms for 10½- or 11½-year olds? Picture Completion has a reliability coefficient of 0.68 at age 10½ and 0.80 at age 11½. Which values should be used for an 11-year-old? I feel it makes the most sense to treat apparently random age-wise fluctuations as chance deviations from the average value and to interpret the average values for all children tested.

In theory, it is desirable to use statistical precision for all mathematical computations pertaining to comparisons among scores. Furthermore, it is undesirable from a theoretical vantage point to rely on positive or negative chance errors when performing the detective work required to generate hypothesized areas of strength or weakness. Practically, however, it makes good sense to use global empirical guidelines as only one facet of profile interpretation. It is also practical to delve into profiles to find support for various hypotheses from subtests that were *not* significant strengths or weaknesses, knowing that the outcome of the detective work is indeed a set of *hypotheses* and nothing more. The potential usefulness and applicability of the derived hypotheses rest on corroboration from supplementary tests and from information about various other aspects of the child's background and behavior.

Hypotheses and Recommendations

The main aim of generating hypotheses from WISC-R profiles is *not* to diagnose an exceptionality or to plan methods for remediating a learning or behavioral disorder, but to help understand the children being evaluated—how they learn best, what they can do relatively well and relatively poorly, how their background and behavior interact with their cognitive functioning, and so forth. From this understanding comes diagnostic hypotheses and remedial suggestions, provided that the WISC-R is supplemented by additional instruments and that standardized testing, in general, is augmented by informal assessment and evaluation in naturalistic settings. It is irrational to suppose that complex disorders such as mental retardation or learning disabilities can be diagnosed, based on an hour or so of 1:1 contact between a strange examiner and apprehensive child. No matter how well rapport is established, the artificiality of the situation is constantly brought to the attention of the child by the stopwatch, the recording of virtually every word uttered by the youngster, and the examiner's dependence on a book to know precisely what to say. The fact that competent examiners with clinical experience and a thorough grounding in psychological theory can gain new insights into children's functioning based on administration of a single instrument such as the WISC-R is indeed impressive; expectations of an instant diagnosis or of automatic recommendations are unreasonable.

Hypotheses generated from WISC-R profiles can aid greatly in understanding children, and this understanding can take many forms. Examiners may find out about well-developed or poorly developed *abilities*, such as memory−reasoning, Spatial−Verbal Conceptualization, or cognition−evaluation. Or they may uncover strong or weak *modes of processing* information, most notably analytic/sequential−holistic/simultaneous. The nature of the *content* to be processed, that is, verbal−nonverbal or meaningful−abstract, may conceivably be isolated as the key distinction for some youngsters. Or, the main finding of a WISC-R administration may be the examiner's awareness of how *nonintellective factors* interact with mental functioning. These nonintellective variables span a wide range from background variables (cultural opportunities at home, speaking Black Dialect) and cognitive style (field dependence−field independence, reflective−impulsive) to characteristic or pervasive behaviors (anxiety, distractibility) and interests or hobbies (reading, solving jigsaw puzzles).

Many of these hypotheses have educational consequences, some of which were discussed or alluded to in Chapter 5. Certainly examiners would anticipate quite different teaching styles being effective for children with good reasoning and poor memory skills as opposed to those with good memory and poor reasoning. Different types of curricular materials are likely to be successful for children whose test performance varies directly with the content of the task. Different learning environments need to be recommended for youngsters with divergent modes of processing information: a structured, rule-governed, logical environment for analytic, left-brained individuals; and an unstructured, flexible, "discovery" environment for right-brained children. Similarly, learning environments need to be adapted to children who are shown to have a specific cognitive style and to children whose intellectual functioning is impeded by extraneous variables such as inability to concentrate, anxiety, or emotional lability. [See Ross (1976) for a research-oriented discussion of these issues, along with excellent remedial suggestions.]

Numerous writers have discussed a variety of recommended educational practices geared specifically to their areas of interest: field-dependent—field-independent cognitive style (Witkin, Moore, et al. 1977), reflective—impulsive cognitive style (Meichenbaum and Goodman 1971), Guilford's SOI model (Meeker 1973), cerebral specialization (Bogen 1975), and children with brain injury (Strauss and Kephart 1955; Strauss and Lehtinen 1947). Other writers, such as Ross (1976), have dealt with a broader base of problems in the cognitive, perceptual, motor, behavioral, and personality domains (Blanco 1972; Farrald and Schamber 1973); Hammill and Bartel 1978; Wallace and Kauffman 1973). Examiners should familiarize themselves with some of these sources to facilitate the translation of hypotheses to meaningful recommendations; particularly valuable is the flexible and comprehensive ADAPT (A Diagnostic and Prescriptive Technique) approach advocated by Farrald and Schamber (1973). The translation of test hypotheses to recommendations will also be an easier task for examiners who are thoroughly knowledgeable about available curricular materials and how to evaluate them. Hammill and Bartel (1978, Chapter 9) offer valuable information for selecting materials and resources and include an annotated list of educational materials in numerous cognitive and perceptual areas.

Crucial educational decisions are sometimes made on the basis of a psychological evaluation, and these decisions should be supported by ample evidence. As has been reiterated throughout this book, hypotheses suggested by a WISC-R profile should be verified by additional measures. In some instances the best recommendations WISC-R examiners can make are the names of supplementary tests or tasks that must be administered, either by the examiners themselves or by other specialized professional personnel. Since reading problems are so frequent as a presenting symptom, an individually administered diagnostic reading battery is often a desirable supplement to an intelligence test. Rarely should direct educational programming follow from an administration of the WISC-R in isolation. Additional data and criteria have to be considered before making suggestions derived from hypotheses that can only be considered as tentative.

Virtually never, in my opinion, should the WISC-R subtests form the specific content areas worthy of remediation. These areas are mere samples of behavior, intended to reflect an individual's abilities and modes of processing information, rather than a criterion-referenced set of topics that have to be mastered. Arguments against the efficacy of treating specific subtests and tasks as measures of a single ability, worthy of direct remediation for low-scoring individuals, have been cogently and logically put forth by Mann (1971), Newcomer and Hammill (1976), and others. Research has apparently not supported the effectiveness of ability training for instruments such as the ITPA or Frostig tests, measures that were developed with specific remediational techniques in mind. Nevertheless, a number of investigators choose to focus on specific educational prescriptions for individuals who perform poorly on different WISC-R subtests (Alcorn and Nicholson 1975; Banas and Wills 1977, 1978; Cutrona 1975; Jacobson and Kovalinsky 1976; Valett 1978), even though Wechsler decidedly did not develop his scales with educational intervention in mind. A number of the educational suggestions made by these investigators are clever and valuable for some children but should *not* be implemented based merely on the results of one or two scaled scores. When additional supportive evidence is available, prudent examiners may wish to borrow some of these recommendations to incorporate into a comprehensive educational plan. However, overvaluation of a single score or of any particular pair of scores is to be avoided. I see as potentially dangerous statements such as: "If Similarities is average or above average, but Object Assembly is weak, this child will usually not be good with a phonetic analysis approach" (Banas and Wills 1977, p. 244).

INTERPRETING SUBTEST SCATTER

A widely used and probably overused and abused term in the clinical vernacular is *subtest scatter*. This term has typically been vague and ill-defined and yet is frequently considered to be a characteristic of a variety of exceptional populations such as the learning disabled or minimally brain dysfunctioned (Clements 1966). How often have we seen examiners attempt to pin a learning disabled label on children primarily because of "considerable scatter in their Wechsler profiles?" Yet how much scatter is considerable? How flat are the WISC-R profiles of normal youngsters? These are the haunting questions that impelled me to investigate the degree of subtest scatter in the profiles of a large sample of normal children (Kaufman 1976b). The results of the study surprised me greatly, as they did numerous clinicians and Wechsler researchers (some quite well known). These results are discussed in the next section.

Normal or Expected Subtest Scatter on the WISC-R

If the scaled scores on the 10 regular WISC-R subtests are rank ordered from high to low for all of the normal children in the standardization sample, what will the *average difference* be between each child's highest and lowest scaled score? That is the question I asked many experienced WISC and WISC-R examiners after I had determined the answer by analyzing the WISC-R standardization data. Their answers soon became predictable: 3 or 4 points, with some bold individuals suggesting a possible range of 5 or 6 points. And yet the answer is 7 *points* (more than 2 SDs!)—based on systematic analysis of the 2200 children in the WISC-R standardization sample (Kaufman 1976b). The 7-point range so surprised me that I had the computer programmer thoroughly recheck the program and rerun the data, and I personally computed the scaled-score range by hand for an entire age group before I was able to accept the results as valid. But 7 points it was, with a standard deviation of 2 points. Two-thirds of all normal children had scaled-score ranges of 7 ± 2. From that perspective, ranges as large as 9 points were within one standard deviation of the mean and hence legitimately termed "normal." Thus the average child had a scaled-score range of 6−13 or 7−14, and even ranges of 3−12 or 9−18 fit easily into the category of normal (i.e., expected) variability. How often have children with scaled-score profiles such as these been diagnosed as learning disabled or neurologically impaired at least in part because of their subtest scatter?

The 7-point range for the WISC-R also undoubtedly characterized the old WISC since the subtest intercorrelation matrices for the two batteries are so similar (Wechsler 1949, 1974), and the magnitude and distributions of V−P discrepancies for the WISC and WISC-R are virtually identical (Kaufman 1976c; Seashore 1951). There is also some empirical support regarding the equality of the WISC and WISC-R scaled-score ranges for two small samples of exceptional children (Anderson, Kaufman, et al. 1976; Weiner and Kaufman in press). Furthermore, the range of 7 ± 2 was observed to hold true regardless of age, sex, race, parental occupation, or intelligence level (Kaufman 1976b). The ranges fluctuated unsystematically between 6.7 and 7.3 for the 11 age groups between 6½ and 16½ years; they equaled 7.1 for males versus 7.0 for females, and 7.0 for whites versus 6.8 for blacks; they were almost identical for each of five categories of parental occupation, fluctuating between 6.8 and 7.1; and they descended gradually from 7.4 for children with Full Scale IQs of 120 and above down to 6.7 for youngsters with Full Scale IQs below 80. Standard deviations also were consistently around 2, ranging from 1.9 to 2.4 for the various groups, with an overall value of 2.1.

The incredible consistency of the scaled-score ranges for a variety of sub-groupings of the normative sample indicates that a single table is sufficient to permit examiners to evaluate the amount of scatter in the profiles of all children tested on the WISC-R. Table 6-5 was developed to fulfill this need and is equipped to help examiners assess scatter within the Verbal, Performance, and Full Scales, regardless of whether five or six subtests are administered per scale.

To use Table 6-5, compute the child's scaled-score ranges separately for the Verbal Scale, Performance Scale, and Full Scale. If all six Verbal or Performance subtests are given, examiners have the option of basing the ranges only on the regular subtests or on all subtests administered. (If 11 subtests are given, examiners have to compute Full Scale ranges based only on the 10 regular subtests.) After computing the three ranges, examiners enter these values into Table 6-5 to determine how unusual the obtained ranges happen to be.

To illustrate the use of Table 6-5, consider Aaron R., whose scaled scores on the five Verbal subtests ranged from 6−11, and whose five Performance scaled

Table 6-5 Percent of Normal Children Obtaining Scaled-score Ranges of a Given Magnitude or Greater (N = 2200)

Scaled-score Range	Regular WISC-R (10 Subtests)			Entire WISC-R (12 Subtests)		
	Verbal (Five Subtests)	Performance (Five Subtests)	Full Scale (10 Subtests)	Verbal (Six Subtests)	Performance (Six Subtests)	Full Scale (12 Subtests)
0	100.0	100.0		100.0		
1	99.9	99.9	100.0	99.9	100.0	
2	97.5	98.6	99.9	99.0	99.6	100.0
3	86.2	92.3	99.6	94.0	97.0	99.9
4	66.7	81.1	97.0	82.1	88.5	99.3
5	45.6	64.1	89.8	62.2	74.9	95.8
6	27.3	45.6	74.7	43.2	57.0	85.9
7	14.3	29.1	56.4	25.9	39.9	70.4
8	6.4	18.0	38.6	13.7	25.9	56.8
9	2.7	10.1	22.6	6.4	14.6	32.9
10	1.2	5.2	12.3	3.0	8.1	19.6
11	0.3	2.6	5.9	1.4	4.1	10.8
12	0.2	1.4	2.9	0.4	2.1	5.3
13	0.0	0.6	1.4	0.1	0.8	2.1
14		0.4	0.5	0.1	0.4	0.6
15		0.1	0.2	0.0	0.1	0.2
16		0.0	0.0		0.0	0.0
Median	4	5	7	5	6	8
Mean	4.5	5.5	7.0	5.3	6.1	7.7
SD	1.9	2.3	2.1	2.0	2.3	2.1

Note: Scaled-score ranges equal children's highest scaled score minus their lowest scaled score on the Verbal, Performance, or Full Scales. Since scores can range from 1 to 19, the maximum possible range equals 18 points.

scores ranged from 8–16. His Verbal range equals 5 (11 minus 6), his Performance range equals 8 (16 minus 8), and his Full Scale range equals 10 (16 minus 6). How unusual is this degree of subtest scatter? Entering the value of 5 into the far-left column in Table 6-5 and reading across to the next column, we see a value of 45.6. This number means that 45.6% of normal children have Verbal scaled-score ranges of 5 or more, which is certainly not an unusual amount of scatter. Next we enter his Performance scaled-score range of 8 into Table 6-5 and find that 18% of normal youngsters have a range of at least 8 points on the Performance Scale. Similarly, a Full Scale range of 10 points or more occurs 12.3% of the time in the population at large.

Are either of the latter two values indicative of substantial scatter in Aaron's WISC-R profile? That depends on the examiner's personal decision of how rare a scaled-score range should be to be considered unusual or worthy of note. I think different values have to be used depending on the purpose of the decision. If examiners are merely looking for an adjective to help describe the scatter in a profile to facilitate communication of the test results, then 15% seems like a reasonable cut-off point between "normal variability" and "substantial scatter"; this value corresponds approximately to scaled-score ranges that are more than one standard deviation from the mean of normal children. However, if examiners are planning to imply that the amount of scatter in a profile is so great that it is deemed *abnormal* and perhaps suggestive of any sort of neurological impairment or psychopathology (to be corroborated by subsequent evaluation), a more stringent criterion is needed. For such purposes, scaled-score ranges occurring less than 5%, or even 2%, in the general population are advisable. Ranges corresponding to various percents of occurrence among children in general, derived from Table 6-5, are tabulated as follows for the 10 regular subtests (as a rule of thumb, add one point to each value if six Verbal, six Performance, or 12 Full Scale subtests are used to compute ranges):

Frequency of Occurrence in Normal Population	Size of Scaled-score Range		
	Verbal (Five Subtests)	Performance (Five Subtests)	Full Scale (10 Subtests)
Less than 15%	7	9	10
Less than 10%	8	10	11
Less than 5%	9	11	12
Less than 2%	10	12	13
Less than 1%	11	13	14

The use of Table 6-5 or the immediately preceding summary table cannot be rigid, but must be flexible and sensible. The Full Scale range will be virtually meaningless for children with sizable V−P IQ discrepancies since a large range for the Full Scale may merely reflect the global V−P difference rather than intersubtest variability. Thus if the Verbal and Performance scaled-score ranges are both of a normal magnitude, a sizable Full Scale range will contribute nothing more than is already known based on the observed V−P discrepancy; in fact, the Full Scale range may be misleading when large V−P IQ differences are obtained. Similarly, an individual can achieve large Verbal, Performance, and Full Scale ranges because of one or two very deviant subtest scores. For example, the child's scores on the Verbal Comprehension and Perceptual Organization subtests may be quite internally consistent, but large ranges may result from very deviant Digit Span and/or Coding scores. Whenever the scatter is produced by one or two subtests that (like Coding and Digit Span) are poor measures of g and have considerable subtest specificity, examiners should give little credence to apparently "significant" subtest scatter.

Primarily because any one index of scatter has to have some flaws, a second index is provided: the number of scaled scores that deviate significantly (±3 points) from the child's own mean. This second index of scatter was also studied empirically and found to be unrelated to age, sex, race, parental occupation, and intelligence level (Kaufman 1976b). Consequently, a single table has been developed to evaluate profile scatter in a second way for all children within the 6−16-year range (see Table 6-6).

To use Table 6-6, compute the number of subtests that deviate significantly (±3 points) from the child's Verbal mean, Performance mean, and Full Scale mean. Examiners may use all six Verbal and Performance subtests if they wish,

Table 6-6   Percent of Normal Children Having at Least a Given Number of Subtest Scores Deviating by 3 or More Points from Their Own Mean Scores ($N = 2200$)

Number of Deviant Subtest Scores	Regular WISC-R (10 Subtests)			Entire WISC-R (12 Subtests)		
	Verbal (Five Subtests)	Performance (Five Subtests)	Full Scale (10 Subtests)	Verbal (Six Subtests)	Performance (Six Subtests)	Full Scale (12 Subtests)
0	100.0	100.0	100.0	100.0	100.0	100.0
1	36.7	53.6	80.7	52.6	65.5	89.5
2	12.0	24.4	51.8	21.3	34.3	65.8
3	1.4	4.5	23.6	4.4	9.6	29.6
4	0.2	1.2	9.2	0.8	2.1	19.8
5	0.0	0.0	3.1	0.1	0.2	8.2
6			1.0	0.0	0.0	2.9
7			0.2			0.7
8			0.0			0.1
9						0.0

and the Full Scale mean may be based on either 10 or 12 subtests. Compute the number of significantly deviating subtest scores, combining strengths and weaknesses. Then use Table 6-6 in the same way as Table 6-5; first enter the table with the child's indices of scatter, and then determine the percent of normal children who had at least that much scatter in their profiles.

Jessica B. was given the 10 regular WISC-R subtests and obtained the following scaled-score profile:

WISC-R Profile

Verbal	Scaled Score	Performance	Scaled Score
Information	9	Picture Completion	5
Similarities	11	Picture Arrangement	14
Arithmetic	6	Block Design	11
Vocabulary	9	Object Assembly	11
Comprehension	6	Coding	6

Verbal IQ = 88.　　Performance IQ = 95.　　Full Scale IQ = 91.

Jessica's Verbal mean equals 8, so a relative strength in Similarities is the only significant discrepancy. Her Performance mean of 9 produces a significant strength in Picture Arrangement and significant weaknesses in Picture Completion and Coding. Based on her Full Scale mean of 9, she has a relative strength in Picture Arrangement and relative weaknesses in Arithmetic, Comprehension, Picture Completion, and Coding. (Notice how somewhat different subtests can emerge as strengths or weaknesses depending on which mean is used as the reference point.)

Jessica thus had *one* deviant score based on her Verbal mean, *three* based on her Performance mean, and *five* based on her Full Scale mean. Entering the value of one into the appropriate Verbal column in Table 6-6, we read 36.7; this value indicates that 36.7% of normal children had at least one significantly deviating scaled score. Entering three into the Performance column, we discover that only 4.5% of the general population had three or more deviant subtest scores, and the value of five for the Full Scale is also a fairly rare phenomenon: only 3.1% of normal youngsters had five or more subtests deviating significantly from their Full Scale means. Again, examiners have to determine what percents they wish to label as rare. Certainly, the 36.7% obtained for the Verbal Scale would not be deemed unusual by any reasonable standard, whereas the values obtained for the Performance and Full Scales would constitute substantial scatter for most examiners.

It is also feasible to determine the scatter in Jessica's profile by computing her scaled-score ranges and entering these indices of scatter into Table 6-5. Her

Verbal range is 5, Performance range is 9, and Full Scale range is 9. Entering Table 6-5 with these values, we find that her Verbal scatter is not unusual, as ranges of 5 or greater occurred for 45.6% of normal children; her Performance scatter is reasonably substantial since only 10.1% of the population had ranges at least as large as Jessica's; and her Full Scale range was equaled or exceeded by a sizable 22.6% of normal youngsters. If a 15% criterion is arbitrarily selected to determine the scatter in Jessica's profile, the scaled-score range method reveals significant scatter only within the Performance Scale. However, the same 15% criterion, if used with the alternative index of scatter (number of deviant subtest scores), indicates significant scatter within *both* the Performance and Full Scales. Which results should examiners heed? Again, they should use their best judgment. Basically, it seems reasonable to compute both indices of scatter and look for commonalities in the findings. In the illustration, there is clear-cut support for Performance Scale scatter, and marginal evidence of Full Scale scatter. Since Jessica's highest and lowest scaled scores both occurred within the Performance Scale, it probably makes the most sense to focus on the scatter among her nonverbal abilities.

However, each index of scatter is particularly sensitive to different kinds of intersubtest fluctuations, and examiners may prefer to focus on one or the other index depending on the profile. The scaled-score range method is sensitive to the existence of a couple of very extreme scores, despite basic consistency in the profile; the deviant-score approach detects scatter when there are several significant subtest fluctuations, even if none is especially sizable. As stated earlier, flexibility and logic have to join with the normative data before decisions can be reached regarding scatter in a profile. And just as the Full Scale subtest-score range is generally inappropriate for children with large V−P IQ discrepancies, so is the number of deviant scores from the Full Scale mean inapplicable for individuals with sizable verbal−nonverbal differences.

Tables 6-5 and 6-6 can be considered as normative tables that provide a *basal level* of scatter, thereby serving as frames of reference for evaluating the scatter in the WISC-R profile of any child referred for testing. The rather large amount of intersubtest variability for normal children should serve as a precaution against overinterpreting peaks and valleys in the scaled-score profiles of children suspected of learning disorders, emotional disturbance, and so on. Since most examiners primarily test individuals who are believed to be abnormal in some way, it is logical for them to have interpreted a subtest-score range of 2−10 or 6−15 as indicative of abnormality. But now we know that ranges such as these are perfectly normal, and our assessment techniques should be adjusted accordingly. The burden is upon researchers to show that various groups of exceptional children really are characterized by considerable subtest scatter. All of the presumptions about scatter in the profiles of learning-disabled children, for example, may be nothing more than clinical speculation that is not borne out by empirical investigation. Two studies suggest the possible truth of the latter statement: a sample of 41 learning-disabled children, diagnosed by a multidisciplinary team of professionals, had scaled-score ranges that did *not* differ significantly from the values for normal youngsters (Anderson, Kaufman, et al. 1976); and a sample of 46 black children referred for learning or behavioral disorders had scaled-score ranges that were virtually identical to the ranges for normal children (Weiner and Kaufman in press). However, these studies do not even scratch the surface, and their results preclude even temporary hypotheses.

Much more investigative research is needed in this crucial area. Based on the increasing number of articles on WISC-R scatter that I have been asked to review for professional journals, on the investigation of empirical indices of WISC-R scatter that are different from the indices described above (Swerdlik and Wilson in press), and on the application to WISC-R subtest scores of a formula to determine the *abnormality* of obtained differences (Piotrowski 1978; Reynolds in press), I feel confident that the necessary research studies are on the horizon. Until new data are available, we should be extremely cautious before inferring that subtest scatter in a WISC-R profile is supportive of a suspected exceptionality—even when state guidelines include Wechsler scatter as part of the legal definition (Swerdlik and Wilson in press). *When we do make such an inference of an association between scatter and an abnormality, we should always be able to justify that the amount of intersubtest variability within the profile is indeed rare when compared to that of normal children.*

Some examiners interpret the research on WISC-R scatter to mean that significant strengths and weaknesses in a profile are unimportant or should be ignored if the amount of overall scatter in the profile is not unusual. Such an interpretation is incorrect. These strengths and weaknesses, even if they are not excessive in number or extraordinarily deviant from the child's own means, provide important information for understanding the child and for making meaningful educational or other practical recommendations. Chapter 5 and the earlier parts of Chapter 6 were devoted to showing how even small (but significant) fluctuations can play dynamic roles in gaining insight into children's abilities, processing styles, characteristic behaviors, and so on. The fact that the amount of scatter may be small does not detract from the potential value of whatever significant peaks and valleys are observed in a profile.

The key distinction here is between diagnosis and educational planning. An unusual amount of scatter is necessary before even beginning to infer a relationship between a WISC-R profile and some abnormal condition; in other words, a *normal* or expected amount of scatter should never be used as part of the diagnostic evidence of an *abnormality*. However, significant fluctuations frequently lead to hypotheses that can affect remediation or other types of educational planning. Even the normal children in the standardization sample, who showed a few significant deviations in their WISC-R profiles, would undoubtedly benefit if these fluctuations (along with corroborating evidence) could be translated into school-related recommendations.

Characteristic Profiles and What They Mean

The notion of characteristic profiles of various exceptional populations was interspersed throughout Chapter 5. Although some examiners may state uncategorically that characteristic profiles for groups have *not* been isolated in the literature, this stereotype is false. The results of profile studies involving groups of children with *personality* disorders or with known *neurological* impairment have certainly been conflicting and inconclusive (Bortner and Birch 1969; Burstein 1976; Dean 1977a; Hamm and Evans 1978; Hopkins 1964; Lewandowski, Saccuzzo, et al. 1977; Morris, Evans et al. 1978; Sattler 1974; Zimmerman and Woo-Sam 1972). However, as indicated in Chapter 5, impressive consistency has emerged in investigations of a wide variety of groups with *school-related* problems: mentally retarded, reading disabled, and learning disabled (Lutey 1977; Rugel 1974b; Silverstein 1968). Using Bannatyne's (1971, 1974) groupings, mentally retarded score relatively high on Spatial subtests and low on Acquired Knowledge tasks; both reading and learning disabled score high on Spatial, low on Sequencing, and low on Acquired Knowledge. Particularly striking for groups of reading-disabled and learning-disabled children is the prevalence of low scores on Information, Arithmetic, Digit Span, and Coding (Ackerman, Dykman, et al. 1976; Lutey 1977; McManis, Figley, et al. 1978; Robeck 1971; Rugel 1974b). Also astounding is the study-by-study consistency in the subtests that emerge as ''easy'' (Picture Completion, Object Assembly, Block Design) or ''hard'' (Arithmetic, Vocabulary, Information) for diverse samples of retarded populations (Kaufman and Van Hagen 1977; Silverstein 1968). Of interest too is Smith's (1978) finding of extreme test−retest stability (7-month interval) of the characteristic profile for learning-disabled children.

Several points require discussion regarding characteristic group profiles. First is whether the existence of predictable peaks and valleys in the profiles of some exceptional populations imply that these profiles are replete with significant scatter. The answer is ''not necessarily''; flat profiles or profiles with substantial variability depend on empirical indices of scatter such as scaled-score range (Kaufman 1976b) or the average of absolute deviations of subtests from the scale mean (Swerdlik and Wilson in press); there are no stipulations, however, regarding *which* subtests are extremely high or low. Thus the learning-disabled sample investigated by Anderson, Kaufman, et al. (1976) earned a relatively high average scaled score on Picture Completion (9.9) and low scaled scores on Similarities (6.4), Information (6.7), and Vocabulary (6.7). Yet despite the one peak and three valleys for this group, they did *not* display significant scatter within their profiles. Their average Verbal, Performance, and Full Scale (10 subtests) scaled-score ranges were 4.8, 5.7, and 7.5—not significantly different from the values for normal children.

A second point that frequently causes confusion is the distinction between group and individual profiles. Group profiles help us learn about the exceptionality in question, but not about specific individuals who are believed to be handicapped. The fact that reading-disabled children have a characteristic Wechsler profile cannot impel us to anticipate that each reading-disabled youngster will manifest virtually the same profile. Such an expectation would imply that both the exceptionality of a reading disability and each particular youngster with this disorder are *unidimensional*. That implication is absurd. Reading disabilities defy a single definition and may be caused by a diversity of factors in the emotional, neurological, or environmental domains. Similarly, reading-disabled children are also black, white, Spanish-speaking, Oriental, and so on; they are attentive or distractible, calm or anxious, impulsive or reflective, confident or insecure; they come from culturally disadvantaged or advantaged homes and have parents who are angry, indifferent, or sympathetic to their reading problem; and so on and so forth. All of these variables affect a child's WISC-R profile in some way, rendering it a unique reflection of the total child, not just of a single aspect of his or her functioning.

In addition, a group profile may mask two or more subprofiles. For example, Lutey (1977, pp. 305–307) identified *three* different subprofiles for reading-disabled children based on a review of numerous WISC studies. Similarly, although Rugel (1974b) found high Spatial and low Sequencing abilities to characterize 22 populations of disabled readers, there were still four of these groups that performed best on Verbal Conceptualization tasks. And whereas a variety of learning-disabled populations have performed rather well on the subtests related both to Bannatyne's Spatial category and Witkin's field-independent cognitive style, at least one investigation has reported seemingly opposite results. Dean (1978, p. 382) compared the WISC-R profiles of emotionally disturbed and learning-disabled children and found that the latter group appeared more field *dependent* and performed more poorly on "those subtests that required nonverbal visual constructive abilities."

Of what value, then, are characteristic group profiles? Mainly, they help us gain greater insight into exceptionalities such as mental retardation or reading disabilities. Consistently high scores by retarded youngsters on Spatial tasks suggest a possible right-brain leaning (holistic processing mode) and/or a field-independent cognitive style. The low Sequencing scores obtained fairly consistently by reading- and learning-disabled children suggest a potential deficiency in their left-brain functioning and/or in their ability to perform successive processing. High WISC-R scores by learning-disabled children on Picture Completion, Object Assembly, and Picture Arrangement may imply a facility to interpret meaningful (as opposed to abstract) visual stimuli. All of these points were raised in Chapter 5. So what if the results do not apply to all children within a given exceptionality? The consistent findings are fruits for future research in special education and school psychology. They also have educational implications for teachers when *group* lessons are given to a mainstreamed class that includes a number of children with school-related difficulties. In a way, the characteristic group profiles are like a significant difference that is found in an experimental study of handicapped versus normal children. For example, a group of learning-disabled children was found to have a deficient long-term memory when compared to normal youngsters (Nolan and Driscoll 1978). No one would interpret this significant difference in an all-or-none fashion (i.e., that every learning-disabled child has a poor long-term memory). Nevertheless, the finding is important and provides another piece of the puzzle in attempting to understand the nature of learning disabilities.

Like significant research findings, characteristic profiles of groups can be regarded as tendencies or trends that become more likely as outcomes for individuals within that group. One would not expect too many reading-disabled children, for example, to score significantly low on most or all of the "valleys" in the group profile, and this expectation is supported by Huelsman's (1970) data. However, logic dictates that a majority of children with a given exceptionality should conform to the overall group profile when the several peaks or valleys in the profile are *averaged* (rather than treated *individually* as was done by Huelsman). This latter contention also has empirical support. Smith, Coleman, et al. (1977b) investigated the Bannatyne profile of each of the 208 learning-disabled children they investigated and found that 70% scored highest on the Spatial category, whereas only 7% achieved their highest scores on the Sequencing subtests. Of the 80 mentally retarded children in the study by Kaufman and Van Hagen (1977), 61% scored higher on the Spatial than Acquired Knowledge category, 16% performed equally in these two areas, and only 23% had higher Acquired Knowledge than Spatial scores.

Thus the apparent trends in the profiles of individuals in a given exceptional category can sometimes provide one piece of evidence to be weighed in the diagnostic process. When there is ample support for a diagnosis from many diverse background, behavioral, test-related (and in some cases medical) criteria, the emergence of a reasonably characteristic profile can be treated as one ingredient in the overall stack of evidence. However, the lack of a characteristic profile should not be considered as disconfirming evidence. In addition, no characteristic profile, in and of itself, should ever be used as the primary basis of a diagnostic decision. We do not even know how many normal youngsters display similar WISC-R profiles. Furthermore, as stated on page 141, the extreme similarity in the relative strengths and weaknesses of the typical profiles for mentally retarded, reading-disabled, and learning-disabled children renders differential diagnosis based primarily on WISC-R subtest patterns a veritable impossibility.

Implications of Scatter for Short Forms

The rapid and frenzied rate of short form development for the WPPSI, WISC, and WAIS (Glasser and Zimmerman 1967; Kaufman 1972; Silverstein 1970; Zimmerman and Woo-Sam 1972) has continued at an exhausting pace for the WISC-R (Goh 1977; Kaufman 1976a; Killan and Hughes 1978; Rasbury, Falgout, et al. 1978; Resnick 1977; Silverstein 1974, 1975). Fascination with short forms stems from a desire to curtail testing time. Some researchers are more impressed by the global IQ than by differential abilities and hence advocate the use of abbreviated versions of the Wechsler scales to make important educational decisions such as special education placement (Levy 1968). Other investigators, myself included, see short forms as useful primarily for screening or research purposes but decidedly *not* as the measure of intelligence for a clinical evaluation.

From the vantage points of current legislation and litigation, and in keeping with the kind of intelligent testing espoused throughout this book, there is certainly no support for the curtailment of testing time; in fact, quite the opposite is necessary for competent assessment. The issue of scatter also enters into the picture. Since children typically exhibit much intersubtest variability, the possibility that the particular subtests included in the short form may, by chance, emphasize an individual's deficits while excluding his or her strengths (or vice versa) is very real. The answer to this problem would seem to be to use a Yudin-type short form, specifically one that includes a sampling of items from all subtests (Yudin 1966). However, I do not believe that this solution is wise for two reasons. First, the investigators associated with the Yudin-type abbreviated forms (Satz, Van De Reit, et al. 1967; Yudin 1966) prefer their approach because it permits clinicians to conduct profile analysis. Interpreting subtests is a difficult and risky enough task with the complete battery; when subtest reliabilities are lowered because of elimination of items, examiners should not be tempted, much less advised, to interpret the profiles. Second, I am not at all convinced that norms derived from administration of complete subtests are applicable when every second or third item is administered. My apprehension is greatest for subtests that require the building up of a response set, such as Similarities and Picture Completion, or that are influenced by actual learning during the task itself (e.g., Block Design). We have all probably seen individuals who, on the Stanford–Binet, failed similarities or digit spans that they passed with ease on an administration of a Wechsler battery. Possibly, the better performance on the Wechsler scale was due to the gradual buildup from easy to hard items in each subtest, as opposed to the Binet format that requires a child to reverse five digits (for example) without first attempting shorter spans. In addition, children who suddenly "catch on" to the Picture Arrangement, Block Design, or Mazes tasks are sometimes seen to pass very difficult items even after, technically, they should have been discontinued. (Naturally, these successes do not count in their scores.) Consequently, examiners who administer *fragmented* subtests in the Yudin-type short forms should weigh the possibility that the normative data (derived from administration of *intact* subtests) are not entirely applicable.

Hence a selection of a few complete subtests may have advantages over the Yudin-type versions when short forms are to be used. Should abbreviated WISC-Rs be avoided altogether in clinical assessment? Ideally, yes. Practically, there are times when screening is necessary or desirable. Clinicians frequently choose brief instruments of homogeneous content to administer (e.g., picture—vocabulary tests) despite poor psychometric properties and/or inadequate norms. They should at least have the option of screening children with a carefully selected group of Wechsler subtests that is brief to administer yet has the advantages of excellent psychometric qualities and a representative, nationwide standardization sample.

When selecting a short form, a number of factors merit careful consideration. These factors, many of which I have discussed in greater detail elsewhere (Kaufman 1972, 1976a, 1977a,b), are listed as follows:

1. *Select equal numbers of Verbal and Performance subtests.* Since significant V−P IQ discrepancies are common, even for normal children, a short form with disproportionate representation of the Verbal and Performance Scales will unfairly penalize a substantial percent of the children evaluated. Triads and pentads, although commonly developed (Goh 1977; Silverstein 1975), are thus not advised. Four-subtest short forms seem to make the most sense in terms of the dual considerations of time reduction and accuracy of estimation. Nevertheless, the Vocabulary—Block Design dyad, which shows promise as a screening tool (Killan and Hughes 1978; Silverstein 1974; Simpson and Bridges 1959) and has been the subject of much investigation by the Public Health Service (Mercer and Smith 1972; Scanlon 1973; Sells 1966), deserves attention.

2. *Use rational, not just empirical, methods for selecting short forms.* There has been too much emphasis in the literature on the "best" WISC-R short form of any given length. Usually a large number of possible abbreviated Wechsler scales correlate about equally well with Full Scale score; the rank orderings are often determined by the third or fourth decimal place, which is trivial for all practical purposes. The data should be used only as *guidelines*, but rationality has to prevail in the selection of short-form subtests. For example, a wide variety of mental operations should be

assessed. No matter how impressive the data for the Information — Comprehension or Information — Vocabulary dyads, combinations of Verbal subtests should be chosen that have less overlap in what they measure; ditto for Performance dyads such as Picture Completion — Object Assembly or Block Design — Object Assembly. The short form should give representation to all three WISC-R factors and should "feel" like a cohesive clinical unit. Other factors to consider include ease of administration and scoring, inclusion of at least one task for "ice breaking" or rapport purposes, the degree to which the tasks are good representatives of their own Scales (Verbal or Performance) rather than of the Full Scale, and research findings regarding typical peaks and valleys for various exceptional populations.

3. *Know the psychometric properties of the short form.* Formulas are readily available to compute reliability and validity data for short forms (Silverstein 1971; Tellegen and Briggs 1967); standard errors of estimate can also be computed or approximated (Kaufman 1972, 1976a). Examiners often demand psychometric information for the tests they use (and rightfully so). Why should less be expected of short forms?

4. *Consider subtest scatter when using a short form for screening, not just the estimated Full Scale IQ.* The short-form estimate of Full Scale IQ is but one piece of information that is yielded by a brief Wechsler test. Rigid cut-off points based on the estimated IQ are to be avoided. Scaled scores on the short-form subtests should be examined for scatter. No formal rules are available, so subjective judgment of substantial scatter must suffice. As general guidelines, the scaled-score ranges for either the regular (five-subtest) Verbal or Performance Scales (see Table 6-5) are adequate for evaluating the scatter in a four-subtest short form. When substantial scatter is deemed to exist in a short-form profile, the child should be "flagged" even if his or her estimated IQ is high.

5. *Always administer the remaining WISC-R subtests to a child flagged by the short form.* Brief Wechsler scales are for screening (or research), not for decision making. Whenever children are flagged, considered to be at risk, and so on, by the results of a short form, the next step should always be to administer the remaining WISC-R subtests. Then decisions can be made about what supplementary test data and what types of subsequent evaluation are needed.

Most of these factors were considered in the Arithmetic — Vocabulary — Picture Arrangement — Block Design short form of the WISC-R that I developed (Kaufman 1976a). This four-subtest short form has several fine features: good reliability, evidence of significant relationships with other intelligence tests, a standard error of estimate of only 5 points, measurement of a diversity of mental operations, and representation of all three WISC-R factors. Yet it also has several flaws. The stability was lowest (0.83) at ages 6½ and 7½, ages for which short forms are most likely to be useful for large-scale screening; the two Verbal subtests are both included in Bannatyne's Acquired Knowledge grouping; and three of the four subtests require a stopwatch, which may be detrimental to an anxious child. The short form should be valuable if used appropriately despite these shortcomings. However, examiners should be aware that all short forms, by definition, have to be lacking in at least some very important areas. Whenever feasible, the complete battery is the instrument of choice.

ILLUSTRATIVE CASE REPORTS

The case reports at the end of Chapter 2 illustrated the interpretation of V−P IQ discrepancies, and the sample reports in Chapter 3 focused on the role of the third factor in WISC-R interpretation. The four reports that follow have as their primary goal the illustration of the principles of detective work and, hence, integration of the teachings of Chapters 4−6. However, since V−P IQ discrepancies are involved for 8-year-old Jill S. and 10½-year-old Cecil Y., the reports are, in effect, a culmination of the approach to WISC-R interpretation presented throughout this book.

Darren B., White Male, Age 6 years 11 months

WISC-R Profile

Verbal	Scaled Score	Performance	Scaled Score
Information	3	Picture Completion	12-S
Similarities	3	Picture Arrangement	4-W
Arithmetic	1-W	Block Design	2-W
Vocabulary	9-S	Object Assembly	8
Comprehension	7	Mazes	6
(Digit Span)	5	(Coding)	11-S
Verbal IQ = 67.	Performance IQ = 75.	Full Scale IQ = 70.	

Referral and Background Information

Darren was referred for evaluation by his school, where he is described as not performing academically, extremely involved in fantasy, and experiencing difficulty getting along with peers. At home he lives with his parents, both of whom hold semiskilled factory jobs, and three older siblings (two brothers and one sister). His development is reported to be normal, except for an accident at age 2 years during which he was briefly unconscious. As a 4-year-old, Darren went through a spell of clinging to his mother and being fearful of all other family members; this problem has completely disappeared. Presently his behavior at home is described as erratic, where he demands his own way, doesn't perform even simple academic tasks, and makes up "wild stories." He is described as similar to his father as a child, and to both parents regarding his lack of school achievement. Previous testing on the Stanford–Binet reported Borderline intellectual functioning at the age of 6½. The purpose of the current evaluation is to more accurately define his cognitive strengths and weaknesses.

Appearance and Behavioral Characteristics

A small boy just weeks short of his seventh birthday, Darren is a very handsome child who came to the testing session shabbily dressed. He was cooperative and genuinely involved with the tasks he attempted, working slowly and thoroughly on them all. Speaking in a scratchy, cracking voice that sounded like that of an old man, Darren offered much spontaneous conversation that showed his potentially mature level of interpersonal communication. His speech was slow, sometimes as slow as one word at a time. He tended to revert to this robot-sounding dysfluency when questioned by the examiner for further elaboration.

Whereas he was able to sit quietly while working on tasks that required him to manipulate concrete objects, Darren displayed no physical control when functioning totally within the auditory–vocal channel. In these circumstances he wiggled, slipped off his chair, and kept taking his shoes off. He also demonstrated poor auditory receptive abilities, probably resulting from a low level of verbal comprehension. On visual–motor tasks Darren evidenced poor fine-muscle coordination. For example, he had great difficulty keeping from knocking puzzle pieces apart when trying to put together cut-up picture puzzles.

Two behavioral strengths clearly outlined Darren's greatest assets during the present evaluation. First, his relative excellence in verbal fluency facilitated a good understanding of what he was thinking as he worked. Thus his talking while completing drawing tasks, for example, gave far more insight into his family life than could the simple pictorial representation alone. Secondly, Darren displayed the love of successful accomplishment. This motivation was on an emotional level, and he vigorously applauded himself when performing visual–motor tasks that gave instant feedback of correct completion.

Tests Administered

WISC-R
Sentence Completion
Kinetic Family Drawing

Test Results and Interpretation

On the WISC-R Darren obtained a Verbal IQ of 67, a Performance IQ of 75, and a Full Scale IQ of 70, which classify his intelligence as Borderline and rank him at about the 2nd percentile for children his age. His true Full Scale IQ is likely (90% chance) to fall in the 65–75 range. The 8-point difference in favor of his Performance IQ is not statistically significant, suggesting that he functions at about the same level whether dealing with concrete objects or expressing himself verbally. However, the Verbal and Performance IQs are not very meaningful for Darren in view of the fluctuations characterizing his profile. Within each separate scale Darren displayed much scatter in his ability spectrum. His scaled scores ranged from 1 in Arithmetic to 9 in Vocabulary on the Verbal Scale and from 2 (Block Design) to 12 (Picture Completion) on the Performance Scale. Thus on some abilities he scored well below the 1st percentile, whereas on others he was above the 50th percentile when compared to his contemporaries. Darren evidenced two main strengths. First, he was able to express his ideas verbally. This skill was apparent from his spontaneous conversation with the examiner as well as in his performance on the WISC-R subtests requiring him to define words and to demonstrate a commonsense understanding of social situations. Second, he performed relatively well on two visual–motor tasks—finding the missing part in pictures and rapidly copying symbols that are paired with numbers. Both of these tests require good visual perception and expressive skills but make little demands on the child's capacity to reason.

When faced with reasoning tasks, however, Darren was markedly deficient. This deficiency was pervasive, spanning both the Verbal and Performance Scales, as he was unable to tell how two things are alike or to arrange pictures to tell a sensible story. Particularly handicapping was his total inability to reason with highly abstract stimuli such as designs or numbers. He could not construct the simplest design out of blocks or solve the most elementary arithmetic problems (i.e., counting). His problem with numbers was even evident in his inability to respond to a simple question such as "How many legs does a dog have?"

Darren responded to all 31 incomplete sentences, although he occasionally made the remark "soon it will be time for me to go, right?" He expressed interest in dogs, awareness of the discipline problems he has caused in school, and positive feelings toward academics coupled with an appropriate amount of lack of confidence. For example, he completed the phrase "I need" with "somebody to help me—with my math, when I grow up, art, English, social studies . . ." Darren said he feels more comfortable at home and talked of his special fondness for his grandmother. He demonstrated cognitive confusion in such statements as "I am happy when *summer comes, 'cause I play in snow*" and by referring to himself in the third person.

The Kinetic Family Drawing Darren drew was a slow, laborious act on which he worked very carefully. He demonstrated detailed activities involving all of his family members, although each one was busy doing his own separate thing—underscoring the lack of communication and open exchange between people. There was evidence of awareness of violent acts, as he drew his oldest brother loading bullets into a large gun pointing to (actually touching) Darren's mother's head. He also drew a huge hammer that his sister was using to kill a spider. The hammer was bigger than his 15-year-old sister.

The total effect of this drawing was of very poor motor coordination. There were several emotional indicators, including transparencies, lack of body-part symmetry, and poor integration of parts of the figures. These particular signs, along with the motor-expressive problem (e.g., ears on all figures were drawn on the tops of their heads, resembling Mickey Mouse ears), the WISC-R scatter, and the specific areas of cognitive deficiency suggest a possible diagnosis of neurological impairment. The immaturity and impulsivity suggest acting-out behavior in addition to brain dysfunction.

Summary and Recommendations

Almost 7 years old, Darren displayed neither the reported fantasy behavior nor poor interpersonal relations. He did, however, demonstrate his academic inadequacies. During the present evaluation he cooperated fully with the demands of the testing situation. Whereas he offered his ideas freely, his voice was raspy and he occasionally assumed a dysfluent, choppy manner of communicating. Darren's activity level varied in accordance with the demands of different tasks, but he showed the greatest degree of restlessness when working without concrete or visual stimuli. Despite his poor fine-muscle coordination, Darren showed pride in successful accomplishment.

Intelligence testing on the WISC-R revealed a Full Scale IQ of 70, which classifies his mental functioning as Borderline. Within both the Verbal and Performance Scales his scaled scores evidenced great scatter, indicating strengths in verbal expression and in nonreasoning visual perceptual skills. On tasks requiring reasoning (especially with abstract stimuli) Darren was markedly deficient. The degree of scatter displayed, the specific areas of deficit, and the additional support gained by examination of his Kinetic Family Drawing all point to possible neurological impairment. On the drawing task his poor motor coordination and many emotional indicators suggest immaturity, impulsivity, and acting-out behavior in addition to the brain impairment.

Darren needs remediation with fine-motor coordination. He works best under structured conditions with concrete materials to help keep both his attention and activity level under control. Darren must begin to acquire some basic facts, both general information and number skills. Verbal expression on Darren's part should be encouraged and used as a medium for teaching him, with care taken to display his successful achievements. He needs conclusions drawn for him; it should not be assumed that he will be able to make inferences for himself. In this manner simple reasoning problems worked on step-by-step may result in some improved ability in this area.

Nadeen L. Kaufman
Psychologist

Jill S., White Female, Age 8 years 3 months

WISC-R Profile

Verbal	Scaled Score	Performance	Scaled Score
Information	5	Picture Completion	12-S
Similarities	4-W	Picture Arrangement	6-W
Arithmetic	7	Block Design	9
Vocabulary	6	Object Assembly	13-S
Comprehension	12-S	Coding	6-W
Digit Span	6		

Verbal IQ = 80.   Performance IQ = 93.   Full Scale IQ = 85.

Referral and Background Information

Jill was referred for evaluation by her teacher, who describes Jill's "sieges of anger" as uncontrollable bursts of violence against whatever is in her way. When the spell is over, Jill appears "drained and limp." At home, Jill lives with her three older sisters and her mother. She often visits her father, who has remarried following a divorce from her mother. Her mother (a beautician) is concerned about Jill's behavior and says that Jill has difficulty controlling and finally releasing her aggression. If not calmed by her mother, Jill goes to her room and sleeps when she is angry. Jill is reported to demand excessive attention and be aggressive to other children. In school there were two incidents of violent attacks on classmates, during which Jill apparently got mad and could not control herself; afterward she said she "didn't mean to" harm anyone. She has also demonstrated self-aggression (e.g., she bites and scratches herself when angry). Jill is currently repeating the second grade and has special troubles with reading.

Appearance and Behavioral Characteristics

Jill is an attractive 8-year-old Caucasian girl who was neatly dressed and well groomed the day of evaluation. She carried a little plastic bag with an orange in it and obligingly came with the examiner to the testing room. She was obviously tense and remained both quiet and frowning for the first several minutes. Her anxiety dissipated as she focused her attention on the drawing test. She worked methodically and deliberately, erasing many times in her attempts to copy the designs presented as perfectly as she was able. Jill acquiescently worked on all tasks the examiner presented. Whereas she exerted her full effort and attention, she showed no emotional involvement with any task. Instead, she neither smiled when successful nor frowned in frustration when faced with more difficult items.

Jill was willing to listen to the examiner's conversation and perform suggested activities, but she offered very little spontaneous verbal expression herself. On frequent occasions she absentmindedly sucked a finger or thumb but did not appear to be receiving much gratification or support from these regressive activities. About halfway through the session she peeled and ate her orange. This was accomplished in a surprisingly neat and nonobtrusive manner and did not interfere with the test administration. In all, Jill was cooperative but maintained rather dull affect throughout the evaluation. Even the stories she created in response to a projective story-telling task were stereotypical and bland.

Tests Administered

WISC-R
Bender—Gestalt
Children's Apperception Test

Test Results and Interpretation

On the WISC-R Jill obtained a Full Scale IQ of 85, which classifies her as Low Average (Dull) and ranks her at the 16th percentile for children her age. The chances are 90% that her true Full Scale IQ is in the 80−90 range. She earned a significantly higher Performance IQ than Verbal IQ (Performance IQ = 93, Verbal IQ = 80), indicating that she functions better when expressing her intelligence via manipulation of concrete nonverbal materials than when confined to verbal comprehension and expression. Thus she demonstrated Average nonverbal skills (32nd percentile) as opposed to Low Average (9th percentile) verbal abilities. Nevertheless, the significant V−P discrepancy is not unusually large in magnitude, with differences of 13 or more points occurring in 28% of the children from comparable socioeconomic backgrounds. In addition, large fluctuations in each scale necessitate going beyond the V−P discrepancy to understand her relative abilities.

Jill demonstrated a significant strength on the Verbal Scale in a task requiring commonsense understanding of social situations (e.g., "What are some reasons why we need policemen?"), as she scored at the 75th percentile for children her age. Her well-developed ability to demonstrate practical information contrasts greatly with the significant weakness (2nd percentile) in a test of abstract conceptual reasoning (e.g., "How are a piano and a guitar alike?"). In other Verbal tasks, assessing skills such as short-term memory and general fund of information, her performance was consistent with her overall Low Average (Dull) skills.

An examination of her Performance tests reveals two significant strengths and two significant weaknesses relative to her Average level of nonverbal ability. She scored at about the 80th percentile in tasks requiring her to find the missing part in a picture and to put together cut-up picture puzzles. Both of these tasks require good spatial ability and knowledge of part—whole relationships. Her relative weaknesses (9th percentile) in the nonverbal area were in tasks requiring her to arrange pictures to tell a logical story and to rapidly copy the abstract symbols that are paired with numbers. These tests have two common elements: they require well-developed visual sequencing skills, and they demand good convergent production of figural stimuli. Furthermore, the picture—story task requires nonverbal reasoning skills; her poorer performance in this task is thus consistent with her low level of ability in the verbal abstract-reasoning test mentioned earlier. Her deficiency in abstract reasoning is also consistent with the fact that her responses tended to be very *concrete*. For example, a hat is something "you can wear," a bicycle is something "you can ride," and a cat and a mouse are alike because they "got long tails." At no time did she respond by giving abstract categories.

The pattern of her test results may have some neurological implications. There is a suggestion that her right hemisphere is far better developed than her left hemisphere in terms of cognitive functioning. Spatial ability and part—whole relationships are predominantly right-brain functions, and these were her areas of excellence. By contrast, verbal abilities, sequencing abilities, and temporal relationships (an ability tapped by the picture—story task) are left-brain functions and represent her major weaknesses. Furthermore, Jill had an above-average amount of scatter on the Verbal Scale, and four out of five of her scaled scores on the Performance Scale deviated significantly from her own mean score. This latter finding indicates extremely great scatter in her nonverbal abilities. It is important to note that subtest scatter is frequently believed to be associated with various types of neurological dysfunction.

One positive note was detected in the pattern of her responses: Jill seemed to benefit greatly from structured help by the examiner. After reversing the legs on a puzzle of a girl, the examiner showed Jill the correct response (as required in the directions for administration). After this feedback she assembled a cut-up horse perfectly, making sure to put the legs in the right place as her first response, and proceeded to solve the other puzzles perfectly as well. In addition, the first four items in the picture—story task require the examiner to give complete or partial feedback if the child makes an error; then a second trial is permitted. For each of these items Jill failed the first trial but then passed every second trial following the examiner's "clues." Thus, even in an area of relative weakness for Jill, she demonstrated good motivation and the ability to benefit from structured help.

Jill's drawings on the Bender—Gestalt earned her a Koppitz error score of 7, which is almost one standard deviation below the mean performance of children her age. Whereas this score still categorizes her visual—motor development as within the average range, it is more representative of the typical 6½-year-old's productions. The errors Jill made have been associated with brain injury; however, most errors made by children past their eighth birthday fall into that category. Nevertheless, some of her errors are considered highly significant as indicators of neurological impairment and lend support to the existence of such a possible condition.

On the Children's Apperception Test, Jill's stories given in response to projective picture stimulus cards were uniformly devoid of the kinds of themes and anxieties usually associated with emotional disturbance. In fact, her consistently bland story descriptions may be regarded as evidence of the defense mechanisms of repression and denial. Jill's overall behavior during the evaluation was in marked contrast to the aggressively violent attacks described as her presenting symptoms. It seems possible that her passive lack of affect may represent a coping technique she has adapted for the control and prevention of these emotional outbursts (which she subsequently acknowledges as occurring in the absence of self-control).

Summary and Recommendations

Jill, an 8-year-old girl described as having violent spells of aggressive outbursts followed by periods of limp exhaustion, revealed none of these behaviors during the present evaluation. Instead, she maintained a manner of dulled affect and quiet cooperation. She did not react emotionally to either frustration or success on test items, or to praise or discipline from the examiner. The WISC-R classifies her level of intelligence as Low Average (Dull) with a Full Scale IQ of 85. There was a significant difference between her Performance IQ (93) and Verbal IQ (80), indicating that she functions somewhat better along nonverbal channels than by expressing her intelligence verbally. In addition, her separate subtest scores revealed much scatter in her individual abilities. On the Bender–Gestalt, Jill made errors associated with neurological impairment, although her overall performance was still within normal limits. The bland stories she made up in response to a projective story-telling task gave insight into her possible coping style of repressing and/or denying her potentially volatile emotions.

Taken individually, the various "soft signs" revealed during this evaluation and listed in the presenting symptoms do not constitute even a presumptive diagnosis of brain dysfunction. Altogether, however, they certainly present a case for such a conclusion. Therefore, it is of primary concern for Jill to be examined by a neurologist and to be given the appropriate medical tests to confirm the possible extent of neurological impairment.

Any remedial program devised to help Jill should use her right-brain strengths of dealing with the holistic aspect of tasks and of working with visual stimuli. This might translate to a reading method focusing on a whole-word configuration rather than, say, a phonetical analysis. An approach that uses concrete visual stimuli (such as Rebus Readers) is also desirable. Her weaknesses in the areas of visual sequencing, temporal relationships, and verbal reasoning need special attention. It would also be of benefit to explore other areas of functioning believed to reside in the right hemisphere which may very well turn out to be strengths for Jill to call upon. For example, the areas of music, art, creativity, and nonverbal communication could easily fit into her academic program. It is also wise to utilize her understanding of social situations, perhaps most effectively as a motivational device.

Nadeen L. Kaufman
Psychologist

Cecil Y., Black Male, Age 10 years 4 months

WISC-R Profile

Verbal	Scaled Score	Performance	Scaled Score
Information	6	Picture Completion	1-W
Similarities	7	Picture Arrangement	1-W
Arithmetic	9	Block Design	8
Vocabulary	6	Object Assembly	4
Comprehension	7	Coding	13-S
(Digit Span)	5	(Mazes)	11-S

Verbal IQ = 81.   Performance IQ = 70.   Full Scale IQ = 74.

Referral and Background Information

Cecil is presently enrolled in a treatment class at a clinic for emotionally disturbed children, where many high-priority problems are being worked on. His most concerning difficulties lie in his urinating on toys and things, setting fires, extreme restlessness, great impulsivity, difficulties in relating to peers, and very poor reading achievement.

At home Cecil lives with his mother and five younger siblings under economically deprived conditions. Cecil's natural father died 4½ years ago. His mother remarried a year later, leading to a life of turbulence and violence for the entire family. Mr. Y. exercised tight control over the family and gave many severe beatings to them all. Cecil, the favorite target of the abuse, began his antisocial behaviors about a year after the remarriage. Six months ago Mr. Y. was imprisoned for armed robbery; divorce proceedings began immediately. Now the family is terrorized by the possibility of his escape, not an unrealistic fear in view of his record of escapes from past imprisonments.

Results of test administrations nine months ago yielded a Stanford−Binet IQ of 84 and a Peabody Picture Vocabulary Test (PPVT) IQ of 62 for Cecil.

Diagnostic hypotheses proposed at a staffing at that time included chronic brain syndrome and adjustment reaction of childhood. Cecil was referred for the present evaluation to gain greater insight into the nature of his cognitive functioning and probable neurological impairment.

Appearance and Behavioral Characteristics

Ten-year-old Cecil arrived in a bright red shirt, his handsome face surrounded by closely cropped curly hair. He maintained an air of friendly cooperation throughout the testing session. At first he spoke little, but as he grew more comfortable he freely exchanged social conversation with the examiner. Using a raspy voice, he asked many personal questions of the examiner and showed a genuine interest in sharing his ideas. When he was unsure of the adequacy of his performance, he glanced up for approval or instructions. Aside from the fact that he sniffed and snorted his nose loudly and often, despite no visible signs of a cold, Cecil acted in an appropriate manner and with no evidence of any of the described behavioral problems. In fact, he evidenced high frustration tolerance, adequate attention span, and positive response to praise.

During tasks involving visual–perceptual abilities, Cecil showed severe and pervasive deficiencies that were dually defined by both test scores achieved and physical behavior. When copying abstract designs he continually rotated both his paper and the stimulus cards. Other compensatory behaviors included much erasing and prolonged studying of the stimulus models. During a task of arranging pictures to tell a sensible story he spontaneously verbalized the logic of the "stories" he created, indicating a total lack of comprehension of the individual picture cards. When solving puzzles, Cecil did not know what object he was supposed to construct for those items where the examiner is not permitted to supply this information. His trial-and-error attempts indicated extremely poor interpretation of the picture-puzzle parts. Amazingly, he managed to put much of the two most difficult puzzles together still not knowing the final goal to be completed. This particularly demonstrates Cecil's difficulty at the *receptive* (as opposed to expressive) level of perceptual functioning.

Tests Administered

WISC-R
Draw-A-Man
Bender–Gestalt
Thematic Apperception Test

Test Results and Interpretation

On the WISC-R Cecil obtained a Verbal IQ of 81, a Performance IQ of 70, and a Full Scale IQ of 74 $\pm$ 5, which place him in the Borderline classification of intelligence and rank him at about the 5th percentile for children his age. The 11-point difference in favor of Verbal IQ is not large enough to be statistically significant, which ordinarily suggests equal intellectual functioning whether dealing with verbal or nonverbal stimuli. In Cecil's case, however, the Performance IQ is meaningless in view of the extremely wide scatter characterizing the Performance Scale (scaled scores ranging from 1 to 13, a degree of scatter occurring in less than 2% of children). Consequently, the $V-P$ discrepancy and the Full Scale IQ have limited meaning; as is discussed in the following paragraphs, Cecil's intelligence is more aptly described as Low Average than Borderline.

When expressing his intelligence verbally, Cecil indicated an equal level of development in a variety of areas. For example, his commonsense understanding of social situations, his fund of general information, and his verbal concept formation were all consistent with his overall Verbal IQ, which surpassed 10% of his contemporaries.

Nonverbally, Cecil displayed relative strengths in two paper-and-pencil tasks—one calling for reasoning and foresight (solving mazes), and one requiring psychomotor speed and clerical ability. On these tasks he scored at about the 75th percentile for children his age, which is above average and certainly far better than his verbal functioning. Conversely, he evidenced marked deficiencies (less than 1st percentile) on two tasks that required him to interpret the significance of pictures of people or things. He was unable to deal effectively with pictures in a holistic sense and showed little analytic ability. This analytic problem does not imply that he cannot reason. Rather, it is a visual perceptual difficulty on a receptive level. His nonverbal reasoning is intact (he solved mazes well), and his visual–motor coordination is certainly adequately developed. His problem, then, would seem to suggest possible neurological dysfunction in the *right* hemisphere of the brain, with particular difficulty perceiving meaningful stimuli. This neurological hypothesis is consistent with the discrepancy in his verbal ability when measured auditorally (Binet IQ = 84, WISC-R Verbal IQ = 81) versus visually (PPVT IQ = 62). Furthermore, despite his adequate performance in an arithmetic task, Cecil showed a complete inability to understand or interpret the face of a watch. Considering that he is almost 10½, this is a significant visuospatial lack.

In view of Cecil's pervasive visual perceptual difficulties, his Low Average scores on the Binet and Verbal IQ are more indicative of his current intellectual functioning than are any other global scores that he has attained. His above-average scores on the two WISC-R paper-and-pencil tasks suggest that his potential may even be higher when the impact of his cultural deprivation and visual receptive problem can be circumvented.

The Bender–Gestalt yielded a Koppitz error score of 8 for Cecil, which is almost 4 SDs below the mean performance for children his age. In fact, his visual–motor development is equivalent to the average 6–6½-year-old child.

Cecil's two relative strengths on the intelligence test both relied heavily on fine-motor coordination; his skill on these paper-and-pencil tasks contrasted with his deficiencies on the Bender reproductions adds heightened credence to the probability of extreme visual receptive impairment. Whereas he was successful in perceiving and copying the simple designs in the WISC-R psychomotor task, he could not cope with the more complex Bender designs. In addition, his errors were almost all highly associated with brain damage in children.

Although there were no emotional indicators in Cecil's Bender drawings, his human figure drawing was replete with signs of emotional disturbance. The figure was grotesque, with a large square head devoid of nose, mouth, ears, and neck. The body was missing arms, hands, and feet. The lack of facial features conveyed the inability (or refusal) to communicate with others, which may serve as a protection from interpersonal relations. In all, there were seven emotional indicators, most of which were omissions of expected developmental items. Most significant is the extremely poor body concept that Cecil reveals, another reflection of his impaired visual perception. He may have merely executed a drawing of the internal body image he has. The Goodenough—Harris scoring system yielded a Standard Score of 64, which was consistent with Koppitz's classification of the drawing at the Mentally Retarded level of functioning. There are several factors that contributed to Cecil's performance on this test: emotional disturbance, intellectual deficiencies, and visual—perceptual/neurological impairment. The degree to which each of these affected the overall outcome is merely speculative, although intelligence probably played the smallest role in his low score.

The stories Cecil told in response to picture-stimulus cards on the Thematic Apperception Test were brief but repetitive in theme. He repeatedly mentioned main characters as being "mad." This anger was undefined in terms of causation or subsequent action. The environment as a whole was described as puzzling, ungratifying, and lonely. Cecil expressed his own desire for friends but seemed thwarted in efforts to attain any. Otherwise, his two-sentence stories did not develop any concrete conflicts that lend themselves to projective interpretation.

Summary and Recommendations

Cecil is a 10-year-old boy who is presently enrolled in a treatment class for emotionally disturbed children. His many high-priority problems include extreme antisocial behaviors. Considered to be suffering from chronic brain syndrome of some unknown or unspecified cause, his socioeconomic deprivation and poor reading achievement compound his difficulties. During the present evaluation Cecil was pleasant and cooperative, revealing none of the characteristic behaviors attributed to him. He did demonstrate visual—perceptual impairment and manifested many compensatory behaviors commonly associated with such type of neurological dysfunction.

Results of WISC-R testing yielded a Verbal IQ of 81, Performance IQ of 70, and Full Scale IQ of 74. Profile analysis suggests that his current functioning is Low Average rather than Borderline, with some skills above average for his age. The pattern of abilities uncovered clearly reveals strengths on tasks of nonverbal reasoning and psychomotor speed. Cecil proved greatly deficient on tasks requiring receptive visual−perceptual skills. This lack was found consistently true in other tests of visual−motor development and perception. Projective devices displayed many emotional indicators, as well as negative feelings of undirected anger and loneliness.

Cecil appears to have neurological dysfunctioning of the right hemisphere of the brain in particular, which is affecting much of his interactions with others. He is experiencing difficulty interpreting many aspects of his environment. The disadvantage that this places on his overall functioning is tremendous, and probably lies at the root of his total lack of reading achievement as well. Cecil most likely is feeling frustrations that he cannot express in a socially acceptable manner. He needs to direct these negative, destructive impulses to other forms of release and to gain positive experiences practicing his new role. In particular, it is recommended that Cecil be given a thorough psychoeducational battery of tests, including the ITPA and diagnostic reading tests, to outline appropriate methodology by which to teach him reading and improve his visual−perceptual ability. Cecil also needs special attention paid to his deficient spatial concepts. For example, he could benefit from structured lessons in achieving competency telling time and correct awareness of body parts.

Nadeen L. Kaufman
Psychologist

Paul H., Black Male, Age 11 years 5 months

WISC-R Profile

Verbal	Scaled Score	Performance	Scaled Score
Information	2-W	Picture Completion	6
Similarities	8-S	Picture Arrangement	5
Arithmetic	4	Block Design	1-W
Vocabulary	4	Object Assembly	6
Comprehension	7	Coding	2
(Digit Span)	2-W		

Verbal IQ = 69   Performance IQ = 61   Full Scale IQ = 63.

Referral and Background Information

Paul was referred for evaluation by his school psychologist, who reports that he has violent temper tantrums, fights with other children, and is experiencing great scholastic difficulties. His teacher describes him as resistant to discipline, demanding of excessive attention, and possessing regressive behaviors such as thumb sucking. Paul has been in an EMR class for three years now, having previously (3½ years ago) achieved an IQ of 70 on the Stanford–Binet. He currently is functioning at close to second-grade level academically. At home Paul is one of 12 children. His mother appears to be incapable of running an organized household, and his oldest sister (age 19) provided the information about the family's extreme poverty and inconsistent supervision by both parents. She also told of Paul's auto accident at the age of 5, when he was taken to the hospital unconscious and remained in intensive care for his internal injuries for a period of 3 months. Some of Paul's siblings have been in trouble with the law, and he appears to lack appropriate identification models.

Subsequent to Paul's referral 3 weeks ago, a social worker trained to administer the AAMD Adaptive Behavior Scale obtained information from Paul's 19-year-old sister and EMR teacher regarding his functioning in various social roles. Independent interviews with his sister and teacher revealed considerable consistency, as both perceived Paul as maladaptive. Paul was rated below the 10th percentile on all domains in Part I of the AAMD Adaptive Behavior Scale, Public School Version, except for Physical Development, using norms for children in regular classes (ages 11–12). He was rated below the 2nd percentile in the areas of Independent Functioning, Language Development, Self-direction, and Socialization. When compared to children his age in EMR classes he ranked near the 50th percentile in five of the ten domains and scored at about the 5th percentile in his very weak areas noted previously.

Appearance and Behavioral Characteristics

Paul came to the testing session with a long pencil stuck through his Afro-style hair and a willing smile on his face. He appeared thin, and the sleeves of his shirt flapped as he was missing both cuff buttons. Paul's tongue tended to protrude through partially opened lips, and he remained quiet except in response to direct questions by the examiner. In general Paul used more manual expression than verbal expression, as he demonstrated his meanings by showing the examiner with his hands what he meant rather than communicating with further words. For example, he "hammered" in a "nail" when defining the word "nail"; he "bowed" a "violin" when telling a projective story about a child reluctant to practice his music, and so on. There were several hints of auditory perceptual difficulty, such as when Paul misinterpreted the examiner's carefully pronounced words (i.e., "fable" was described as "flavor"; "diamond" was defined as a "studded dog collar"; "thief" was interpreted as "nose"; "charity" was heard and responded to as "child"). It is certainly a possibility that his Black Dialect may have interfered with the communicative process in this case, however.

Using slow, methodical trial-and-error thought processes, Paul was able to concentrate for long periods of time, revealing both a good, nondistractible attention span as well as high frustration tolerance. He obviously enjoyed a task requiring him to put together cut-up puzzles, and he hummed softly while working on this activity even beyond time limits. Whereas he demonstrated good eye contact, he continued to yawn frequently throughout the evaluation. Most of his answers were on a concrete level of thought, and he exhibited maximum difficulty on abstract tasks. There were indications of a sequencing problem on a task requiring him to rapidly copy abstract symbols into numbered boxes. He did not even know to look at the beginning of the number line provided to find a 1 or a 2, and for each new number a complete visual search was required. Similarly, he was totally unable to repeat digits presented by the examiner—an imitative task—yet he did have some skill when repeating stimulus numbers backward. One hypothesis may be that Paul is limited when an *automatic* response is required, but that when he can call on his *representational* level of organization he performs more adequately.

Tests Administered

WISC-R
Bender—Gestalt
Draw-A-Man
Kinetic Family Drawing
Thematic Apperception Test

Test Results and Interpretation

On the WISC-R Paul, age 11½, obtained IQs in the Mentally Deficient range of intelligence (Verbal IQ = 69, Performance IQ = 61, Full Scale IQ = 63), as he ranked at about the 1st percentile for children his age. There is a 90% chance that his true Full Scale IQ is in the range 58–68. No significant difference was evident between his Verbal and Performance IQs, indicating that Paul functions at the same low level whether dealing with concrete nonverbal materials or expressing his ideas verbally.

On the Verbal Scale Paul's pattern of performance revealed the effects of environmental deprivation on his functioning. Although his performance on all Verbal tasks was well below average, he scored at about the 20th percentile on reasoning tasks (concept formation and social judgment), but only at about the

1st percentile on achievement-oriented and school-related tasks. In addition, Paul performed very poorly on a Verbal task requiring him to repeat digits spoken by the examiner, as indicated previously.

Another interesting pattern emerged in Paul's nonverbal abilities. On visual—motor tasks involving *concrete* stimuli (people and things) he scored at about the 8th percentile; however, on the Performance tasks stressing *abstract* stimuli (symbols and designs) he scored well below the first percentile. Coupled with his extremely poor performance on the memory subtest on the Verbal Scale and his unimpressive score on an oral arithmetic task, his pattern of severe deficiencies suggests a pervasive difficulty in the manipulation of abstract forms and symbols, pointing to the feasibility of neurological involvement.

Thus we get a picture of a boy whose current functioning is mentally retarded. His presenting symptoms of immature and regressive behavior, along with his poor adaptive behavior, are consistent with his intellectual level. In addition, his other presenting symptoms of violent temper tantrums and lack of frustration tolerance with other children may well be related to his possible organic brain dysfunction. Paul's extremely deprived home environment and his failure to achieve academically have obviously compounded his poor performance on the WISC-R. However, Paul is apparently multiply handicapped, as he seems to be both mentally retarded (even if it has been culturally induced) and neurologically impaired.

Paul's Bender—Gestalt performance provides additional evidence of his likely brain dysfunction. His Koppitz error score of 11 is equivalent to the average 5½-year-old's level of visual—motor development. For his own chronological age of 10½, Paul's performance is 4½ SDs below the mean. All of Paul's errors (mostly rotations) are consistent with the types of errors made by brain-injured children; in fact, they are the specific errors that discriminate most significantly between brain-injured and normal children. Two of his errors were highly significant, occurring almost exclusively in brain-injured groups.

The man Paul drew earned a Goodenough—Harris Standard Score of 102, which is good for a child with the problems he is experiencing. Human-figure drawings are less affected by cultural environment and scholastic achievement than are intelligence tests, and Paul's performance suggests that his actual potential may be higher than his functional retardedness indicates. As with his Bender productions, Paul's drawing here revealed no significant emotional indicators. There were, however, a few areas uncovering potential conflict: erased, folded arms are usually connected with suspicious hostile feelings. His person drawing, as well as the members of his family in the Kinetic Family Drawing, all have heavily emphasized belts. This has been viewed as a suggestion of conflict between expression and control of sex or impulse. Paul's Kinetic Family Drawing included only his mother and three sisters who were seen "playing in a car." Coming from such a large family and omitting so many siblings (as well as his father) connotes Paul's negative or rejecting attitude toward these "forgotten" members. This symbolic elimination included his own self, furthering an image of low self-esteem. Interestingly, his three sisters were all tiny figures, yet he put one of them in the car's driver's seat rather than his mother who was drawn playing too. All figures lacked arms. The composite drawing depicts Paul's lack of strength and support emanating from a diminished family unit.

On a projective story-telling task (Thematic Apperception Test) Paul's responses transformed even passive and peaceful stimulus pictures into tales of violence and aggression. His perception of the world appears to be turbulent and filled with danger. The stories tended to reveal Paul's antiauthority attitude, underscored by lack of parental nurturance. His weak superego fosters an acting-out coping style in dealing with his feelings of inadequacy. Most noteworthy about his performance on this test was the degree of Paul's social awareness of adult topics. He describes real-life situations with a style that hints at some first-hand knowledge. He presumably has either seen or heard much about adult life and happenings. In telling these stories he demonstrated sound, logical reasoning and apparent understanding of mature themes. This flavor is evident in a short excerpt: "That night she got kidnapped, tied up, and raped; two white guys who got her drunk. She had a baby. It didn't look like her husband. It died because she had no milk."

Summary and Recommendations

Paul is an 11½-year-old boy who is presently experiencing difficulties in his EMR class where he is reported to exhibit no self-control over his violent temper and to lack goal-oriented scholastic behavior. His home life is described as economically deprived, and there is little parental organization provided for the household's 12 children. Paul was recently found to have poor adaptive behavior, as rated by his older sister and EMR teacher.

Unlike his limited attention span in school, Paul proved capable of long periods of concentration during the evaluation. His WISC-R Full Scale IQ of 63 places him in the Mentally Deficient category of intelligence, and there was no significant difference between his verbal comprehension and expression and his nonverbal reasoning with concrete materials. He proved highly inadequate when dealing with abstract stimuli (designs and symbols); when performing tasks involving concrete stimuli (people and things), he fared much better—but still well below average. The pattern of his abilities closely resembles that of a child with organic brain syndrome; this was repeated in significant findings on Paul's Bender productions. It is possible that the apparent brain injury may have occurred at the time of a serious auto accident Paul recovered from at age 5. He is thus functioning as a mentally retarded child who additionally seems to be neurologically impaired. Projective measures uncover Paul's lack of support from his family, low self-esteem, and a mature level of awareness of the harsh realities of adult life. He appears to have a weak superego and possesses an antiestablishment attitude in an environment perceived as hostile.

Paul needs a therapeutic program to help him direct his inner angers into constructive outlets. Most importantly, he needs to develop self-control. One way for him to find appropriate models with whom to identify is through a sponsoring organization like a boys club or a sports-related group. He may also find new sources of approval there. At home Paul's behavior might improve with more structure and greater consistency. Under these circumstances he would be better able to make predictions about the day's routine, helping to prepare him for any stressful events likely to occur.

Paul appears capable of understanding things seen as relevant to his life; this should pave the way for new kinds of academic stimulation. School activities and learning situations should bring meaningful examples into focus to help motivate Paul's work output. His teacher should be using concrete materials whenever dealing with abstract concepts. For example, arithmetic problems should be worked with actual objects that can be manipulated when computational skills are being taught. Correspondingly, his reading acquisition might be facilitated if pictures and objects were available. Paul is not likely to learn how to read well in a straightforward fashion that is adapted for an EMR class only in its slow presentation; he needs programs that incorporate knowledge of his apparent neurological impairment as well. In addition, it is suggested that Paul undergo a neurological examination to corroborate this examiner's findings.

Nadeen L. Kaufman
Psychologist

References

Abrahams, R. D., The advantages of Black English, in J. S. De Stephano (Ed.), *Language, Society, and Education: A Profile of Black English,* Charles A. Jones, Worthington, Ohio, 1973.

Ackerman, P. T., Dykman, R. A., and Peters, J. E., Hierarchical factor patterns on the WISC as related to areas of learning deficit, *Perceptual and Motor Skills,* **42,** 583−615 (1976).

Alcorn, C. L., and Nicholson, C. L., A technique for programming interpretations and educational recommendations based on the WISC-R. Paper presented at the meeting of the National Association of School Psychologists, Atlanta, Ga., April 1975 [*NASP Proceedings,* 208 (1974−1975)].

Aliotti, N. C., Alternative assessment strategies in a pluralistic society, *School Psychology Digest,* **6,** 6−12 (1977).

Aliotti, N. C., Strategies for making assessments less biased: Testing-the-limits, WISC-R subtest recategorizations, and creativity tests. Paper presented at the meeting of the National Association of School Psychologists, New York City, March 1978.

Allen, G. A., Mahler, W. A., and Estes, W. K., Effects of recall tests on long-term retention of paired associates, *Journal of Verbal Learning and Verbal Behavior,* **8,** 463−470 (1969).

Altus, G. T., WISC patterns of a selective sample of bilingual school children, *Journal of Genetic Psychology,* **83,** 241−248 (1953).

American Psychological Association. Psychology and mental retardation, *American Psychologist,* **25,** 267−268 (1970).

Ames, L. B., A low intelligence quotient often not recognized as the chief cause of many learning difficulties, *Journal of Learning Disabilities,* **1,** 45−58 (1968).

Anastasi, A., *Psychological Testing,* 4th ed., Macmillan, New York, 1976.

Anderson, M., Kaufman, A. S., and Kaufman, N. L., Use of the WISC-R with a learning disabled population: Some diagnostic implications, *Psychology in the Schools,* **13,** 381−386 (1976).

Andrew, J. M., Delinquency, the Wechsler P > V sign, and the I-level system, *Journal of Clinical Psychology,* **30,** 331−335 (1974).

Anglin, J. M., *The Growth of Word Meaning,* MIT Press, Cambridge, Mass., 1970.

Angoff, W. H., A technique for the investigation of cultural differences, in *Test Bias:*

Interactions between Test Scores, Test Items, Criterion Scores, and Population Subgroups. Symposium presented at the meeting of the American Psychological Association, Honolulu, September 1972.

Arthur, G., *A Point Scale of Performance, Revised From II: Manual for Administering and Scoring the Tests*, Psychological Corporation, New York, 1947.

Baker, H. J., and Leland, B., *Examiner's Handbook: Detroit Tests of Learning Aptitude*, rev. ed., Bobbs-Merrill, Indianapolis, 1967.

Banas, N., and Wills, I. H., Prescriptions from WISC-R patterns, *Academic Therapy*, **13**, 241–246 (1977).

Banas, N., and Wills, I. H., Prescriptions from WISC-R patterns, *Academic Therapy*, **13**, 365–370 (1978).

Bannatyne, A., *Language, Reading, and Learning Disabilities,* Charles C Thomas, Springfield, Ill., 1971.

Bannatyne, A., Diagnosis: A note on recategorization of the WISC scaled scores, *Journal of Learning Disabilities,* **7**, 272–274 (1974).

Baratz, J. C., Teaching reading in an urban Negro school system, in F. Williams (Ed.), *Language and Poverty,* Markham, Chicago, 1970, pp. 11–22.

Bauman, R., An ethnographic framework for the investigation of communicative behaviors. *Asha,* **13**, 334–340 (1971).

Baumeister, A. A., and Bartlett, C. J., A comparison of the factor structure of normals and retardates on the WISC, *American Journal of Mental Deficiency,* **66**, 641–646 (1962a).

Baumeister, A. A., and Bartlett, C. J., Further factorial investigation of WISC performance of mental defectives, *American Journal of Mental Deficiency,* **67**, 257–261 (1962b).

Baumeister, A. A., Bartlett, C. J., and Hawkins, W. F., Stimulus trace as a predictor of performance, *American Journal of Mental Deficiency,* **67**, 726–729 (1963).

Bender, L., *Bender Motor Gestalt Test: Cards and Manual of Instruction,* American Orthopsychiatric Association, New York, 1946.

Benton, A. L., *Revised Visual Retention Test,* 3rd ed., The State University of Iowa, Iowa City, 1963.

Berry, K., and Sherrets, S., A comparison of the WISC and WISC-R for special education students, *Pediatric Psychology,* **3**, 14 (1975).

Bersoff, D. N., Silk purses into sow's ears: The decline of psychological testing and suggestion for its redemption, *American Psychologist,* **28**, 892–899 (1973).

Bever, T. G., Cerebral asymmetries in humans are due to the differentiation of two incompatible processes: Holistic and analytic, in D. Aaronson and R. Rieber (Eds.) *Developmental Psycholinguistics and Communication Disorders,* New York Academy of Sciences, 1975.

Biggs, J. B., Genetics and education: An alternative to Jensenism, *Educational Researcher,* **7**, 11–17 (1978).

Binder, L. M., Hemispheric specialization, *Journal of Pediatric Psychology,* **1**, 34–37 (1976).

Birch, J. W., *Mainstreaming: Educable Mentally Retarded Children in Regular Classes,* Council for Exceptional Children, Reston, Va., 1974.

Black, F. W., Patterns of cognitive impairment in children with suspected and documented neurological dysfunction, *Perceptual and Motor Skills,* **39**, 115–120 (1974a).

Black, F. W., WISC Verbal–Performance discrepancies as indicators of neurological dysfunction in pediatric patients, *Journal of Clinical Psychology,* **30**, 165–167 (1974b).

Black, F. W., Cognitive, academic, and behavioral findings in children with suspected and documented neurological dysfunction, *Journal of Learning Disabilities,* **9**, 182–187 (1976).

Blanco, R. F., *Prescriptions for Children with Learning and Adjustment Problems,* Charles C Thomas, Springfield, Ill., 1972.

Bogen, J. E., The other side of the brain: Parts I, II, and III, *Bulletin of the Los Angeles Neurological Society,* **34**, 73–105; 135–162; 191–203 (1969).

Bogen, J. E., Some educational aspects of hemispheric specialization, *UCLA Educator,* **17**, 24–32 (1975).

Bogen, J. E., De Zure, R., Tenhouten, N., and Marsh, J., The other side of the brain IV: The A/P ratio, *Bulletin of the Los Angeles Neurological Society,* **37**, 49–61 (1972).

Bogen, J. E., Fischer, E. D., and Vogel, P. J., Cerebral commisurotomy: A second case report, *Journal of the American Medical Association,* **194**, 1328–1329 (1965).

Bortner, M., and Birch, H. G., Patterns of intellectual ability in emotionally disturbed and brain-damaged children, *Journal of Special Education,* **3**, 351–369 (1969).

Bortner, M., Hertzig, M. E., and Birch, H. G., Neurological signs and intelligence in brain-damaged children, *Journal of Special Education,* **6**, 325–333 (1972).

Bosma, B., The NEA testing moratorium, *Journal of School Psychology,* **11**, 304–306 (1973).

Bower, G. H., and Winzenz, D., Group structure, coding, and memory for digit series, *Journal of Experimental Psychology Monograph,* **80**, (2, part 2), 1–17 (1969).

Brannigan, G. R., and Ash, T., Cognitive tempo and WISC-R performance, *Journal of Clinical Psychology,* **33**, 212 (1977).

Bransford, L. A., Social issues in special education, *Phi Delta Kappan,* **55**, 530–532 (1974).

Brooks, C. R., WISC, WISC-R, S-B L & M, WRAT: Relationships and trends among children ages six to ten referred for psychological evaluation, *Psychology in the Schools,* **14**, 30–33 (1977).

Brooks, L. R., Treating verbal stimuli in a novel manner. Paper presented at the meeting of the Eastern Psychological Association, Washington, D. C., April 1973.

Bryan, T. H., Learning disabilities: A new stereotype, *Journal of Learning Disabilities,* **7**, 304–309 (1974).

Bryan, T. H., and Bryan, J. H., *Understanding learning disabilities,* Alfred, Port Washington, N. Y., 1975.

Bryden, M. P., and Allard, F., Visual hemifield differences depend on typeface, *Brain and Language,* **3**, 191−200 (1976).

Budoff, M., Measuring learning potential: An alternative to the traditional intelligence test, in G. R. Gredler (Ed.), *Ethical and Legal Factors in the Practice of School Psychology,* Proceedings of the First Annual Conference in School Psychology, Temple University, Philadelphia, 1972.

Burgemeister, B. B., Blum, L. H., and Lorge, I., *Columbia Mental Maturity Scale,* 3rd ed., Harcourt Brace Jovanovich, New York, 1972.

Buriel, R., Cognitive styles among three generations of Mexican American children, *Journal of Cross-Cultural Psychology,* **6**, 417−429 (1975).

Buriel, R., Relationship of three field-dependence measures to the reading and math achievement of Anglo American and Mexican American children, *Journal of Educational Psychology,* **70**, 167−174 (1978).

Burstein, A., Schizophrenic patterns on the WISC and their validity for white, black, and Hispanic children (doctoral dissertation, Fordham University), University Microfilms, Ann Arbor, Mich., 1976, No. 76−17, 894.

Bush, W. J., and Waugh, K. W., *Diagnosing Learning Disabilities,* 2nd ed., Charles E. Merrill, Columbus, Ohio, 1976.

Canavan, D., Field dependence in children as a function of grade, sex, and ethnic group membership. Paper presented at the meeting of the American Psychological Association, Washington, D. C., August 1969.

Cardon, B. W., Law, professional practice, and university preparation: Where do we go from here, in B. W. Cardon, P. J. Kuriloff, and B. N. Phillips (Eds.), *Law and the School Psychologist: Challenge and Opportunity.* Human Sciences Press, New York; special issue of *Journal of School Psychology,* **13**, 377−386 (1975).

Carmon, A., and Nachson, I., Ear asymmetry in perception of emotional non-verbal stimuli, *Acta Psychologica,* **37**, 351−357 (1973).

Carter, C., Prospectus on black communications, *School Psychology Digest,* **6**, 23−30 (1977).

Catron, D. W., and Catron, S. S., WISC-R vs. WISC: A comparison with educable mentally retarded children, *Journal of School Psychology,* **15**, 264−266 (1977).

Cattell, R. B., Theory of fluid and crystallized intelligence: A critical experiment, *Journal of Educational Psychology,* **54**, 1−22 (1963).

Cattell, R. B., The theory of fluid and crystallized general intelligence checked at the 5−6 year-old level, *British Journal of Educational Psychology,* **37**, 209−224 (1967).

Cattell, R. B., Are I.Q. tests intelligent, *Psychology Today,* **2**, 56−62 (1968).

Cattell, R. B., *Abilities: Their Structure, Growth, and Action,* Houghton-Mifflin, Boston, 1971.

Christiansen, T., and Livermore, G., A comparison of Anglo−American and Spanish−American children on the WISC, *Journal of Social Psychology,* **81**, 9−14 (1970).

Cleary, T. A., Test Bias: Prediction of grades of Negro and white students in integrated colleges, *Journal of Educational Measurement,* **5**, 115−124 (1968).

Cleary, T., A., Humphreys, L. G., Kendrick, S. A., and Wesman, A. G., Educational uses of tests with disadvantaged students, *American Psychologist,* **30,** 15−41 (1975).

Clements, S. D., *Minimal Brain Dysfunction in Children: Terminology and Identification–Phase One* (NINDB Monograph No. 3, U. S. Public Health Service Publication No. 1415), Department of Health, Education, and Welfare, Washington, D.C., 1966.

Coates, S., Field independence and intellectual functioning in preschool children, *Perceptual and Motor Skills,* **41,** 251−254 (1975).

Cohen, B. D., Berent, S., and Silverman, A. J., Field dependence and lateralization of function in the human brain, *Archives of General Psychiatry,* **28,** 165−167 (1973).

Cohen, J., The factorial structure of the WAIS between early adulthood and old age, *Journal of Consulting Psychology,* **21,** 283−290 (1957).

Cohen, J., The factorial structure of the WISC at ages 7−6, 10−6, and 13−6, *Journal of Consulting Psychology,* **23,** 285−299 (1959).

Cohen, R., Conceptual styles: Cultural conflict and non-verbal tests of intelligence, *American Anthropologist,* **71,** 825−856 (1969).

Cole, S., and Hunter, M., Pattern analysis of WISC scores achieved by culturally disadvantaged children, *Psychological Reports,* **29,** 191−194 (1971).

Coleman, J. S., Campbell, E. Q., Hobson, C. J., McPartland, J., Mood, A. M., Weinfeld, F. D., and York, R. L., *Equality of Educational Opportunity.* Washington, D. C.: Department of Health, Education, and Welfare, Office of Education, Washington, D.C., 1966 (U.S. Government Printing Office Superintendent of Documents Catalog No. FS 5.238: 38000).

Conger, A. J., and Conger, J. C., Reliable dimensions for WISC profiles, *Educational and Psychological Measurement,* **35,** 847−863 (1975).

Costa, L. D., The relation of visuospatial dysfunction to digit span performance in patients with cerebral lesions, *Cortex,* **11,** 31−36 (1975).

Cronbach, L. J., How can instruction be adapted in individual differences? in R. Gagne (Ed.), *Learning and Individual Differences,* Charles E. Merrill, Columbus, Ohio, 1967.

Cronbach, L. J., *Essentials of Psychological Testing,* 3rd ed., Harper & Row, New York, 1970.

Cronbach, L. J., Equity in selection—where psychometrics and political philosophy meet, *Journal of Educational Measurement,* **13,** 31−41 (1976).

Cronbach, L. J., *Educational Psychology,* 3rd ed., Harcourt Brace Jovanovich, New York, 1977.

Cronbach, L. J., and Snow, R. E., *Aptitudes and Instructional Methods: A Handbook for Research on Interactions,* Irvington, New York, 1977.

Crowl, T. K., and MacGinitie, W. H., The influence of students' speech characteristics on teachers' evaluations of oral answers, *Journal of Educational Psychology,* **66,** 304−308 (1974).

Cummins, J., Systems of mediation in memory and reasoning. Paper presented at the meeting of the Canadian Psychological Association, Victoria, Canada, June 1973.

Cutrona, M. P., *A Psychoeducational Interpretation of the Wechsler Intelligence Scale for Children—Revised*, 2nd ed., Cutronics Publications, Belleville, N. J., 1975.

Das, J. P., Patterns of cognitive ability in nonretarded and retarded children, *American Journal of Mental Deficiency*, **77**, 6–12 (1972).

Das, J. P., Cultural deprivation and cognitive competence, in N. R. Ellis (Ed). *International Review of Research in Mental Retardation*, Vol. 6, Academic Press, New York, 1973a.

Das, J. P., Structure of cognitive abilities: Evidence for simultaneous and successive processing, *Journal of Educational Psychology*, **65**, 103–108 (1973b).

Das, J. P., Kirby, J., and Jarman, R. F. Simultaneous and successive syntheses: An alternative model for cognitive abilities, *Psychological Bulletin*, **82**, 87–103 (1975).

Das, J. P., and Molloy, G. N., Varieties of simultaneous and successive processing in children, *Journal of Educational Psychology*, **67**, 213–220 (1975).

Davis, E. E., Matched pair comparison of WISC and WISC-R scores, *Psychology in the Schools*, **14**, 161–166 (1977).

Davis, F. B., Interpretation of differences among averages and individual test scores, *Journal of Educational Psychology*, **50**, 162–170 (1959).

Davis, F. B., *Standards for Educational and Psychological Tests.*, American Psychological Association, Washington, D.C., 1974.

Day, M. E., An eye movement phenomenon relating to attention, thought, and anxiety, *Perceptual and Motor Skills*, **19**, 443–446 (1964).

Dean, R. S., Patterns of emotional disturbance on the WISC-R, *Journal of Clinical Psychology*, **33**, 486–490 (1977a).

Dean, R. S., Reliability of the WISC-R with Mexican–American children, *Journal of School Psychology*, **15**, 267–268 (1977b).

Dean, R. S., Distinguishing learning-disabled and emotionally disturbed children on the WISC-R, *Journal of Consulting and Clinical Psychology*, **46**, 381–382 (1978).

De Avila, E. A., I.Q. and the minority child, *Journal of the Association of Mexican American Educators*, **1**, 34–38 (1973).

De Boer, D. L., Kaufman, A. S., and McCarthy, D., *The Use of the McCarthy Scales in Identification, Assessment and Deficit Remediation of Preschool and Primary Age Children*, symposium presented at the meeting of the Council for Exceptional Children, New York, April 1974.

De Horn, A., and Klinge, V., Correlations and factor analysis of the WISC-R and the Peabody Picture Vocabulary Test for an adolescent psychiatric sample, *Journal of Consulting and Clinical Psychology*, **46**, 1160–1161 (1978).

Denckla, M. B., Development of motor coordination in normal children, *Developmental Medicine and Child Neurology*, **16**, 729–741 (1974).

Denney, D. R., Relationship of three cognitive style dimensions to elementary reading abilities, *Journal of Educational Psychology*, **66**, 702–709 (1974).

Diana v. *State Board of Education*, Civil Action No. c-70-37RFP (N. D. Cal. 1970).

Doppelt, J. E., and Kaufman, A. S., Estimation of the differences between WISC-R and WISC IQs, *Educational and Psychological Measurement*, **37**, 417–424 (1977).

Education for All Handicapped Children Act, PL 94–142 (U.S., November 29, 1975).

Ellis, N. R., The stimulus trace and behavioral inadequacy, in N. R. Ellis (Ed.), *Handbook of Mental Deficiency,* McGraw-Hill, New York, 1963.

Engin, A. W., Leppaluoto, J. R., and Petty, S. Z. (Eds.), *Multifactored Unbiased Assessment,* special issue of *School Psychology Digest,* **6** (3) (1977).

Estes, W. K., An associative basis for stimulus coding, in A. W. Melton and E. Martin (Eds.), *Coding Processes in Human Memory,* Academic Press, New York, 1972.

Estes, W. K., Learning theory and intelligence, *American Psychologist,* **29**, 740–749 (1974).

Faglioni, P., Scotti, G., and Spinnler, H., Impaired recognition of written letters following unilateral hemispheric damage, *Cortex,* **5**, 120–133 (1969).

Fairweather, H., and Butterworth, G., The WPPSI at four years: A sex difference in Verbal–Performance discrepancies, *British Journal of Educational Psychology,* **47**, 85–90 (1977).

Farrald, R. R., and Schamber, R. G., *A Diagnostic and Prescriptive Technique: Handbook I: A Mainstream Approach to Identification, Assessment and Amelioration of Learning Disabilities,* 2nd ed., Adapt Press, Sioux Falls, S. D., 1973.

Fedio, P., and Mirsky, A. F., Selective intellectual deficits in children with temporal lobe or centrencephalic epilepsy, *Neuropsychologia,* **7**, 287–300 (1969).

Fitch, M. J. Verbal and performance test scores in bilingual children (doctoral dissertation, Colorado State College), University Microfilms, Ann Arbor, Mich., 1966, No. 66–12, 168.

Flaugher, R. L., Bias in testing: A review and discussion (TM Report 36), ERIC Clearinghouse on Tests, Measurements, and Evaluation, Princeton, N. J., 1974.

Flaugher, R. L., The many definitions of test bias, *American Psychologist,* **33**, 671–679 (1978).

Flynn, J. T., Vitelli, R. J., and Goldblatt, R., The TARDOR interpretive system. Paper presented at the meeting of the National Association of School Psychologists, New York, March 1978 [*NASP Proceedings,* 115–116 (1978)].

Freides, D., Do dichotic listening procedures measure lateralization of information processing or retrieval strategy?, *Perception and Psychophysics,* **21**, 259–263 (1977).

Frostig, M., Maslow, P., Lefever, D. W., and Whittlesey, J. R. B., *The Marianne Frostig Developmental Test of Visual Perception,* Consulting Psychologists Press, Palo Alto, Calif., 1964.

Gagne, R. M., *Conditions of Learning,* 3rd ed., Holt, Rinehart & Winston, New York, 1977.

Galin, D., Implications for psychiatry of left and right cerebral specialization, *Archives of General Psychiatry,* **31**, 78–82 (1974).

Galin, D., Educating both halves of the brain, *Childhood Education,* **53**, 17–20 (1976).

Galin, D., and Ornstein, R., Individual differences in cognitive style I: Reflective eye movements, *Neuropsychologia,* **12**, 367–376 (1974).

Gazzaniga, M. S., *The Bisected Brain,* Appleton-Century-Crofts, New York, 1970.

Gazzaniga, M. S., Recent research on hemispheric lateralization of the human brain:

Review of the split-brain, *UCLA Educator,* **17**, 9−12 (1975).

Gazzaniga, M. S., and Sperry, R. W., Language after section of the cerebral commissures, *Brain,* **90**, 131−148 (1967).

Gerken, K. C., Performance of Mexican American children on intelligence tests, *Exceptional Children,* **44**, 438−443 (1978).

Gibson, A. R., Dimond. S., and Gazzaniga, M., Left-field superiority for word matching, *Neuropsychologia,* **10**, 463−466 (1972).

Gibson, E., Learning to read, *Science,* **148**, 1066−1072 (1965).

Gironda, R. J., A comparison of WISC and WISC-R results of urban educable mentally retarded students, *Psychology in the Schools,* **14**, 271−275 (1977).

Glasser, A. J., and Zimmerman, I. L., *Clinical Interpretation of the WISC,* Grune & Stratton, New York, 1967.

Goh, D. S., Validity of short forms of the Wechsler Intelligence Scale for Children—Revised. Paper presented at the meeting of the National Association of School Psychologists, Cincinnati, March 1977.

Goldman, R. D., and Hartig, L. K., The WISC may not be a valid predictor of school performance for primary-grade minority children, *American Journal of Mental Deficiency,* **80**, 583−587 (1976).

Goldstein, K., *Aftereffects of Brain Injuries in War, their Evaluation and Treatment,* Grune & Stratton, New York, 1948.

Goodenough, D. R., and Karp, S. A., Field dependence and intellectual functioning, *Journal of Abnormal and Social Psychology,* **63**, 241−246 (1961).

Guadalupe Organization, Inc., v. *Tempe Elementary School District No. 3,* Stipulation and Order (January 24, 1972).

Guilford, J. P., *The Nature of Human Intelligence,* McGraw-Hill, New York, 1967.

Guilford, J. P., and Hoepfner, R., *The Analysis of Intelligence,* McGraw-Hill, New York, 1971.

Guzman, M. D. C., A comparative study of the WISC-Revised, the Spanish WISC (Escala de Inteligencia Wechsler para Ninos), PPVT (English version), PPVT (Spanish version), and the CMMS on Mexican−American children (doctoral dissertation, Texas Woman's University) University Microfilms, Ann Arbor, Mich., 1976, No. 77−742.

Hale, R. L., The WISC-R as a predictor of Wide Range Achievement Test performance, *Psychology in the Schools,* **15**, 172−175 (1978).

Halpern, F. C., Clinicians must listen, in G. J. Williams and S. Gordan (Eds.), *Clinical Child Psychology,* Behavioral Publications, New York, 1974, pp. 324−325.

Hamm, H. A., and Evans, J. G., WISC-R subtest patterns of severely emotionally disturbed students, *Psychology in the Schools,* **15**, 188−190 (1978).

Hamm, H., Wheeler, J., McCallum, S., Herrin, J., Hunter, D., and Catoe, C., A comparison between the WISC and WISC-R among educable mentally retarded students, *Psychology in the Schools,* **13**, 4−8 (1976).

Hammill, D. D., and Bartel, N. R., *Teaching Children with Learning and Behavior Problems,* 2nd ed., Houghton-Mifflin, Boston, 1978.

Hammill, D. D., and Larsen S., The effectiveness of psycholinguistic training: A reaffirmation of position, *Exceptional Children,* **44**, 402−414 (1978).

Hardy, J. B., Welcher, D. W., Mellits, E. D., and Kagan, J., Pitfalls in the measurement of intelligence: Are standard intelligence tests valid instruments for measuring the intellectual potential of urban children?, *Journal of Psychology,* **94**, 43−51 (1976).

Hartlage, L. C., and Steele, C. T., WISC and WISC-R correlates of academic achievement, *Psychology in the Schools,* **14**, 15−18 (1977).

Hebb, D. O., *The Organization of Behavior,* Wiley, New York, 1949.

Hilliard, A. G., The strengths and weaknesses of cognitive tests for young children, in J. D. Andrews (Ed.), *One Child Indivisible,* National Association for the Education of Young Children, Washington, D. C., 1975, pp. 17−33.

Hilliard, A. G., Discussion, in M. C. Reynolds (Ed.), *Mainstreaming: Origins and Implications,* University of Minnesota, Minneapolis, 1976, pp. 38−41.

Hirshoren, A., and Kavale, K., Profile analysis of the WISC-R: A continuing malpractice, *The Exceptional Child,* **23**, 83−87 (1976).

Hively, W., and Reynolds, M. C., *Domain Referenced Testing in Special Education,* University of Minnesota, Minneapolis, 1975.

Hobbs, N. (Ed.), *The Futures of Children,* Jossey-Bass, San Francisco, 1975a.

Hobbs, N. (Ed.), *Issues in the Classification of Children, Vol. 2,* Jossey-Bass, San Francisco, 1975b.

Hodges, W. F., and Spielberger, C. D., Digit Span: An indicant of trait or state anxiety, *Journal of Consulting and Clinical Psychology,* **33**, 430−434 (1969).

Hoffman, C., and Kagan, S., Lateral eye-movements and field-dependence−independence, *Perceptual and Motor Skills,* **39**, 153−154 (1974).

Holland, W. R., Language barrier as an educational problem of Spanish speaking children, *Exceptional Children,* **27**, 42−47 (1960).

Holroyd, J., and Wright, F., Neurological implications of WISC Verbal−Performance discrepancies in a psychiatric setting, *Journal of Consulting Psychology,* **29**, 206−212 (1965).

Hopkins, K. D., Empirical analysis of efficacy of the WISC in diagnosis of organicity in children of normal intelligence, *Journal of Genetic Psychology,* **105**, 163−172 (1964).

Horn, J. L., Organization of abilities and the development of intelligence, *Psychological Review,* **75**, 242−259 (1968).

Horn, J. L., Organization of data on life-span development of human abilities, in L. R. Goulet and P. B. Baltes (Eds.), *Life-span Developmental Psychology,* Academic Press, New York, 1970.

Horn, J. L., and Cattell, R. B., Refinement and test of the theory of fluid and crystallized intelligence, *Journal of Educational Psychology,* **57**, 253−270 (1966).

Huelsman, C. G., The WISC subtest syndrome for disabled readers, *Perceptual and Motor Skills,* **30**, 535−550 (1970).

Hunt, E., Quote the Raven? Nevermore, in L. Gregg (Ed.), *Knowledge and Cognition,* Erlbaum, Hillsdale, N. J., 1974.

Hunt, J. McV., *The Challenge of Incompetence of Poverty*, Illinois U. P., Urbana, 1969.

Hunter, E. J., and Lewis, H. M., The dyslexic child—two years later, *Journal of Psychology*, **83**, 163–170 (1973).

Hunter, J. E., and Schmidt, F. L., Critical analysis of the statistical and ethnical implications of various definitions of test bias, *Psychological Bulletin*, **83**, 1053–1071 (1976).

Ilg, F. L., and Ames, L. B., *School Readiness*, new ed., Harper & Row, New York, 1972.

Jackson, G. D., On the report of the ad hoc committee on educational uses of tests with disadvantaged students: Another psychological view from the Association of Black Psychologists, *American Psychologist*, **30**, 88–93 (1975).

Jacobson, S., and Kovalinsky, T., *Educational Interpretation of the Wechsler Intelligence Scale for Children—Revised (WISC-R)*, Remediation Associates, Linden, N. J., 1976.

Jensen, A. R., How much can we boost I.Q. and scholastic achievement?, *Harvard Educational Review*, **39**, 1–123 (1969).

Jensen, A. R., Test bias and construct validity, *Phi Delta Kappan*, **58**, 340–346 (1976).

Jensen, A. R., and Figueroa, R. A., Forward and backward digit-span interaction with race and I.Q., *Journal of Educational Psychology*, **67**, 882–893 (1975).

Johnson, N. F., The role of chunking and organization in the process of recall, in G. H. Bower (Ed.), *The Psychology of Learning and Motivation*, Vol. 4, Academic Press, New York, 1970.

Kagan, J., Reflection—impulsivity and reading ability in primary grade children, *Child Development*, **36**, 609–628 (1965).

Kagan, J., Reflection—impulsivity: The generality and dynamics of conceptual tempo, *Journal of Abnormal Psychology*, **71**, 17–24 (1966).

Kagan, J., and Klein, R. E., Cross-cultural perspectives on early development, *American Psychologist*, **28**, 947–961 (1973).

Kagan, S., and Zahn, G. L., Field dependence and the school achievement gap between Anglo—American and Mexican—American children, *Journal of Educational Psychology*, **67**, 643–650 (1975).

Kagan, S., Zahn, G. L., and Gealy, J., Competition and school achievement among Anglo—American and Mexican—American children, *Journal of Educational Psychology*, **69**, 432–441 (1977).

Kaltsounis, B., Race, socioeconomic status and creativity, *Psychological Reports*, **35**, 164–166 (1974).

Karp, S. A., Field dependence and overcoming embeddedness, *Journal of Consulting Psychology*, **27**, 294–302 (1963).

Kaufman, A. S., A short form of the Wechsler Preschool and Primary Scale of Intelligence, *Journal of Consulting and Clinical Psychology*, **39**, 361–369 (1972).

Kaufman, A. S., Analysis of the McCarthy Scales in terms of Guilford's structure of intellect model, *Perceptual and Motor Skills*, **36**, 967–976 (1973).

Kaufman, A. S., Factor analysis of the WISC-R at eleven age levels between 6½ and 16½ years, *Journal of Consulting and Clinical Psychology*, **43**, 135–147 (1975).

Kaufman, A. S., A four-test short form of the WISC-R, *Contemporary Educational Psychology*, **1**, 180–196 (1976a).

Kaufman, A. S., A new approach to the interpretation of test scatter on the WISC-R, *Journal of Learning Disabilities*, **9**, 160–168 (1976b).

Kaufman, A. S., Verbal-Performance IQ discrepancies on the WISC-R, *Journal of Consulting and Clinical Psychology*, **44**, 739–744 (1976c).

Kaufman, A. S., A McCarthy short form for rapid screening of preschool, kindergarten, and first-grade children, *Contemporary Educational Psychology*, **2**, 149–157 (1977a).

Kaufman, A. S., Should short form validity coefficients be corrected?, *Journal of Consulting and Clinical Psychology*, **45**, 1159–1161 (1977b).

Kaufman, A. S. Cerebral specialization and intelligence testing, *Journal of Research and Development in Education* (in press a).

Kaufman, A. S., The role of speed on WISC-R performance across the age range, *Journal of Consulting and Clinical Psychology* (in press b).

Kaufman, A. S., and Di Cuio, R. F., Separate factor analyses of the McCarthy Scales for groups of black and white children, *Journal of School Psychology*, **13**, 10–18 (1975).

Kaufman, A. S., and Doppelt, J. E., Analysis of WISC-R standardization data in terms of the stratification variables, *Child Development*, **47**, 165–171 (1976).

Kaufman, A. S., and Hollenbeck, G. P., Comparative structure of the WPPSI for blacks and whites, *Journal of Clinical Psychology*, **30**, 316–319 (1974).

Kaufman, A. S., and Kaufman, N. L., Black–white differences at ages 2½–8½ on the McCarthy Scales of Children's Abilities, *Journal of School Psychology*, **11**, 196–206 (1973).

Kaufman, A. S., and Kaufman, N. L., *Clinical Evaluation of Young Children with the McCarthy Scales*, Grune & Stratton, New York, 1977.

Kaufman, A. S., and Van Hagen, J., Investigation of the WISC-R for use with retarded children: Correlation with the 1972 Stanford–Binet and comparison of WISC and WISC-R profiles, *Psychology in the Schools*, **14**, 10–14 (1977).

Kaufman, A. S., and Waterstreet, M. A., Determining a child's strong and weak areas of functioning on the Stanford–Binet: A simplification of Sattler's SD method, *Journal of School Psychology*, **16**, 72–78 (1978).

Keislar, E. R., and Stern, C., Differentiated instruction in problem solving for children of different mental ability levels, *Journal of Educational Psychology*, **61**, 445–450 (1970).

Keogh, B. K., and Hall, R. J. WISC subtest patterns of educationally handicapped and educable mentally retarded pupils, *Psychology in the Schools*, **11**, 296–300 (1974).

Keogh, B. K., Wetter, J., McGinty, A., and Donlon, G., Functional analysis of WISC performance of learning-disordered, hyperactive, and mentally retarded boys, *Psychology in the Schools*, **10**, 178–181 (1973).

Kershner, J. R., and King, A. J., Laterality of cognitive functions in achieving hemiplegic children, *Perceptual and Motor Skills*, **39**, 1283–1289 (1974).

Killan, J. B., and Hughes, L. C., A comparison of short forms of the Stanford–Binet and the Wechsler Intelligence Scale for Children—Revised in the screening of gifted referrals, *Gifted Child Quarterly,* **22,** 111–115 (1978).

Kimura, D., Dual function asymmetry of the brain in visual perception, *Neuropsychologia,* **4,** 275–285 (1966).

Kinsbourne, M., and Smith, W. L. (Eds.), *Hemispheric Disconnection and Cerebral Function,* Charles C Thomas, Springfield, Ill., 1974.

Kirby, J. R., and Das, J. P., Reading achievement, IQ, and simultaneous successive processing, *Journal of Educational Psychology,* **69,** 564–570 (1977).

Kirby, J. R., and Das, J. P., Information processing and human abilities, *Journal of Educational Psychology,* **70,** 58–66 (1978).

Kirk, S. A., and Kirk, W. D., *Psycholinguistic Learning Disabilities,* Illinois U. P., Urbana, 1971.

Kirk, S. A., McCarthy, J. J., and Kirk, W. D., *Examiner's Manual: Illinois Test of Psycholinguistic Abilities,* rev. ed., Illinois U. P., Urbana, 1968.

Kitzinger, H., and Blumberg, E., Supplementary guide for administering and scoring the Wechsler–Bellevue Intelligence Scale (Form I), *Psychological Monographs,* **65,** 1–20 (1951).

Klausmeier, H. J., Morrow, R. G., and Walter, J. E., *Individually Guided Education in the Multiunit School,* Wisconsin Research and Development Center for Cognitive Learning, Madison, 1968.

Klinge, V., Rodziewicz, T., and Schwartz, L., Comparison of the WISC and WISC-R on a psychiatric adolescent sample, *Journal of Abnormal Child Psychology,* **4,** 73–81 (1976).

Klonoff, H., Factor analysis of a neuropsychological battery for children aged 9 to 15, *Perceptual and Motor Skills,* **32,** 603–616 (1971).

Knight, G. P., Kagan, S., Nelson, W., and Gumbiner, J., Acculturation of second- and third-generation Mexican American children, *Journal of Cross-Cultural Psychology,* **9,** 87–97 (1978).

Krashen, S. D., The left hemisphere, *UCLA Educator,* **17,** 17–23 (1975).

Krashen, S., Seliga, R., and Hartnett, D., Two studies in adult second language learning, *Kritikon Litterarum,* **3,** 220–228 (1973).

Labov, W., The logic of Nonstandard English, in F. Williams (Ed.), *Language and Poverty,* Markham, Chicago, 1970, pp. 153–189.

Lambert, N. M., Legal challenges to testing—Larry P.: A case in point, in *Intelligence Testing Today in the Light of Legal Challenges,* Symposium presented at the meeting of the American Psychological Association, Toronto, August 1978.

Lambert, N., Windmiller, M., Cole, L., and Figueroa, R., *Manual for the AAMD Adaptive Behavior Scale, Public School Version,* 1974 rev. ed., American Association on Mental Deficiency, Washington, D.C., 1975.

Laosa, L. M., Reform in educational and psychological assessment: Cultural and linguistic issues, *Journal of the Association of Mexican American Educators,* **1,** 19–24 (1973).

Larrabee, G. J., and Holroyd, R. G., Comparison of WISC and WISC-R using a sample of highly intelligent children, *Psychological Reports,* **38**, 1077−1080 (1976).

Larry P., M. S., M. J., et al. v. *Riles,* Civil Action No. C-71-2270 (N D Cal. 1972).

Lennon, R. T., Perspective on intelligence testing. Invited address, National Council on Measurement in Education, Toronto, March 1978.

Lesser, G. (Ed.), *Psychology and Educational Practice,* Scott, Foresman, New York, 1971.

Leton, D. A., A factor analysis of ITPA and WISC scores of learning-disabled pupils, *Psychology in the Schools,* **9**, 31−36 (1972).

Levy, P., Short form tests: A methodological review, *Psychological Bulletin,* **69**, 410−416 (1968).

Lewandowski, N. G., Saccuzzo, D. P., and Lewandowski, D. G., The WISC as a measure of personality types, *Journal of Clinical Psychology,* **33**, 285−291 (1977).

Lezak, M. D., *Neuropsychological Assessment.* Oxford U. P., New York, 1976.

Lombard, T. J., and Riedel, R. G., An analysis of the factor structure of the WISC-R and the effect of color on the Coding subtest, *Psychology in the Schools,* **15**, 176−179 (1978).

Lund, K. A., Foster, G. E., and McCall-Perez, F. C., The effectiveness of psycholinguistic training: A reevaluation, *Exceptional Children,* **44**, 310−319 (1978).

Luria, A. R., *Human Brain and Psychological Processes,* Harper & Row, New York, 1966.

Luria, A. R., and Simernitskaya, E. G., Interhemispheric relations and the function of the minor hemisphere, *Neuropsychologia,* **15**, 175−178 (1977).

Lutey, C., *Individual Intelligence Testing: A Manual and Sourcebook,* 2nd and enlarged ed., Carol L. Lutey Publishing, Greeley, Colo., 1977.

Mann, L., Psychometric phrenology and the new faculty psychology: The case against ability assessment and training, *Journal of Special Education,* **5**, 3−14 (1971).

Marwit, S. J., Marwit, K. L., and Boswell, J. J., Negro children's use of nonstandard grammar, *Journal of Educational Psychology,* **63**, 218−224 (1972).

Marwit, S. J., and Neumann, G., Black and white children's comprehension of standard and nonstandard English passages, *Journal of Educational Psychology,* **66**, 329−332 (1974).

Massey, J. O., *WISC Scoring Criteria,* Consulting Psychologists Press, Palo Alto, Calif., 1965.

Matarazzo, J. D., *Wechsler's Measurement and Appraisal of Adult Intelligence,* 5th ed., Williams & Wilkins, Baltimore, 1972.

Mayman, M., Schafer, R., and Rapaport, D., Interpretation of the WAIS in personality appraisal, in H. H. Anderson and G. L. Anderson (Eds.), *An Introduction to Projective Techniques,* Prentice-Hall, New York, 1951, pp. 541−580.

McCarthy, D., *Manual for the McCarthy Scales of Children's Abilities,* Psychological Corporation, New York, 1972.

McDonald, K. G., and Crookes, T. G., The WAIS Picture Arrangement test in British psychiatric patients, *Journal of Social Clinical Psychology,* **6**, 72 (1967).

McManis, D. L., Figley, C., Richert, M., and Fabre, T., Memory-for-Designs, Bender—Gestalt, Trail Making Test, and WISC-R performance of retarded and adequate readers, *Perceptual and Motor Skills* **46**, 443–450 (1978).

Meeker, M. N., *The Structure of Intellect,* Charles E. Merrill, Columbus, Ohio, 1969.

Meeker, M. N., Individualized curriculum based on intelligence test patterns, in R. H. Coop and K. White (Eds.), *Psychological Concepts in the Classroom,* Harper & Row, New York, 1973.

Meeker, M. N., *Glossary for SOI Factor Definitions: WISC-R Analysis,* Available from SOI Institute, 214 Main St., El Segundo, Calif. (1975a).

Meeker, M. N., *WISC-R Template for SOI Analysis,* Available from SOI Institute, 214 Main St., El Segundo, Calif. (1975b).

Meeker, M. N., Mestyanek, L., Shadduck, R., and Meeker, R., *S.O.I. Learning Abilities Test,* Available from SOI Institute, 214 Main St., El Segundo, Calif. (1975).

Meeker, M. N., and Shadduck, R. D., *Evaluation: SOI Abilities Workbook,* Institute for Applied SOI Studies, Manhattan Beach, Calif. (1973).

Meichenbaum, D. H., and Goodman, J., Training impulsive children to talk to themselves: A means of developing self-control, *Journal of Abnormal Psychology,* **77**, 115–126 (1971).

Meisgeier, C., A review of critical issues underlying mainstreaming, in L. Mann and D. Sabatino (Eds.), *The Third Review of Special Education,* Grune & Stratton, New York, 1976, pp. 245–269.

Mercer, J. R., *Labeling the Mentally Retarded,* California U. P., Berkeley and Los Angeles, 1973.

Mercer, J. R., Latent functions of intelligence testing in the public schools, in L. P. Miller (Ed.), *The Testing of Black Students: A Symposium for the American Educational Research Association,* Prentice-Hall, Englewood Cliffs, N. J., 1974.

Mercer, J. R., The struggle for children's rights: Critical juncture for school psychology, *School Psychology Digest,* **6**, 4–19 (1977).

Mercer, J. R., and Lewis, J. F., *System of Multicultural Pluralistic Assessment (SOMPA),* Psychological Corporation, New York, 1978.

Mercer, J. R., and Smith, J. M., *Subtest Estimates of the WISC Full Scale IQ's for Children,* U. S. Department of Health, Education, and Welfare, Public Health Service, Vital and Health Statistics (Series 2, No. 47), DHEW Publication No. (HSM) 72-1047, 1972.

Merz, W. R., A factor analysis of the Goodenough-Harris drawing test across four ethnic groups (doctoral dissertation, University of New Mexico), University Microfilms, Ann Arbor, Mich., 1970, No. 70–19, 714.

Messer, S. B., Reflection-impulsivity: A review, *Psychological Bulletin,* **83**, 1026–1052 (1976).

Miele, J. A., Sex differences in intelligence: The relationship of sex to intelligence as measured by the Wechsler Adult Intelligence Scale and the Wechsler Intelligence Scale for Children (doctoral dissertation, New York University), University Microfilms, Ann Arbor, Mich., 1958, No. 58–2129.

Miller, C. K., and Chansky, N. M., Psychologists' scoring of WISC protocols, *Psychology in the Schools,* **9**, 144−152 (1972).

Miller, C. K., Chansky, N. M., and Gredler, G. R., Rater agreement on WISC protocols, *Psychology in the Schools,* **7**, 190−193 (1970).

Mishra, S. P., and Hurt, M., Jr., The use of Metropolitan Readiness Tests with Mexican−American children, *California Journal of Educational Research,* **21**, 182−187 (1970).

Mitchell, B. C., Predictive validity of the Metropolitan Readiness Tests and the Murphy−Durrell Reading Readiness Analysis for white and for Negro pupils, *Educational and Psychological Measurement,* **27**, 1047−1054 (1967).

Molloy, G. N., Age, socioeconomic status and patterns of cognitive ability (Unpublished doctoral dissertation, University of Alberta) 1973.

Montessori, M., *The Montessori Method,* Shocken, New York, 1964.

Morris, J. D., Evans, J. G., and Pearson, D. R., The WISC-R subtest profile of a sample of severely emotionally disturbed children, *Psychological Reports,* **42**, 319−325 (1978).

Myers, P. I., and Hammill, D. D., *Methods for Learning Disorders,* 2nd ed., Wiley, New York, 1976.

Myklebust, H. R., Bannochie, M. N., and Killen, J. R., Learning disabilities and cognitive processes, in H. R. Myklebust (Ed.), *Progress in Learning Disabilities,* Vol. 2, Grune & Stratton, New York, 1971.

Nebes, R. D., Hemispheric specialization in commisurotomized man, *Psychological Bulletin,* **81**, 1−14 (1974).

Newcomer, P. L., and Hammill, D. D., *Psycholinguistics in the Schools,* Charles E. Merrill, Columbus, Ohio, 1976.

Nolan, J. D., and Driscoll, R. L., Memory deficits in learning disabled children. Paper presented at the meeting of the American Psychological Association, Toronto, August 1978.

Oakland, T. (Ed.), *Psychological and Educational Assessment of Minority Children,* Brunner/Mazel, New York, 1977.

Oakland, T., and Matuszek, P., Using tests in nondiscriminatory assessment, in T. Oakland (Ed.), *Psychological and Educational Assessment of Minority Children,* Brunner/Mazel, New York, 1977, pp. 52−69.

Ornstein, R., *The Psychology of Consciousness,* Freeman, San Francisco, 1972.

Ornstein, R. (Ed.), *The Nature of Human Consciousness,* Freeman, San Francisco, 1973.

Ornstein, R., The split and the whole brain, *Human Nature* (May 1978).

Oros, J. A., Johnson, J. J., and Lewis, M. L., The effect of induced anxiety on the Wechsler Intelligence Scale for Children, *Psychology in the Schools,* **9**, 388−392 (1972).

Osgood, C. E., *Method and Theory in Experimental Psychology,* Oxford U. P., New York, 1953.

Osgood, C. E., and Miron, M. S. (Eds.), *Approaches to the Study of Aphasia,* Illinois U. P., Urbana, 1963.

Palmer, M., and Graffney, P. D., Effects of administration of the WISC in Spanish and English and relationship of social class to performance, *Psychology in the Schools,* **9,** 61−64 (1972).

Pask, G., and Scott, B. C. E., Learning strategies and individual competence, *International Journal of Man−Machine Studies,* **4,** 217−253 (1972).

Phillipus, M. J., *Test Prediction of School Success of Bilingual Hispano–American Children,* Denver Department of Health and Hospitals, Denver, Colo., 1967 (ERIC Document Reproduction Service No. ED 036 577).

Piaget, J., and Inhelder, B., *The Child's Conception of Space,* Norton, New York, 1967.

Pines, M., *The Brain Changers,* Harcourt Brace Jovanovich, New York, 1973.

Piotrowski, R. J., Abnormality of subtest score differences on the WISC-R, *Journal of Consulting and Clinical Psychology,* **46,** 569−570 (1978).

Piotrowski, R. J., and Grubb, R. D., Significant subtest score differences on the WISC-R, *Journal of School Psychology,* **14,** 202−206 (1976).

Pirozzolo, F. J., Cerebral asymmetries and reading acquisition, *Academic Therapy,* **13,** 261−266 (1978).

Pirozzolo, F. J., and Rayner, K., Hemispheric specialization in reading and word recognition, *Brain and Language,* **4,** 248−261 (1977).

Plomin, R., and Buss, A., Reflection−impulsivity and intelligence, *Psychological Reports,* **33,** 726 (1973).

Polley, D., The relationship of the channels of communication of the Illinois Test of Psycholinguistic Abilities to the Wechsler Intelligence Scale for Children. (doctoral dissertation, University of Northern Colorado), University Microfilms, Ann Arbor, Mich., 1971, No. 72−3298.

Quay, L. C., Language, dialect, reinforcement, and the intelligence test performance of Negro children, *Child Development,* **42,** 5−15 (1971).

Quay, L. C., Negro dialect and Binet performance in severely disadvantaged black four-year-olds, *Child Development,* **43,** 245−250 (1972).

Ramirez, M., *Current Educational Research: The Basis for a New Philosophy for Educating Mexican−Americans,* Teacher Corps Assistance Project, Center for Communication Research, University of Texas, School of Communication, Austin, 1972.

Ramirez, M., and Castaneda, A., *Cultural Democracy, Bicognitive Development and Education,* Academic Press, New York, 1974.

Ramirez, M., and Price-Williams, D. R., Cognitive styles of three ethnic groups in the United States, *Journal of Cross-Cultural Psychology,* **5,** 212−219 (1974).

Rapaport, D., Gill, M. M., and Schafer, R., *Diagnostic Psychological Testing,* Year Book Publishers, Chicago, 1945−1946.

Rasbury, W. C., Falgout, J. C., and Perry, N. W., A Yudin-type short form of the WISC-R: Two aspects of validation, *Journal of Clinical Psychology,* **34,** 120−126 (1978).

Raskin, L. M., Bloom, A. S., Klee, S. H., and Reese, A., The assessment of developmentally disabled children with the WISC-R, Binet and other tests, *Journal of Clinical Psychology,* **34,** 111−114 (1978).

Raven, J. C., *Guide to Using the Coloured Progressive Matrices*, rev. ed., H. K. Lewis, London, 1956.

Raven, J. C., *Guide to Using the Standard Progressive Matrices*, H. K. Lewis, London, 1960.

Reed, H. B. C., Pediatric neuropsychology, *Journal of Pediatric Psychology*, **1**, 5–7 (1976).

Reitan, R. M., Methodological problems in clinical neuropsychology, in R. M. Reitan and L. A. Davison (Eds.), *Clinical neuropsychology: Current status and applications*, Wiley, New York, 1974, pp. 19–46.

Reschly, D. J., WISC-R factor structures among Anglos, Blacks, Chicanos, and Native-American Papagos, *Journal of Consulting and Clinical Psychology*, **46**, 417–422 (1978).

Reschly, D. J., and Reschly, J. E., Validity of WISC-R factor scores in predicting achievement and attention for four sociocultural groups, *Journal of School Psychology* (in press).

Reschly, D. J., and Sabers, D. L., Analysis of test bias in four groups with the regression definition, *Journal of Educational Measurement* (in press).

Resnick, R. J., An abbreviated form of the WISC-R: Is it valid?, *Psychology in the Schools*, **14**, 426–429 (1977).

Reynolds, C. R., Interpreting the index of abnormality (A_d) when the distribution of scores is known: Comment on Piotrowski, *Journal of Consulting and Clinical Psychology* (in press).

Reynolds, C. R., and Hartlage, L. C., Comparison of WISC and WISC-R racial regression lines. Paper presented at the meeting of the Southeastern Psychological Association, Atlanta, March 1978.

Reynolds, C. R., and Kaufman, A. S., Conjugate lateral eye movements in preschool and primary grade children. Paper presented at the meeting of the Southeastern Psychological Association, Atlanta, March 1978.

Reynolds, M. C., Educating exceptional children in regular classes. Paper presented at the meeting of the Leadership Training Institute, Chicago, October 1974.

Reynolds, M. C., Trends in special education: Implications for measurement, in W. Hively and M. C. Reynolds (Eds.), *Domain-referenced Testing in Special Education*, University of Minnesota, Minneapolis, 1975, pp. 15–28.

Riley, R. T., and Denmark, F. L., Field independence and measures of intelligence: Some reconsiderations, *Social Behavior and Personality*, **2**, 25–29 (1974).

Roach, E. G., and Kephart, N. C., *The Purdue Perceptual–Motor Survey*, Charles E. Merrill, Columbus, Ohio, 1966.

Robeck, M. C., Identifying and preventing reading disabilities, in J. A. R. Wilson (Ed.), *Diagnosis of Learning Difficulties*, McGraw-Hill, New York, 1971.

Ross, A. O., *Psychological Aspects of Learning Disabilities and Reading Disorders*, McGraw-Hill, New York, 1976.

Rourke, B. P., and Telegdy, G. A., Lateralizing significance of WISC Verbal–Performance discrepancies for older children with learning disabilities, *Perceptual and Motor Skills*, **33**, 875–883 (1971).

Rourke, B. P., Young, G. C., and Flewelling, R. W., The relationships between WISC Verbal−Performance discrepancies and selected verbal, auditory−perceptual, visual−perceptual, and problem-solving abilities in children with learning disabilities, *Journal of Clinical Psychology,* **27**, 475−479 (1971).

Royer, F. L., Information processing of visual figures in the digit symbol substitution test, *Journal of Experimental Psychology,* **87**, 335−342 (1971).

Rudel, R. G., and Teuber, H. L., Spatial orientation in normal children and in children with early brain injury, *Neuropsychologia,* **9**, 401−407 (1971).

Rudel, R. G., Teuber, H. L., and Twitchell, T. E., Levels of impairment of sensorimotor functions in children with early brain damage, *Neuropsychologia,* **12**, 95−108 (1974).

Rudman, H., The standardized test flap, *Phi Delta Kappan,* **59**, 179−185 (1977).

Rugel, R. P., The factor structure of the WISC in two populations of disabled readers, *Journal of Learning Disabilities,* **7**, 581−585 (1974a).

Rugel, R. P., WISC subtest scores of disabled readers: A review with respect to Bannatyne's recategorization, *Journal of Learning Disabilities,* **7**, 48−55 (1974b).

Rumelhart, D. E., Lindsay, P. H., and Norman, D. A., A process model for long-term memory, in E. Tulving and W. Donaldson (Eds.), *Organization of Memory,* Academic Press, New York, 1972, pp. 197−246.

Russell, E. W., WAIS factor analysis with brain-damaged subjects using criterion measures, *Journal of Consulting and Clinical Psychology,* **39**, 133−139 (1972).

Ryan, L. E., An investigation of the relationship between the scores earned by selected Negro and white children on the Wechsler Intelligence Scale for Children and the Wide Range Achievement Test (doctoral dissertation, Mississippi State University) University Microfilms, Ann Arbor, Mich., 1973, No. 73−25, 711.

Sage, W., The split brain lab, *Human Behavior,* **5**, 24−28 (1976).

Samples, R. E. Are you teaching only one side of the brain?, *Learning,* **3**, 24−30 (1975).

Sanders, M., Scholz, J. P., and Kagan, S., Three social motives and field independence− field dependence in Anglo American and Mexican American children, *Journal of Cross-Cultural Psychology,* **7**, 451−461 (1976).

Sattler, J. M., Analysis of functions of the 1960 Stanford−Binet Intelligence Scale, Form L-M, *Journal of Clinical Psychology,* **21**, 173−179 (1965).

Sattler, J. M., *Assessment of Children's Intelligence,* rev. ed., Saunders, Philadelphia, 1974.

Sattler, J. M., and Winget, B. M., Intelligence testing procedures as affected by expectancy and IQ, *Journal of Clinical Psychology,* **26**, 446−448 (1970).

Satz, P., Van De Reit, H., and Mogel, S., An abbreviation of the WISC for clinical use, *Journal of Consulting Psychology,* **31**, 108 (1967).

Saunders, D. R., A factor analysis of the Information and Arithmetic items of the WAIS, *Psychological Reports,* **6**, 367−383 (1960).

Scanlon, J., *Intellectual Development of Youths as Measured by a Short Form of the Wechsler Intelligence Scale,* U.S. Department of Health, Education, and Welfare,

Public Health Service, Vital and Health Statistics (Series 11, No. 128), DHEW Publication No. (HRA) 74-1610, 1973.

Schwarting, F. G., A comparison of the WISC and WISC-R, *Psychology in the Schools,* **13**, 139–141 (1976).

Schwarting, F. G., and Schwarting, K. R., The relationship of the WISC-R and WRAT: A study based upon a selected population, *Psychology in the Schools,* **14**, 431–433 (1977).

Schwebel, M., and Raph, J. (Eds.), *Piaget in the Classroom,* Basic Books, New York, 1973.

Seashore, C. E., Lewis, D., and Saetveit, J. G., *Seashore Measures of Musical Talents,* Psychological Corporation, New York, 1960.

Seashore, H. G., Differences between verbal and performance IQs on the WISC, *Journal of Consulting Psychology,* **15**, 62–67 (1951).

Sechrest, L., Fay, T. L., and Zaidi, S. M. H., Problems of translation in cross-cultural research, *Journal of Cross-cultural Psychology,* **3**, 41–56 (1972).

Sells, S. B., *Evaluation of Psychological Measures Used in the Health Examination Survey of Children Ages 6–11,* U.S. Department of Health, Education, and Welfare, Public Health Service, Vital and Health Statistics, Publication No. 1000 (Series 2, No. 15), 1966.

Seth, G., Eye–hand coordination and handedness: A developmental study of visuo-motor behavior in infancy, *British Journal of Educational Psychology,* **43**, 35–49 (1973).

Shapiro, R., A computerized WISC report: Rules for making descriptive statements of intellectual functioning (doctoral dissertation, Long Island University) University Microfilms, Ann Arbor, Mich., 1974, No. 74–17, 713.

Shellenberger, S., A cross-cultural investigation of the Spanish version of the McCarthy Scales of Children's Abilities for Puerto Rican children (unpublished doctoral dissertation, University of Georgia, 1977).

Shellenberger, S., and Lachterman, T., Usability of the McCarthy Scales of Children's Abilities in the intellectual assessment of the Puerto Rican child. Paper presented at the meeting of the National Association of School Psychologists, Kansas City, Mo., March 1976.

Shiek, D. A., and Miller, J. E., Validity generalization of the WISC-R factor structure with 10½-year-old children, *Journal of Consulting and Clinical Psychology,* **46**, 583 (1978).

Silverstein, A. B., WISC subtest patterns of retardates, *Psychological Reports,* **23**, 1061–1062 (1968).

Silverstein, A. B., Reappraisal of the validity of the WAIS, WISC, and WPPSI short forms, *Journal of Consulting and Clinical Psychology,* **34**, 12–14 (1970).

Silverstein, A. B., A corrected formula for assessing the validity of WAIS, WISC, and WPPSI short forms, *Journal of Consulting and Clinical Psychology,* **27**, 212–213 (1971).

Silverstein, A. B., Factor structure of the Wechsler Intelligence Scale for Children for three ethnic groups, *Journal of Educational Psychology,* **65**, 408–410 (1973).

Silverstein, A. B., A short-short form of the WISC-R for screening purposes, *Psychological Reports,* **35**, 817–818 (1974).

Silverstein, A. B., Validity of WISC-R short forms, *Journal of Clinical Psychology,* **31**, 696–697 (1975).

Silverstein, A. B., Variance components in the subtests of the WISC-R, *Psychological Reports,* **39**, 1109–1110 (1976).

Simensen, R. J., and Sutherland, J., Psychological assessment of brain damage: The Wechsler scales, *Academic Therapy,* **10**, 69–81 (1974).

Simpson, W. H., and Bridges, C. C., A short form of the Wechsler Intelligence Scale for Children, *Journal of Clinical Psychology,* **15**, 424 (1959).

Smith, M. D., Stability of WISC-R subtest profiles for learning disabled children, *Psychology in the Schools,* **15**, 4–7 (1978).

Smith, M. D., Coleman, J. M., Dokecki, P. R., and Davis, E. E., Intellectual characteristics of school labeled learning disabled children, *Exceptional Children,* **43**, 352–357 (1977a).

Smith, M. D., Coleman, J. M., Dokecki, P. R., and Davis, E. E., Recategorized WISC-R scores of learning disabled children, *Journal of Learning Disabilities,* **10**, 444–449 (1977b).

Snow, R. E., Consequences for instruction: The state and art of individualizing, in M. C. Reynolds (Ed.), *Mainstreaming: Origins and Implications,* University of Minnesota, Minneapolis, 1976, pp. 23–31.

Snow, R. E., Individual differences and instructional theory, *Educational Researcher,* **6**, 10–15 (1977).

Sobotka, R., and Black, F. W., A procedure for the rapid computation of WISC-R factor scores, *Journal of Clinical Psychology,* **34**, 117–119 (1978).

Solly, D. C., Comparison of WISC and WISC-R scores of mentally retarded and gifted children, *Journal of School Psychology,* **15**, 255–258 (1977).

Solway, K. S., Fruge, E., Hays, J. R., Cody, J., and Gryll, S., A comparison of the WISC and WISC-R in a juvenile delinquent population, *Journal of Psychology,* **94**, 101–106 (1976).

Spence, A. G., Mishra, S. P., and Ghozeil, S., Home language and performance on standardized tests, *Elementary School Journal,* **71**, 309–313 (1971).

Sperry, R. W., Hemisphere deconnection and unity in conscious awareness, *American Psychologist,* **23**, 723–733 (1968).

Spitz, H. H., The role of input organization in the learning and memory of mental retardates, in N. R. Ellis (Ed.), *International Review of Research in Mental Retardation,* Vol. 2, Academic Press, New York, 1966.

Spitz, R. A., and Wolf, K. M., Anaclitic depression; an inquiry into the genesis of psychiatric conditions in early childhood, II, in A. Freud et al. (Eds.), *The Psychoanalytic Study of the Child,* Vol. II, International Universities Press, New York, 1946, pp. 313–342.

Stanley, J. C., George, W. C., and Salano, C. H. (Eds.), *The Gifted and the Creative: A Fifty Year Perspective,* Johns Hopkins U. P., Baltimore, 1977.

Stedman, J. M., Lawlis, G. F., Cortner, R. H., and Achterberg, G., Relationships between WISC-R factors, Wide-Range Achievement Test Scores, and visual–motor maturation in children referred for psychological evaluation, *Journal of Consulting and Clinical Psychology,* **46**, 869–872 (1978).

Stewart, W. A., Toward a history of American Negro Dialect, in F. Williams (Ed.), *Language and Poverty,* Markham, Chicago, 1970, pp. 351–379.

Strauss, A. A., and Kephart, N. C., *Psychopathology and Education of the Brain-injured Child,* Vol. 2, Grune & Stratton, New York, 1955.

Strauss, A. A., and Lehtinen, L., *Psychopathology and Education in the Brain-injured Child,* Vol. 1, Grune & Stratton, New York, 1947.

Street, R. F., *A Gestalt Completion Test. Contributions to Education,* No. 481, Bureau of Publications, Teachers College, Columbia University, New York, 1931.

Swade, R. E., Relationship of the Block Design subtest of the WISC to reading achievement (doctoral dissertation, Temple University) University Microfilms, Ann Arbor, Mich., 1971, No. 71–26, 530.

Swanson, E., and Deblassie, R., Interpreter effects on the WISC performance of first grade Mexican–American children, *Measurement and Evaluation in Guidance,* **4**, 172–175 (1971).

Swerdlik, M. E., A comparison of the WISC and WISC-R for children referred to school psychologists because of concerns about their intellectual ability (unpublished doctoral dissertation, Michigan State University, 1976).

Swerdlik, M. E., The question of the comparability of the WISC and WISC-R: Review of the research and implications for school psychologists, *Psychology in the Schools,* **14**, 260–270 (1977).

Swerdlik, M. E., Comparison of WISC and WISC-R scores of referred black, white, and Latino children, *Journal of School Psychology* (in press).

Swerdlik, M. E., and Schweitzer, J., A comparison of factor structures of the WISC and WISC-R, *Psychology in the Schools,* **15**, 166–172 (1978).

Swerdlik, M., and Wilson, F. R., A comparison of WISC and WISC-R subtest scatter and implications for special education programs for the learning disabled, *Journal of Learning Disabilities* (in press).

Talerico, M., and Brown, F., Intelligence test patterns of Puerto Rican children seen in child psychiatry, *Journal of Social Psychology,* **62**, 57–66 (1963).

Taylor, E. M., *Psychological Appraisal of Children with Cerebral Defects,* Harvard U. P., Cambridge, Mass., 1959.

Tellegen, A., and Briggs, P. F., Old wine in new skins: Grouping Wechsler subtests into new scales, *Journal of Consulting Psychology,* **31**, 499–506 (1967).

Terman, L. M., and Merrill, M. A., *Stanford–Binet Intelligence Scale: Manual for the Third Revision, Form L–M,* Houghton Mifflin, Boston, 1973.

Thomas, A., Hertzig, M. E., Dryman, I., and Fernandez, P., Examiner effect in IQ testing of Puerto Rican working-class children, *American Journal of Orthopsychiatry,* **41**, 809–821 (1971).

Thorndike, E. L., *Measurement of Intelligence,* Teacher's College, Columbia University, New York, 1926.

Thorndike, R. L., Concepts of culture-fairness, *Journal of Educational Measurement,* **8,** 63–70 (1971).

Thorndike, R. L., and Hagen, E., *Measurement and Evaluation in Psychology and Education,* 4th ed., Wiley, New York, 1977.

Thorne, J. L. H., An analysis of the WISC and ITPA and their relationships to school achievement, socioeconomic status, and ethnicity (doctoral dissertation, University of Houston) University Microfilms, Ann Arbor, Mich., 1974, No. 75-1026.

Thurstone, L. L., Primary mental abilities, *Psychometric Monographs,* (1) (1938).

Todd, J., Coolidge, F., and Satz, P., The Wechsler Adult Intelligence Scale discrepancy index: A neuropsychological evaluation, *Journal of Consulting and Clinical Psychology,* **45,** 450–454 (1977).

Torrance, E. P., *Torrance Tests of Creative Thinking: Directions Manual and Scoring Guide,* Ginn & Company, Lexington, Mass., 1974.

Torrance, E. P., *Discovery and Nurturance of Giftedness in the Culturally Different,* Council for Exceptional Children, Reston, Va., 1977.

Tucker, J. A., Operationalizing the diagnostic-intervention process, in T. Oakland (Ed.), *Psychological and Educational Assessment of Minority Children,* Brunner/Mazel, New York, 1977, pp. 91–111.

Tulving, E., Theoretical issues in free recall, in T. R. Dixon and D. L. Horton (Eds.), *Verbal Behavior and General Behavior Theory,* Prentice-Hall, Englewood Cliffs, N. J., 1968.

Tulving, E., Episodic and semantic memory, in E. Tulving and W. Donaldson (Eds.), *Organization of Memory,* Academic Press, New York, 1972, pp. 381–403.

Tuma, J. M., Appelbaum, A. S., and Bee, D. E., Comparability of the WISC and the WISC-R in normal children of divergent socioeconomic backgrounds, *Psychology in the Schools,* **15,** 339–346 (1978).

Undheim, J. O., Ability structure in 10–11-year-old children and the theory of fluid and crystallized intelligence, *Journal of Educational Psychology,* **68,** 411–423 (1976).

Valett, R. E., *Developing Cognitive Abilities,* Mosby, St. Louis, 1978.

Vance, H. B., and Engin, A., Analysis of cognitive abilities of black children's performance on WISC-R, *Journal of Clinical Psychology,* **34,** 452–456 (1978).

Vance, H. B., Gaynor, P., and Coleman, M., Analysis of cognitive abilities for learning disabled children, *Psychology in the Schools,* **13,** 477–483 (1976).

Vance, H. B., and Wallbrown, F. H., The structure of intelligence for black children: A hierarchical approach, *Psychological Record,* **28,** 31–39 (1978).

Van Hagen, J., and Kaufman, A. S., Factor analysis of the WISC-R for a group of mentally retarded children and adolescents, *Journal of Consulting and Clinical Psychology,* **43,** 661–667 (1975).

Varma, V. P., and Williams, P. (Eds.), *Piaget, Psychology and Education,* F. E. Peacock, Itasca, Ill., 1976.

Vernon, P. E., *The Structure of Human Abilities*, (rev. ed.), Methuen, London, 1960.

Volle, F. O., A proposal for "testing the limits" with mental defectives for purposes of subtest analysis of the WISC Verbal scale, *Journal of Clinical Psychology*, **13**, 64−67 (1957).

Wadsworth, B. J., *Piaget for the Classroom Teacher*, Longman, New York, 1978.

Wallace, G., and Kauffman, J. M., *Teaching Children with Learning Problems*, Charles E. Merrill, Columbus, Ohio, 1973.

Wallbrown, F., Blaha, J., Wallbrown, J., and Engin, A., The hierarchical factor structure of the Wechsler Intelligence Scale for Children-Revised, *Journal of Psychology*, **89**, 223−235 (1975).

Watson, B. L., Field dependence and early reading achievement (doctoral dissertation, University of California, Los Angeles), University Microfilms, Ann Arbor, Mich., 1969, No. 70-14, 335.

Wechsler, D., *The Measurement of Adult Intelligence*, 3rd ed., Williams & Wilkins, Baltimore, 1944.

Wechsler, D., *Manual for the Wechsler Intelligence Scale for Children*, Psychological Corporation, New York, 1949.

Wechsler, D., *Measurement and Appraisal of Adult Intelligence*, 4th ed., Williams & Wilkins, Baltimore, 1958.

Wechsler, D., *Manual for the Wechsler Preschool and Primary Scale of Intelligence*, Psychological Corporation, New York, 1967.

Wechsler, D., *Manual for the Wechsler Intelligence Scale for Children-Revised*, Psychological Corporation, New York, 1974.

Weems, L., Assessment issues concerning minority children. Symposium presented at the meeting of the National Association of School Psychologists, Atlanta, April 1975.

Weinberg, J., Diller, L., Gerstman, L., and Schulman, P., Digit span in right and left hemiplegics, *Journal of Clinical Psychology*, **28**, 361 (1972).

Weiner, S. G., and Kaufman, A. S., WISC-R vs. WISC for black children suspected of learning or behavioral disorders, *Journal of Learning Disabilities* (in press).

Wender, P. H., *Minimal Brain Dysfunction in Children*, Wiley-Interscience, New York, 1971.

Wener, B. D., and Templer, D. I., Relationship between WISC Verbal−Performance discrepancies and motor and psychomotor abilities of children with learning disabilities, *Perceptual and Motor Skills*, **42**, 125−126 (1976).

Wepman, J. M., Jones, L. V., Bock, R. D., and Van Pelt, D., Studies in aphasia: Background and theoretical formulations, *Journal of Speech and Hearing Disorders*, **25**, 323−332 (1960).

Wesman, A. G., Aptitude, intelligence, and achievement, *Test Service Bulletin, (51)* (December 1956).

Wesman, A. G., Intelligent testing, *American Psychologist*, **23**, 267−274 (1968).

West, D. E., The relationship between intelligence structure and psycholinguistic abilities in learning-disabled children (doctoral dissertation, North Texas State University), University Microfilms, Ann Arbor, Mich., 1973, no. 74-14, 833.

Williams, R. L., Abuses and misuses in testing black children, in R. L. Jones (Ed.), *Black Psychology,* Harper & Row, New York, 1972.

Williams, R. L., From dehumanization to black intellectual genocide: A rejoinder, in G. J. Williams and S. Gordon (Eds.), *Clinical Child Psychology,* Behavioral Publications, New York, 1974a, pp. 320–323.

Williams, R. L., Scientific racism and IQ: The silent mugging of the black community, *Psychology Today,* **7**, 32 ff. (1974b).

Witelson, S. F., Sex and the single hemisphere: Specialization of the right hemisphere for spatial processing, *Science,* **193**, 425–427 (1976).

Witelson, S. F., Developmental dyslexia: Two right hemispheres and none left, *Science,* **195**, 309–311 (1977).

Witkin, H. A., Dyk, R. B., Faterson, H. G., Goodenough, D. R., and Karp, S. A., *Psychological Differentiation,* Erlbaum, Potomac, Md., 1974.

Witkin, H. A., Faterson, H., Goodenough, D. R., and Birnbaum, J., Cognitive patterning in mildly retarded boys, *Child Development,* **37**, 301–316 (1966).

Witkin, H. A., and Goodenough, D. R., Field dependence and interpersonal behavior, *Psychological Bulletin,* **84**, 661–689 (1977).

Witkin, H. A., Moore, C. A., Goodenough, D. R., and Cox, P. W., Field-dependent and field-independent cognitive styles and their educational implications, *Review of Educational Research,* **47**, 1–64 (1977).

Witkin, H. A., Oltman, P. K., Raskin, E., and Karp, S. A., *A Manual for the Embedded Figures Tests,* Consulting Psychologists Press, Palo Alto, Calif., 1971.

Woo-Sam, J., and Zimmerman, I. L., Speed as a variable on three WISC Performance subtests, *Perceptual and Motor Skills,* **34**, 451–455 (1972).

Yudin, L. W., An abbreviated form of the WISC for use with emotionally disturbed children, *Journal of Consulting Psychology,* **30**, 272–275 (1966).

Zaidel, E., Linguistic competence and related functions in the right cerebral hemisphere of man following commissurotomy and hemispherectomy (doctoral dissertation, California Institute of Technology), University Microfilms, Ann Arbor, Mich., 1973, No. 73-26, 481.

Zaidel, E., and Sperry, R. W., Performance on the Raven's Coloured Progressive Matrices Test by subjects with cerebral commisurotomy, *Cortex,* **9**, 34–39 (1973).

Zimmerman, I. L., and Woo-Sam, J., Research with the Wechsler Intelligence Scale for Children: 1960–1970, *Psychology in the Schools,* **9**, 232–271 (1972).

Zimmerman, I. L., and Woo-Sam, J. M., *Clinical Interpretation of the Wechsler Adult Intelligence Scale,* Grune & Stratton, New York, 1973.

Zimmerman, S. F., Whitmyre, J. W., and Fields, F. R. J., Factor analytic structure of the Wechsler Adult Intelligence Scale in patients with diffuse and lateralized cerebral dysfunction, *Journal of Clinical Psychology,* **26**, 462–465 (1970).

Zingale, S. A., and Smith, M. D., WISC-R patterns for learning disabled children at three SES levels, *Psychology in the Schools,* **15**, 199–204 (1978).

Author Index

Subject Index